God's Reflections

God's Reflections

Biblical Insight from America's Story

Historical Narratives by
Ronald Ian Phillips

Biblical Insights by
Ernest Schmidt,
David Grotzke, Seth Grotzke,
and Ronald Ian Phillips

WIPF & STOCK · Eugene, Oregon

GOD'S REFLECTIONS
Biblical Insight from America's Story

Copyright © 2022 Ronald Ian Phillips, Ernest Schmidt, David Grotzke, and Seth Grotzke. All rights reserved. Except for brief quotations in critical publications or reviews, no part of this book may be reproduced in any manner without prior written permission from the publisher. Write: Permissions, Wipf and Stock Publishers, 199 W. 8th Ave., Suite 3, Eugene, OR 97401.

Wipf & Stock
An Imprint of Wipf and Stock Publishers
199 W. 8th Ave., Suite 3
Eugene, OR 97401

www.wipfandstock.com

PAPERBACK ISBN: 978-1-6667-3572-7
HARDCOVER ISBN: 978-1-6667-9310-9
EBOOK ISBN: 978-1-6667-9311-6

03/22/22

Unless otherwise marked, Scripture quotations are taken from the King James Version of the Holy Bible.

Scripture quotations marked NIV are taken from the Holy Bible, New International Version®, NIV© 1973, 1978, 1984, 2011 by Biblica, Inc. Used by permission. All rights reserved.

Scripture quotations marked ESV are taken from ESV® Bible (The Holy Bible, English Standard Version®), copyright © 2001 by Crossway, a publishing ministry of Good News Publishers. Used by permission. All rights reserved.

Scripture quotations marked NKJV are taken from the New King James Version®. Copyright © 1982 by Thomas Nelson. Used by permission. All rights reserved.

Contents

Acknowledgments | ix
Introduction | xi

1 Discovery of the United States of America: Into the Unknown | 1
   Biblical Insight: The Way to a New World

2 The Mayflower on Its Way to a City on a Hill | 6
   Biblical Insight: Religious Freedom—What Does It Mean?

3 The Great Awakening: 1730–60 | 10
   Biblical Insight: Ruth's Ruin to Redemption

4 The Father of the United States of America: George Washington | 15
   Biblical Insight: In the Face of Doubt and Uncertainty

5 Paul Revere's Midnight Ride | 20
   Biblical Insight: Cause for Courage

6 Alexander Hamilton: Fatally Flawed Founding Father | 24
   Biblical Insight: Do Not Let Anger Destroy You

7 It's Just a Flag | 28
   Biblical Insight: The Winning Side

8 Lewis and Clark Expedition: The Importance of Being Prepared | 32
   Biblical Insight: Paul's World-Impacting Expeditions

9 The Adams Family | 37
   Biblical Insight: Uncelebrated Legacy

10 Go West, Young Man | 43
    Biblical Insight: A Mansion over a Hilltop

11 Soapy Smith: A Master of Deception | 48
    Biblical Insight: A Heartless Deceiver

12 Abraham Lincoln: A Cause Worth Fighting for | 51
    Biblical Insight: We Are Not the Light, Just the Reflection if We Stand Close Enough to the Source

13 The High Price of Freedom | 56
    Biblical Insight: Freedom is not Free

14 Failure Is Not an Option | 59
    Biblical Insight: Perseverance through Failure and Great Responsibilities

15 The Gilded Age: Exceptionally Good, Exceptionally Bad | 63
    Biblical Insight: Almost Persuaded

16 Thomas Nast's Sharp Pencil | 68
    Biblical Insight: Well Done, Good and Faithful Servant

17 Liberty Enlightening the World | 73
    Biblical Insight: Longing to Belong—Heaven Bound

18 Fanny Crosby: "All the Way My Savior Leads Me" | 77
    Biblical Insight: Is Blindness Really a Blight?

19 Alexander Graham Bell: A Problem-Solver | 81
    Biblical Insight: God Hears and Opens Doors

20 P. T. Barnum: The Greatest Showman on Earth | 85
    Biblical Insight: The Center of Attention

21 The Great Flood of 1889 | 90
    Biblical Insight: Whose Fault?

22 Not One of the Idle Rich: John D. Rockefeller | 94
    Biblical Insight: Serving God by Serving Others

23 Their Fate Was Sealed | 98
    Biblical Insight: Life after Certain Death

24 Carry A Nation | 102
    Biblical Insight: Barking at What Jesus Doesn't Like

25 Annie Oakley: A Sure Shot | 107
    Biblical Insight: Surprising Transformation

26 Shadow of Death: Theodore Roosevelt | 111
    Biblical Insight: Perseverance

27 Mary Jane (Blight) Phillips: An Immigrant's Story | 115
    Biblical Insight: Sacrificial Love

28 Sinking of the Lusitania: He Will Direct Your Paths | 121
    Biblical Insight: God Works in Unique Ways

29 Unprepared for a Pandemic | 125
    Biblical Insight: Be Prepared for the Worst

30 Death-Defying Harry Houdini | 130
    Biblical Insight: Avoiding the Occult

31 Trial by Fire: The Glenn Cunningham Story | 134
    Biblical Insight: Fiery Trials

32 The Lost Generation in the Roaring 20s | 138
    Biblical Insight: Taking the Christian Family Name

33 The Scopes Monkey Trial | 143
    Biblical Insight: Teach Your Children Well

34 Thomas Midgley Jr.: Just Because You Can Doesn't Mean You Should | 149
    Biblical Insight: Good Stewards of God's Creation

35 Amelia Earhart: A High-Flyer Who Lost Her Way | 153
    Biblical Insight: God Wants a Safe Arrival for His Children

36 Mount Rushmore: Bigger Than Life | 158
    Biblical Insight: A Test for Greatness in God's Kingdom

37 Compassion for the Forgotten | 164
    Biblical Insight: Hope in the Midst of Silence

38 Huey Long: America's Dictator, or a Progressive Populist? | 168
    Biblical Insight: A Failure of Leadership

39 Consider Your Ways | 175
    Biblical Insight: Stewardship of God's Creation

40 Don't Believe Everything You Hear: War of the Worlds | 179
   Biblical Insight: A False Narrative (Fake News)

41 Ashes to Ashes: The 1939–40 New York World's Fair | 183
   Biblical Insight: We Have a Bright Future

42 General Douglas MacArthur: The Right Leader for the Right Time? | 186
   Biblical Insight: Godly Leadership

43 The G. I. Bill: When Government Got It Right | 192
   Biblical Insight: Benefit Others by Benefiting Yourself

44 Norman Rockwell Paintings of America's Best | 196
   Biblical Insight: The Artistry of God

45 Dwight David Eisenhower: A Man of Remarkable Deeds and Character | 201
   Biblical Insight: What Will Be Your Legacy?

46 Life in the Suburbs: A Proud Sense of Community | 207
   Biblical Insight: The Ideal Church

47 A Struggle for Human and Civil Rights | 213
   Biblical Insight: Before the Throne

48 Sandra Day O'Connor: A Day in Court | 219
   Biblical Insight: How to Recognize a Wise Person

49 The Supreme Court: Equal Justice Under Law | 223
   Biblical Insight: God's Law, Man's Law, My Law

50 Endless Wars | 229
   Biblical Insight: Neither Will They Learn War Anymore

51 In God We Trust | 234
   Biblical Insight: Whom Can We Trust?

52 A Journey to the Heavens | 239
   Biblical Insight: Heaven

Bibliography | 245

Acknowledgments

ABOVE ALL I WOULD like to thank my wife, Shelby, for reading the early to final drafts, suggesting changes for clarity, and spending countless hours supporting me in this arduous, wonderful adventure. I owe you everything as not only my early editor, proofreader, and sounding board, but also for your love, support, and for being my best friend.

Words do not suffice to express my gratitude to my three co-authors, Dr. Ernest Schmidt, Rev. David Grotzke, and Rev. Seth Grotzke. Their knowledge of Scripture, proclaiming the gospel of God, and encouraging others by sound doctrine is evident in the biblical insights they wrote. My debt of gratitude extends to their wives—Gen Schmidt, Cindy Grotzke, and Crystal Grotzke—who I realize are these co-authors' lifelong partners in this and every ministry they do for God's glory.

I am particularly grateful to Mr. Matthew Wimer and his team at Wipf and Stock for publishing this work and providing invaluable assistance.

Finally, I would like to acknowlege my late father who was the inspiration for much of this book. Shelby and I were on vacation in Florida when we got the call that my dad had passed away. We were not prepared to hear that he was gone. I wished I could talk to him one more time, give him a hug, and tell him how much I will miss him. As we quickly started packing up to come home, I said, "Let's go for a walk on the beach one more time." Walking along, Shelby said, "Just like that, your dad is in Heaven today."

And I said, "Yes. and he met Jesus today, was in the presence of God the Father and talked to the angels."

We started listing all the people he probably met on his first day in Heaven like Adam, Noah, the disciples, and loved ones.

We might not have been prepared for my father to leave this earth, but he was. He had spent his whole life preparing for that instant when his last breath left him, and just that quickly he would awake in Heaven.

So much had been taken from him as his earthly body wore out, but like the 23rd Psalm says, the Lord restored his soul on March 19th 2013. For 98½ years, dad walked by faith with the hope of things to come. He doesn't need his faith anymore because Jack Phillips's permanent address is now Heaven.

Ronald Ian Phillips

Introduction

GOD'S REFLECTIONS IS A thoroughly researched and captivating account of fifty-two biblical and American history stories: one for each week of the year. This unique and groundbreaking approach combines religion and history, two widely read subject matters that now intricately weave America's exceptionalism with God's truths. The life-giving honesty of each American story is paired with one life-shaping application of the gospel, bridging the gaps and connecting two individually and highly researched topics.

The belief in God and biblical principles has been intricately intertwined with the history of the United States of America from its earliest beginnings. The First Amendment's establishment clause separates church and state, but simultaneously acknowledges the need for God in governing and individual worship. As evidence of the nation's religious heritage, "God" or "the Divine" is mentioned in the Declaration of Independence, each of the nation's fifty state constitutions, the Pledge of Allegiance, America's national anthem, and is printed on American currency.

God's Reflections—Biblical Insight from America's Story highlights the unique privilege of being both an American citizen and a child of God. People by the millions come to America every year to take advantage of the special opportunities this exceptional country provides to build a successful life and to openly worship. The authors navigate through authentic accounts of human frailties, failures, and triumphs in America's past, while connecting them with biblical stories that provide hope and strength for a brighter future.

Nothing exists that does not owe its existence to God the Creator. Our every breath on this earth and our hope and assurance of life in eternity are dependent on God, who created and sustains this world and the next in all its richness, diversity, and order.

Today's national discourse of what should be taught in public schools was originally argued in the 1920s Scopes Monkey Trial. The authors have merged this multifaceted debate with biblical insights from the book of Daniel, which teaches Christians how to respond to government authority when it contradicts their own beliefs.

An inspirational account of political cartoonist Thomas Nast using his talents to sway presidential elections, bring corrupt politicians to justice, and influence the outcome of the American Civil War is documented to exemplify Jesus' parable of the talents.

The adventurous life of Amelia Earhart, the experienced aviator who lost her way, is skillfully woven with biblical insights showing God's desire for his children's safe arrival in Heaven.

A college/seminary president, a missionary, and a preacher with five decades in God's ministry joined in this collaborative accomplishment with a historian scholar who has taught over 11,000 students in the past forty years. This unique team achievement reflects the broad scope of their knowledge, wisdom, experience, background, and collective expertise. *God's Reflections* was created by four individuals that researched, trained, and dedicated their lives over the course of decades to arrive at an accurate account of American history and biblical validity.

If *God's Reflections* was the only source to understand American history or biblical principles, it would be a great foundation to build upon. But this innovative approach provides more than just the bedrock principles of American history and biblical foundations.

Read through the centuries of American history found in *God's Reflections* and reflect upon the biblical truths that impacted each event. *God's Reflections* gives proper perspective to the past, purpose for the present, and assurance of eternal peace and joy for the future. Let this book brighten your understanding of how God's word continues to be heard throughout American history. Learn what God has planned for you, and how these plans will make a difference in your life.

Ronald Ian Phillips

1

Discovery of the United States of America
Into the Unknown

THE HISTORY OF THE present-day United States mainland begins with the settlement of indigenous people thousands of years before any European explorers came to the New World. These early inhabitants soon diversified into hundreds of culturally distinct nations and tribes.[1] But who was the first European to cross the Atlantic Ocean and discover this land?

How can it be such a mystery to discover which European first set foot on what is now the continental United States of America? Ask reasonably well-educated Americans and it is almost certain they will not know the answer, or they will get it wrong.

Children across America learned that Christopher Columbus discovered America by reciting: "In fourteen hundred ninety-two Columbus sailed the ocean blue." But did he? One might think so considering fifty-four United States counties, cities, and other municipalities, including the Nation's capitol of Washington DC, are named in his honor.[2] President Franklin Delano Roosevelt designated Columbus Day a national holiday in 1934, and in 1968 Congress added Columbus Day, now the second Monday of October, as an official public holiday.

Long before Christopher Columbus left the shores of Spain in August of 1492, well-educated people, and even those who did not pay attention in their university studies, knew the world was not flat.[3] As

1. Garcia et al., *Creating America*, 32.
2. Lawson, *Discovery of Florida*, 29–32.
3. Russell, *Inventing the Flat Earth*, 3.

fifteenth-century sailors took one last longing look, they could see the lower part of the city they were sailing from was invisible. They attributed this phenomenon to the Earth's curvature, which led them to conclude the Earth was round. Pythagoras, Anaxagoras, and Aristotle, among others, all made observations that led them to believe the earth was a sphere,[4] but hundreds of years earlier it had already been recorded in the book of Isaiah. A study of the Holy Bible would have led them to this truth recorded in Isaiah 40:22: "He sits enthroned above the circle of the earth, and its people are like grasshoppers. He stretches out the heavens like a canopy, and spreads them out like a tent to live in."

The real danger for sailors in these small ships, crossing vast stretches of the Atlantic Ocean, was not falling off the edge of a flat Earth, but turbulent seas, coping with disease, and having ample food and water until they reached land.

After receiving the rank of "Admiral of the Ocean Sea," and funds for his voyage from Spain's King Ferdinand & Queen Isabella, also known as the Catholic Monarchs, Columbus set out to find a direct water route west from Europe to Asia. Instead after a several thousand-mile voyage across the Atlantic Ocean lasting six and a half weeks, Columbus and his exhausted crew sighted a small group of islands in the archipelago known today as the Bahamas, the Dominican Republic, and Cuba, and went ashore. The "Indians" of the Bahamas, and in fact all whom Columbus encountered on his first voyage, belonged to the so-called Taino culture of the Arawak language group. On first seeing the Europeans, they plunged into the sea, swam to the boat, and climbed on board to see if Columbus and his crew had come from heaven.[5] The Tainos, whom Columbus found so gentle and hospitable, are long since extinct.

Christopher Columbus changed the world by initiating the permanent European colonization of the Americas as the result of his four voyages to Central America, South America, and the Caribbean between 1492 and 1502. Columbus shattered the unknown and the obscurity between the Old and New Worlds, but he never set foot in North America or discovered land that is now the United States.

The Americas were named after another Italian explorer, Amerigo Vespucci.[6] Vespucci made his voyage a decade after Columbus first

---

4. Thompson, "Astronomy 161."
5. Morison, *Admiral of the Ocean Sea*, 232–35.
6. Fernández-Armesto, *Amerigo*, 185–86.

crossed the Atlantic Ocean. Christopher Columbus opened the new world for Europeans, but Vespucci is credited with recognizing that they were not exploring India but an entirely new continent. While Columbus underestimated the earth's circumference by approximately 6,000 miles, Amerigo Vespucci predicted the circumference within fifty miles. But like Columbus, Vespucci never entered North America.

Norse sailor Leif Erikson is believed to be the first known European to set foot on continental North America in AD 1000.[7] Five hundred years before Columbus's and Vespucci's voyages to the new world, Erikson reached the island of Newfoundland in modern-day Canada.[8] Erikson's discovery was a relatively unknown Viking saga for centuries until the Americas were visited again by Columbus when he reached the Bahamas on October 12, 1492. On June 24, 1497, John Cabot, commissioned by Henry VII of England, repeated Erikson's accomplishment and paved the way for England's colonization of most of North America. However, neither Leif Erikson nor John Cabot entered land currently in the United States.[9]

So if Columbus, Vespucci, Erikson, and Cabot didn't actually explore what is now the continental United States of America, who did? The answer is Juan Ponce de León.[10] In 1513, he is credited as the first known European to reach the present-day United States mainland, arriving on the coast of Florida near the present-day city of St. Augustine.[11] Supposedly Ponce de León was searching for the Fountain of Youth, but modern historians believe that is a myth. In 1521, Ponce de León attempted to establish a permanent settlement on the west coast of Florida. The indigenous people did not put out the welcome mat but instead repulsed his expedition, and Ponce de León was struck by an arrow and died from his wounds.[12]

Sailing into the unknown was fraught with the dangers of starvation, turbulent seas, and sickness. It led to mutiny as the voyagers were terrified they might have reached the point of no return. They felt the utter hopelessness of no promise of land in sight. Knowledge, courage,

---

7. Calkins, *Story of America*, 16.
8. Tellier, *Urban World History*, 341.
9. Waxman, "Troubling History."
10. Hazen, "Episode 6: Early Maps of Florida."
11. Lawson, *Discovery of Florida*, 29–32.
12. Grunwald, *Swamp*, 25.

perseverance, and faith were all needed for the explorers to safely arrive in the new world.

Biblical Insight: The Way to a New World

by Ronald Ian Phillips

Whatever can be said about the early discoverers, they were brave, and their goals were ambitious. They risked their lives for riches, new trade routes, and new lands to expand their home countries' power and influence, as well as to proselytize their religion. They didn't know where they were going or how long it would take, but they did have New-World aspirations.

Explorers, led by Christopher Columbus and others, ventured out into the vast ocean where storms and its waves could have capsized their small, crowded ships. Starvation or disease might have killed them long before they reached their destination. Homesickness, in-fighting, and mutiny were common.

You might be thinking these explorers were incredibly courageous, but a journey to a new world is not a trip I want to take. You might be saying, "I want a cruise ship with a balcony and a buffet." But you might have more in common with the Old-World discoverers than you think.

We are already on a voyage to a new world. It began at the time of our birth and will continue until our life on earth ends. Like these early explorers, we need to plan for the arduous journey, and we need to prepare for a life at the end of our journey. Like the explorers, we know where we want to end up—in Heaven—but we may not be sure how to get there or how long it will take. Alexandre Dumas, who wrote *The Count of Monte Cristo*, is widely quoted as writing: "Life is a storm, my young friend. You will bask in the sunlight one moment, be shattered on the rocks the next. What makes you a man is what you do when that storm comes."[13]

When the storms of life shatter us on the rocks, there is a way of escaping to safety. The Bible reveals God's plan to help us navigate through life's journey and enter Heaven. Inspired by God, the Bible is the bestselling book of all time, with well over 5 billion copies sold and distributed.[14] As recorded in 2 Timothy 3:16, "All Scripture is given by inspiration of

---

13. Dumas, "Alexandre Dumas Quotes," para. 4.
14. Guinness World Records, "Best-Selling Book," paras. 1–5.

God, and is profitable for doctrine, for reproof, for correction, for instruction in righteousness." "Inspired" literally means "God-breathed."

The only human eyewitness to Heaven—God's son, Jesus, who was both God and man—clearly explains the only way to Heaven in John 14:2–6:

> "In My Father's house are many mansions; if it were not so, I would have told you. I go to prepare a place for you. And if I go and prepare a place for you, I will come again and receive you to Myself; that where I am, there you may be also. And where I go you know, and the way you know."
>
> Thomas said to Him, "Lord, we do not know where You are going, and how can we know the way?"
>
> Jesus said to him, "I am the way, the truth, and the life. No one comes to the Father except through Me." (NKJV)

Once we accept this free gift of salvation by accepting Jesus as our Savior, we have assurances of God's love and guidance through life's journey to Heaven. Deuteronomy 31:8 states, "The Lord himself goes before you and will be with you; he will never leave you nor forsake you. Do not be afraid; do not be discouraged" (NIV). Proverbs 3:5–6 says, "Trust in the Lord with all thine heart; and lean not unto thine own understanding. In all thy ways acknowledge Him, and He shall direct thy paths."

We do not have any miraculous exemption from the frequent sorrows and trials of life. But we do not have to take life's journey alone. We can be guided by One who knows the future and has a plan for our lives. Psalm 139:8–10 assures us, "If I go up to the heavens, You are there; if I make my bed in the depths, You are there. If I rise on the wings of the dawn, if I settle on the far side of the sea, even there Your hand will guide me, Your right hand will hold me fast" (NIV).

2

The Mayflower on Its Way to a City on a Hill

Religious Freedom

INSCRIBED ON A BLOCK of wood on the oval office desk of President John F. Kennedy was the old Breton prayer, "Oh God thy sea is so great and my boat is so small." This could have been the prayer of every puritan and pilgrim that made their historic journey to America aboard the Mayflower. Violent storms, seasickness, and scurvy were common. With no fresh water to wash clothes, the passengers wore the same clothes the entire voyage. There were no bathrooms and only a compass and instruments to align the stars to guide the ship.

John Howland boarded the cramped Mayflower for its three-month journey across the Atlantic Ocean at the height of storm season. A second ship, the Speedwell, set sail for America with the Mayflower in August of 1620, but twice had to return to England after taking on water. Now early September, the decision was made to abandon the Speedwell. Some of its passengers boarded the already crowded Mayflower with their belongings and set sail to the New World.[1]

John Howland joined over 100 puritans who called themselves saints or separatists and pilgrims who were also referred to as strangers. More than half would be dead within a year. Once well out to sea, Howland was almost one of the first to die. He was swept overboard in a storm but miraculously was saved by grabbing and hanging on to a

---

1. Philbrick, *Mayflower*, 32–37.

rope for hoisting or lowering a sail until he could be rescued.² Howland eventually outlived all but two of the male Mayflower passengers, dying at the age of eighty years old. How fortunate for the millions of his descendants, including Mrs. Theodore Roosevelt, and Presidents George H. and George W. Bush.³

When the pilgrims and puritans first stepped off the Mayflower in November of 1620, they were not the first on the eastern shores of the North American continent. Indian tribes greeted them, and Vikings and French, Spanish, and even English travelers came before them. Other Europeans in settlements like Roanoke and Jamestown came for economic opportunities, not with the intent to stay like the pilgrims.

What also set the Mayflower saints apart from others who had earlier crossed the Atlantic Ocean was they migrated for religious freedom. They felt ordained by God to build a city on a hill to be a beacon of light for Christians everywhere. But it wasn't all brotherly love.

The Mayflower landed in Massachusetts, 200 miles north of where they were supposed to according to the puritans' contract with King James of England and the Virginia Company. Some pilgrims argued they were no longer bound by any rules or governing body. To quell a potential mutiny, the pilgrims signed the Mayflower Compact which created laws for democratically governing themselves.⁴ Many believe this document influenced the Declaration of Independence and the US Constitution. The Mayflower Compact was essential for the Plymouth colonists enduring their first winter, which claimed half the colonists' lives due to poor shelter, starvation, and illness.

After a year, the pilgrims, with help from their Native American neighbors, were able to celebrate the providence of God with a three-day Thanksgiving celebration.⁵ Under the leadership of William Bradford and others, the Plymouth Colony flourished. Soon more settlers came and created towns which formed the beginnings of America's democratic republic.

---

2. Philbrick, *Mayflower*, 32–37.
3. Johnson, "John Howland."
4. Young, *Chronicles of the Pilgrim Fathers*, 117–24.
5. Roach, "For Pilgrims," paras. 1–10.

Biblical Insight: Religious Freedom—What Does It Mean?

by Ernest Schmidt

The pilgrims believed religious freedom was worth the risk of death as they traveled to the unknown. They had experienced the heavy hand of civil and church persecution for worshiping and serving God in the manner they were convinced the Scriptures taught, so they were ready to sacrifice everything for their religious freedom. The guide to a person's relationship with the Lord is the Bible, so the believer should follow its teaching and directives. To be refused ownership of the Bible or to be denied the right to follow it is the ultimate in deprivation. Clergy or governments are not to be the sole gatekeeper of God's word or to dictate the will of God in an individual's life. This is intolerable for one who loves God and is conscience-bound to honor him. So, like pilgrims the believer will risk everything to freely worship God.

A critical question needs to be considered: Is religious freedom for everyone, including those we believe are in radical error? This needs to be addressed, because some who came to America for religious liberty actually persecuted others who did not hold their same convictions. While this seems contradictory in the extreme, it is a fact.

Religious liberty must be for all. A distinction may help. There is a difference between pluralism and religious freedom. Pluralism holds all religious beliefs to be equal, that is, there is no absolute truth intended for everyone. To pluralists, statements like "I am the way, the truth, and the life. No one comes to the Father except through me" (John 14:6) are invalid.

How then can there be religious freedom in a pluralistic society if we believe in absolute truth? Religious liberty allows false beliefs, but does not consider all of them accurate. It is tolerated but does not need to be accepted or promoted. That does sound contradictory, but it is biblically sound. According to the New Testament, a relationship to God is not forced upon an individual by government or a church.

Establishing the right relationship with the Lord requires a free-will decision. "But as many as received Him, to them He gave the right to become children of God, to those who believe in His name" (John 1:12). "For God so loved the world that He gave His only begotten Son, that whoever believes in Him should not perish but have everlasting life" (John 3:16). Each individual must be personally responsible in their relationship with the Lord.

A nation or church may make people conform, but they cannot force a genuine spiritual decision. A law that requires people to conform to state-approved church/worship, even if it is theologically accurate does not replace one's personal responsibility to believe.

The basis for all this is that religious liberty is built into the fabric of mankind. It is not a matter that is endorsed by government. As the Declaration of Independence states, "We hold these truths to be self-evident, that all men are created equal, that they are endowed by their creator with certain inalienable rights, that among these are life, liberty, and the pursuit of happiness . . ."

If government gives it, it can easily be removed. If God is the author of religious liberty, it is a fact that cannot be altered. Praise the Lord for religious freedom. Enjoy it and do all you can to assure it is provided for all.

3

The Great Awakening

1730–60

THE GREAT AWAKENING WAS a Protestant religious revival in Great Britain and its thirteen American colonies from the 1730s through the 1760s.[1] Over 100 years had passed since the Mayflower arrived in America with puritans seeking religious freedom. These New England puritans required that church members undergo a conversion experience that they could describe publicly.

As their lives and those of their descendants became more prosperous, they turned away from worshiping and serving God. The pursuit of prosperity replaced piety. The American colonists became inattentive, uninterested, and bored with church services. A Halfway Covenant was offered to those who wanted to become church members but lacked a public testimony of conversion or personal relationship with Jesus Christ.[2]

The downward spiral continued in puritan (Congregationalists) and Church of England (Anglican) church membership, dropping from 40 percent of American congregations in 1760 to under 2.5 percent by 1790.[3] In many areas there was no separation between church and state. Virginia formally established the Church of England in 1619 as the official religion in the colony, and it would remain so until it was disestablished shortly after the American Revolution.[4] Local taxes paid

1. Kamensky et al., *People and a Nation*, 109.
2. Severance, "What Was the Great Awakening?," para. 4.
3. "Significance of the Great Awakening," para. 2.
4. Bell, *Empire, Religion and Revolution*, 140.

for church expenses. The official church in Virginia was controlled by the Bishop of London, who sent priests and missionaries to preside over the colonial churches.

Many felt true religion had been corrupted and manipulated by religious authorities for their personal gain and power. The Great Awakening was a rebellion against such authoritarian religious rule. Colonists increasingly rejected the belief that God's will was to be interpreted by monarchs or priests.

Enlightenment philosophical rationalism spread its influence among the educated classes further, leading colonists to abandon seeking God's guidance through prayer and studying the Bible. A number of Founding Fathers were influenced by Deism that relied on personal experiences and science rather than believing in the Bible or revelation.[5]

The deadness of churches in America was shocking to the early great revivalist ministers. One of the most famous was Jonathan Edwards, who delivered his sermon, "Sinners in the Hands of an Angry God" on July 4, 1741. Edward preached that true religion must affect the heart, not just the mind. A personal conversion from a state of sin to a "new birth" through preaching of the Holy Bible was needed. He taught that Jesus is the Son of God and the Savior of people, and a believer's life would evidence a love of God and his fellow man.[6]

Evangelical preachers during the Great Awakening "sought to include every person in conversion, regardless of gender, race, and status."[7] Throughout the North American colonies, especially in the South, the revival movement increased the number of African slaves and free blacks who were exposed and subsequently converted to Christianity. The most influential and famous evangelist of the Great Awakening was the Anglican minister George Whitefield. He was born in England and educated at Oxford. Breaking through denominational barriers, Whitefield preached that, "all who enter Heaven are Christians—believers in Christ, who have been overcome by the blood of the Lamb.[8] During his life, he made seven tours of the colonies and preached 18,000 sermons.[9]

---

5. Holmes, "Founding Fathers, Deism, and Christianity."
6. Severance, "What Was the Great Awakening?" paras 9–12.
7. Lawson and Lawson, *Race and Ethnicity in America*, 7.
8. Going, *Christian Library*, 2:489.
9. Evers, "George Whitefield."

This emphasis on a personal relationship with God opened the way for the First Great Awakening. It pulled people away from the established church. By the 1760s, Presbyterians, Baptists, and Methodists were growing rapidly, while Anglicans, Quakers, and Congregationalists were left behind.[10]

Eventually this religious movement turned into a political revolution with sentiments of self-governance. Observing the American quest for independence, William Knox, a British statesman, wrote, "Every man being thus allowed to be his own Pope, he becomes disposed to wish to become his own King."[11] John Adams gave credit to The Great Awakening as the motivation behind the American Revolutionary War. God did not work exclusively through kings or bishops, clergy or magistrates, but through people themselves.[12] The Great Awakening contributed to the colonists' belief in individualism and exceptionalism and directly planted the seeds of independence and self-governance that resulted in the American Revolution.

Biblical Insight: Ruth's Ruin to Redemption

by Ronald Ian Phillips

The Great Awakening's spiritual revival during colonial times led to America's exceptionalism. God has blessed the United States of America perhaps more than any other nation in history. Critics who see only America's past injustices, inequities, and inequalities seldom correctly identify the cause of these failures as the times when America moved away from God and toward secular humanism.

When Benjamin Franklin was the United States Ambassador to France, he often attended the Infidels' Club, a group of intellectuals who read literary masterpieces but scorned the Bible. One day Franklin read from the book of Ruth but changed the names so it would not be recognized as a book of the Bible. When be finished, they praised the book as a compassionate love story masterpiece and begged him to print it. "It is already in print," said Franklin. "It is a part of the Bible you ridicule."[13]

---

10. "Religion and the Founding."
11. Huckabee and Feazel, *Three Cs*, 11–13.
12. Gullotta, "Great Awakening."
13. Garrett, "Ruth 1:1–5," paras. 1–13.

The book of Ruth has only four chapters and a total of eighty-five verses. It was written during the time of the Judges, where the Israelites seemed to have a never-ending cycle of ruin, repentance, revival, and redemption.

Elimelech, a man of Bethlehem, along with his wife Naomi and his two sons, Mahlon and Chilion, left a famine in Judea and traveled to Moab about forty miles away but far away from God. From the heights of Bethlehem, Elimelech may have looked eastward across the Dead Sea and seen the mountains of Moab from which Moses had earlier viewed the promised land before his death (Deut 34:1–5). Like those before The Great Awakening who turned away from worshiping and serving God to pursue prosperity and self-interests, Elimelech's family left God's people and the promised land for the pagan land of Moab.

Judges 17:6 says, "In those days there was no king in Israel: every man did that which was right in his own eyes." The famine referred to in Ruth 1:1 may have been a judgment of God upon Israel for its sins. The famine gave Elimelech an opportunity to show he had faith in God, but his fear and self-reliance brought about his failure. Proverbs 14:12 tells us, "There is a way that seems right to a man, but its end is the way of death." And so Elimelech moved his family to Moab and soon died, leaving his wife and his two sons in a foreign, pagan land.

The widowed Naomi and her sons did not turn back to Bethlehem. Instead they settled in Moab, a land of idolatry, where the sons married Moabite women, Orpah and Ruth. A decade later, the sons also died (Ruth 1:4–5). Hearing the famine in Judah had ended, Naomi decided to return home.

These three destitute widows were about to take three different paths. Ruth 1:19–21 tells us Naomi became bitter in her grief and blamed God for her misfortunes and insisted her friends call her Mara, meaning "bitter," instead of Naomi, meaning "pleasant." Orpah started to leave Moab for Bethlehem but turned "back to her people and to her gods" (Ruth 1:15). Ruth faced the same desperate situation as the other widows but made the right choice. When her mother-in-law Naomi insisted she also turn back to Moab, Ruth replied: "Don't urge me to leave you or to turn back from you. Where you go I will go, and where you stay I will stay. Your people will be my people and your God my God" (Ruth 1:16 NIV).

The two women arrived in Bethlehem at the beginning of barley harvest in dire poverty. Ruth immediately went to work gleaning the fields of the godly landowner Boaz, unaware that he was a wealthy kinsman of

Elimelech. When Boaz visited the field and heard of Ruth's loyalty to his relative Naomi, he instructed his workers to leave additional grain for her.

Eventually Ruth and Boaz married and had a son, Obed, who "was the father of Jesse, father of David" (Ruth 4:17). So God had a plan for Ruth even in her darkest hour. He directed the paths of this virtuous gentile woman to give birth to a son and be included in the earthly lineage of the Redeemer, Jesus Christ (Matt 1:5–16).

The words "redeem" or "redemption" are found twenty-three times in the book of Ruth. Whether it's a nation like colonial America during The Great Awakening, or an individual like Ruth, the first steps back from ruin to redemption are when we start moving toward God. "For I know the plans I have for you," declares the Lord, "plans to prosper you and not to harm you, plans to give you hope and a future. Then you will call on me and come and pray to me, and I will listen to you. You will seek me and find me when you seek me with all your heart" (Jer 29:11–13 NKJV).

4

The Father of the United States of America
George Washington

WHEN GEORGE WASHINGTON DIED in 1799, just two years after leaving the United States presidency, he was eulogized by Harry "Light Horse" Lee, who said Washington was "First in war, first in peace, and first in the hearts of his countrymen."[1] It can be a challenge to sort the myths from the legends of the man sometimes referred to as the "Father of the United States of America."[2]

Over two centuries after his death, stories continue to circulate of his wooden teeth which were actually made out of hippopotamus bone, lead, and ivory.[3] The fictional story about Washington chopping down a cherry tree and, when confronted by his father, saying he could not tell a lie was fabricated by his biographer Parson Mason Locke Weems.[4] And George Washington did not throw a silver dollar across the Potomac River which is about a mile wide.

Most historians do agree, however, with Robert E. Lee's father Harry, that George Washington was "Pious, just, humane, temperate, and sincere; uniform, dignified, and commanding; his example was as edifying to all around him as were the effects of that example lasting."[5]

1. Grizzard, *George Washington*, 110.
2. Ferling, *Setting the World Ablaze*, 188.
3. Grizzard, *George Washington*, 103–5.
4. "'I Can't Tell a Lie, Pa,'" para. 9.
5. Ferling, *Ascent of George Washington*, 2–3.

Washington is recognized around the world as the paragon of a benevolent national founder.

George was eleven years old when his father, Augustine Washington, died, leaving him a 280-acre family farm and ten slaves. Washington had little formal education and became an apprentice surveyor by his seventeenth birthday.[6] At age sixteen, George had moved into his half-brother Lawrence's estate, called Mount Vernon on the Potomac River, just fifteen miles south of present-day Washington DC. Three years later he traveled to Barbados to find a cure for Lawrence, who was dying from tuberculosis.[7] Instead George contracted smallpox and Lawrence was dead within a year, leaving George Washington the Mt. Vernon estate.

When the French and Indian War broke out in 1754, George Washington volunteered and was the youngest lieutenant colonel in the British army. He was ambitious but lacked experience. Washington suffered a humbling defeat when he was forced to surrender a Pennsylvania outpost.[8] Later in the war he had two horses shot out from under him and a number of bullet holes in his coat from bullets that somehow missed him.[9] The lessons learned in this conflict, however, greatly prepared him for his role as the Commander-in-Chief of the Continental Army during the American Revolutionary War (1775–83).

In 1759, Washington married Martha Curtis, a very wealthy widow with two children. At the age of twenty-seven, Martha owned 17,500 acres of land and 300 slaves.[10] She and Washington did not have children together, but they were totally devoted to her children and each other.

With what was described by Ralph Waldo Emerson as the "shot heard round the world,"[11] the battles of Lexington and Concord propelled the American colonies into the American Revolutionary War and George Washington into the role of America's top military commander. His fortitude, tenacity, and leadership eventually won victories at Trenton in 1776, Yorktown in 1781, and independence for America. The American

---

6. Wood, *Empire of Liberty*, 98–99.
7. Chernow, *Washington*, 24.
8. Ferling, *Setting the World Ablaze*, 23–25.
9. "10 Things You Really Ought to Know about George Washington."
10. Fields, *Worthy Partner*, xx–xxviii.
11. Emerson, quoted in "Shot Heard Round the World."

Revolutionary War, which had lasted seven years, officially ended with the signing of the Treaty of Paris on September 3, 1783.[12]

Favoring a democratic republic, the Continental Congress thought, "Who better to become America's first President than George Washington?"[13] He was the only United States President to be elected by unanimous electoral vote in 1789 and again in 1793.

Whereas the current presidential cabinet includes sixteen members, George Washington's had just four members when he established the cabinet within the executive branch. Washington surrounded himself with incredible talent, including John Adams as Vice President, Thomas Jefferson as Secretary of State, and Alexander Hamilton as Secretary of Treasury. He set important precedents by limiting the presidency to two terms, not relying on seniority to fill Supreme Court positions, and introducing a policy of neutrality relating to foreign wars.[14]

Many admire America's founding father most for what he did not do. George Washington preserved American democracy by leaving the presidency after just two terms at a time when monarchs, despots, dictators, and politicians for life were common.[15] As he stepped down in 1796, George Washington used his thirty-two-page, handwritten farewell address to warn against long-term alliances or entanglements with foreign nations.[16]

Washington also urged his fellow Americans to avoid political party and geographical rancorous divisions. One of the Senate's most enduring traditions is the annual reading of his farewell address. With political discourse seemingly at new heights, these wise words will hopefully resonate today, not only in Washington DC, but throughout all of these United States of America.[17]

12. Wood, *Empire of Liberty*, 553–57.
13. Fisher, *Washington's Crossing*, 428–32.
14. Wood, *Empire of Liberty*, 89.
15. Ellis, *Founding Brothers*, 121–22.
16. "President George Washington's Farewell Address."
17. Terry, *How a Senate Tradition*, 1–2.

Biblical Insight: In the Face of Doubt and Uncertainty

by Seth Grotzke

We often grasp and fight for recognition, clawing at the importance that others might place upon our identity, job, or accomplishments. But even the highest praise and most sincere recognition fade. There really is only one opinion that matters and endures, and it can't be earned. It is given.

George Washington's position in history at the beginning of the independence of the United States of America places him at the headwaters of our national identity. He represents, in some way, a larger collective idea of who we are as Americans, no matter our ethnic background. Thankfully, his character is one which is worthy of honor and emulation.

In a similar way, the Scriptures repeatedly point back to the headwaters of the Jewish people. Abraham stands as the forefather, the spring from which all the Jewish people would come, culminating in the Messiah. Abraham is remembered for his faith in God, his bravery in battle, his humility in dealing with conflict, and his generosity, kindness, and hospitality (Gen 12–25). Second Chronicles 20:7 (NKJV) acknowledges the depth of God's relationship with Abraham: "Are You not our God, who drove out the inhabitants of this land before Your people Israel, and gave it to the descendants of Abraham, Your friend forever?"

But looking back at those in our national history, like George Washington, or our spiritual heritage, like Abraham, we are left to wonder: How could someone ever attain to the level of these people? Their mark is left so high; the personality is larger than life. After we see the self-control and self-sacrifice of individuals like them, we see no possibility of following their example. What enabled them to be so sure of themselves that they could do what was right even when the whole world seemed to be saying something different?

George Washington demonstrated the wisdom to be able to move forward after humiliating defeats and then to step away from leadership even when popular opinion was high. He was secure in his personal identity in the context where he was operating. He learned from history, from others, and from his own mistakes, and the fact that he was able to see himself clearly allowed him to live in a way which defied the clamoring voices around him. Although his own religious beliefs were kept very private, we do know he was not swayed merely by popular opinion, but directed by a deep-seated understanding of who he was and what was required of him.

When we look at the life of Abraham we see someone who consistently, although not flawlessly (Gen 20), lived according to his identity and purpose. He believed God's promises and left his home to look for the home God would provide (Heb 11). He was willing to lay everything he cherished on the altar as a sacrifice to God (Gen 22). He charged into battle (Gen 14). He sacrificed for others (Gen 13).

Abraham possessed what we desperately need in order to live our lives in obedience to God. Without it we risk drowning in the surging waters of popular opinion. How do you think God would describe your relationship with him? The only way we will ever be able to live a life of obedience and meaning is when our identity is secure. The extent to which an individual looks to their Creator and King for their identity and purpose will determine their ability to withstand the onslaught of personal doubt and the world's opposition.

We, too, will face humiliating defeats. There will be times of personal doubt and uncertainty. We will question God's promises and his presence. We, too, will hear the fickle voices of the crowd, shifting from ridicule to praise and back again. At times we will be encouraged to do what we believe is wrong. What passages from Scripture do you go to in order to remind yourself of what God thinks about you?

What does the example of Abraham, and others in the faith, lead us to do? James 2:23 states, "Abraham believed God, and it was credited to him as righteousness, and he was called a friend of God." Isaiah 41:8 (NKJV) confirms this everlasting friendship with God: "But you, Israel, are My servant, Jacob whom I have chosen, the descendants of Abraham My friend." It is a comfort to know that every true believer is a friend of God as we find our identity and purpose in Jesus Christ.

Jesus sees me. He knows me. He knows all I have ever done. He knows all I will ever do. And even though he knows all of that, he died for me even while I was still a sinner (Rom 5:8). My identity, acceptance, and future could not be more secure. I may boldly follow my King even though I am regularly tripped by my own sinfulness or enemies because Jesus loves me. This I know.

5

Paul Revere's Midnight Ride

IT HAD BEEN A contentious year and a half since the Boston Tea Party when eighty patriots, poorly disguised as Native Americans, boarded three British ships and dumped 342 tea chests into the harbor to protest British taxation.[1] The British monarchy decided it was time to crush the Massachusetts colonists it viewed as treasonous revolutionaries.

While King George III became more insistent that colonial America submit to England, many of the colonists were equally spoiling for a fight. They were tired of the British army roaming their streets, and the Quartering Act of 1765 that forced the colonists to provide provisions and barracks for the troops.[2] The rally cry "No taxation without representation!" grew louder with the Stamp Act of 1775, which required colonies to fund the cost of British armies in America.[3]

As night fell on the evening of April 18, 1775, the British troops were on the move. The order was given to capture the military supplies stored at Concord, Massachusetts, and arrest the rebel Sons of Liberty leaders Sam Adams and John Hancock at Lexington. As an active member of the Sons of Liberty, Paul Revere arranged for a signal of one lantern to shine from Christ Church (also known as the Old North Church in Boston) if the British were attacking by land, or two if by sea. Patriots watched

---

1. Alexander, *Samuel Adams*, 125–26.
2. Unger, *French War against America*, 43.
3. Reid, *Constitutional History*, 206.

from across the Charles River and at 10 p.m. two lanterns appeared in the church steeple.

Revere borrowed a horse and began his historic midnight ride to warn the colonists that the British Regulars were coming. Danger enveloped him as he rode at full gallop through the night. He could feel the advancing British troops on his heels and the Tories, or loyalists to the crown, surrounding him on his fifteen-mile ride northwest of Boston to Lexington.

Paul Revere could have stayed home the night of his historic midnight ride. He had many responsibilities and much more to lose than most. Sarah, his first wife, died just two years earlier, leaving him with eight children. He had remarried and was well on his way to fathering eight more children with his second wife, Rachel.[4] Revere was a prominent Boston silversmith, illustrator, dentist, and engraver. But above all, he was a patriot and willing to risk his life to warn his countrymen.

After warning many en route, Paul Revere made it to Lexington around midnight. A sentry asked that he not make so much noise. "Noise!" cried Revere, "You'll have noise enough before long. The regulars are coming out!"[5]

Hancock and Adams were warned and escaped, but as Revere rode on to Concord seven miles away, he was captured. Although he escaped within hours, it was Dr. Samuel Prescott, riding with him, who managed to make it to Concord and alert the patriots. By morning the next day the "shot heard round the world" had been fired and the American Revolutionary War had begun.

When he died at the age of eighty-three, Paul Revere was relatively unknown.[6] Then, over forty years later, Henry Wadsworth Longfellow wrote the poem "Paul Revere's Ride." Longfellow wrote that Paul Revere's cry of alarm that went through the night was a cry of defiance and not of fear.[7] This brave patriot became rightly recognized as a national hero who risked all for freedom and a new democratic republic.

---

4. Fischer, *Paul Revere's Ride*. 15.
5. "Real Story of Revere's Ride."
6. "Later Years."
7. Longfellow, "Paul Revere's Ride."

Biblical Insight: Cause for Courage

by Ernest Schmidt

We all have memories of crucial aspects in our past. For instance, I recall my wife reminding our children that there were some things worth giving one's life for, if necessary. Paul Revere demonstrated that truth whether he learned this from family or not. He believed in a cause he deemed more even important than his own safety and life. We read of him with admiration, but are we ready to follow his example in action?

We are familiar with the Bible's account of David and Goliath, but there is a detail you may not remember. David was sent by his father with a "care package" and instructions to see how his military brothers were doing (1 Sam 17:17–18). While he was there Goliath appeared with his challenge. David was shocked that no one accepted the challenge. Eliab, his oldest brother, overheard David asking about the reward for taking on Goliath. The part we may have forgotten is Eliab angrily reprimanding David for asking why no one was willing to fight the giant. David responded to his brother, "Is there not a cause?" (1 Sam 17:28–29). David then risked his life and defeated Goliath.

Both David and Paul Revere illustrate that the cause must be valid. We all know there are zealots that follow or seek to create causes that are less than valid or are actually a detriment to others' well-being. They are often careless or calloused about the concerns of, or effects on, others. They merely want to accomplish their agenda. Obviously we want to avoid that approach to life. So how do we know what is a worthy cause?

Paul the apostle gives a concrete illustration of a worthy cause. In each city he visited on his way to Jerusalem he was warned that persecution awaited him (Acts 20:22–23). His response reveals his life's purpose was more important to him than convenience, comfort, or life itself: "But none of these things move me; nor do I count my life dear to myself, so that I may finish my race with joy, and the ministry which I received from the Lord Jesus, to testify to the gospel of the grace of God" (Acts 20:24).

Paul is not showing a casual attitude toward his future, but a commitment to his passion for the Lord Jesus Christ, his plan for him, and those he influenced. Paul considered doing God's will more important than his life. His goal was to finish the race of sharing the gospel of God's grace in an effective manner. It was easy for him to say, because he lived it as written in 2 Corinthians 11:22–28.

He went through these trials because he was dedicated to the cause of Christ for the sake of others. How did it turn out? Paul's summary of his life recorded in 2 Timothy 4:7 showed he personally fulfilled his goal and cause. In Acts 20:24, Paul states he wanted to finish his race with joy. The phrase "I have finished the race" assures us he successfully accomplished the task for which he risked his life.

A question remains for us: Is there not a cause? Yes, there is. But the ultimate question is: Am I willing to dedicate my life for the cause of Christ?

6

Alexander Hamilton
Fatally Flawed Founding Father

ALEXANDER HAMILTON DEFINITELY HAD anger issues.[1] He looks so distinguished and composed on the US $10 bill. Yet, a dozen times he had squared off in a duel although shots were never exchanged.[2] Then came that fateful day in July of 1804 when the Vice President of the United States, Aaron Burr, shot Hamilton in the abdomen with a 54 caliber bullet.[3] As he lay bleeding on the rocky shore of New Jersey he may have wondered how his life could have begun and ended in such tragedy. Three years earlier, his eldest son Philip died in a duel in almost this same exact spot.[4] As a result of Philip's death, Alexander's seventeen-year-old daughter suffered a mental breakdown and never recovered.

Hamilton certainly experienced trauma in childhood which may have made him quick tempered. Alexander was born out of wedlock on the small Caribbean island of Nevis.[5] After leaving her first husband and child without a divorce, his mother moved in with James Hamilton and gave birth to Alexander and his brother.[6] Shortly afterward, Alexander's father abandoned the family. By the time Alexander was thirteen, his mother contracted yellow fever and died, leaving him orphaned. The

1. Kennedy, *Burr, Hamilton, and Jefferson*, 23.
2. Good, "That Time When Alexander Hamilton," para. 1.
3. Chernow, *Alexander Hamilton*, 558–60.
4. Roberts, *Place in History*, 135.
5. Kennedy, *Burr, Hamilton, and Jefferson*, 38–40.
6. Chernow, *Alexander Hamilton*, 8.

Hamilton brothers were briefly cared for by their cousin, but when he committed suicide the brothers were separated and Alexander was on his own at the age of fourteen.[7]

Young Hamilton's fortune seemed to change when he was taken in by a wealthy merchant and eventually sent to New York to pursue his education. His studies did not always come easy. Alexander worked hard to eventually become a talented writer and a student of mathematics. When the American Revolutionary War began in 1775, Alexander was about twenty years old and eager to join the cause. He played a vital role, both on the battlefield and as a senior aide to General George Washington. When the war ended, Hamilton was elected to the Congress of the Confederation,[8] from which he eventually resigned to practice law and later established the Bank of New York.[9]

As one of the leading advocates for a strong national government, Hamilton wrote the majority of the Federalist Paper essays.[10] The primary purpose of these essays was to explain the US Constitution. Even after the Constitution was signed on September 17, 1787, it still needed to be ratified by the states. Hamilton believed individuals and states must yield their interest to the higher authority of a federal government. Furthermore, he proposed a United States President and Senators for life, contingent upon "good behavior" and subject to removal for corruption or abuse. He also wanted to take self-government out of the Constitution and claimed only the "rich and well born" should hold power.[11] Thomas Jefferson held an opposite view and eventually drafted the United States Bill of Rights to protect individual rights.

American colonists knew what type of government they did not want under the British, but it was far from decided what they wanted as victors in the American Revolution. Monarchs and clergy in the 1600s and 1700s still told people how to behave, believe, and bow to a higher earthly power. Anti-Federalists like Jefferson rejected this collectivism, which they believed led to an authoritarian state. Jefferson thought the newfound independence in America championed inalienable individual rights to life, liberty, property, and the pursuit of happiness.

---

7. Chernow, *Alexander Hamilton*, 25–30.
8. Wood, *Empire of Liberty*, 90–91.
9. Ellis, *American Creation*, 174.
10. Chernow, *Alexander Hamilton*, 246–47.
11. Steward, *Madison's Gift*, 33.

Federalists like Hamilton believed this might lead to mob rule and unrestrained personal freedom. So Federalists favored a strong central government. Battle lines were drawn that still bring contentious debate on this topic today.

Thomas Jefferson and his anti-Federalist allies, James Madison, John Adams, and James Monroe, won the day with public support for a small-town agrarian America. But it was Hamilton's brilliance that laid the groundwork and vision for America to evolve into a modern industrial, financial, cosmopolitan, democratic republic.

Alexander Hamilton's lasting accomplishments in the formative years of the United States are almost unparalleled even for the founding fathers. As the first treasury secretary, he formed the financial system of the United States and was the guiding inspiration for Wall Street. He is remembered as the principal architect of the federal government and the two-party system. Hamilton established the US Customs Service and was the father of the US Coast Guard.[12]

His courage on the battlefield and boundless passion for the new republic led to tremendous achievements. Yet the deadly duel revealed Hamilton's fatally flaw—anger—which not only shortened his life but denied him the credit he deserves, until quite recently, as one of America's greatest Founding Fathers.

Biblical Insight: Do Not Let Anger Destroy You

by Ernest Schmidt

Alexander Hamilton reminds us that even though we make contributions to others, we can let anger destroy us and our influence. The physical effects are serious, but the relational effects are very serious. The rupture in a relationship is emotionally and spiritually debilitating.

Ephesians 4:26 tells us to "be angry and do not sin." That may seem to be a contradiction, but it is possible. The way to do that is to be angry at sin. Mark 3:5 states Jesus "looked around at them in anger." Why would the Lord Jesus give an angry look? The rest of the verse gives the answer: "being grieved by the hardness of their hearts." Calloused religious leaders knew there was a deformed man in the synagogue, but they were not concerned for him. They were seeking to trap Jesus into breaking

---

12. Howell, "Alexander Hamilton," 1–2.

man-made Sabbath regulations. Jesus responded with righteous indignation at their hypocrisy.

Consider what the Bible describes as causes for anger. Judges 9:30 illustrates how our choice of words can create anger. Proverbs 15:1 reminds us our attitude does the same. People become angry when others function contrary to the angry person's ideas (1 Sam 20:30; Luke 15:28; John 7:23). Sometimes people respond in anger to preaching because it hits too close to home (2 Chr 16:10)! The prosperity of the wicked can be an occasion for anger for those who cannot seem to get ahead, even though they are doing what is right (Ps 37:7–8). A very sobering cause of anger is the provocation of impatient or overbearing fathers (Eph 6:4).

The Bible gives insight into the remedy for anger. Proverbs 22:24 warns us to avoid an angry person, so we do not "pick up on" the attitude of anger. Since anger usually involves verbal interaction, anger can be nipped in the bud by a calm response (Judg 8:3; Prov 15:1). Colossians 3:8 instructs us to "put off all of these . . ." and lists "anger" as a sin to delete. The way to do that is to "put on the new man." The putting on refers to conversion and its results. As a believer, the ultimate solution is self-control (Prov 15:18; 16:32; 19:11). Submitting to the Holy Spirit enables us to exercise self-control (Gal 5:22–23).

If you look up all the references to anger, you will be surprised. While there are many that deal with human anger, 50 percent or more of references deal with God's anger. God's anger is not an uncontrolled outburst of impatience. The truth is he is longsuffering with people (1 Tim 1:16; 2 Pet 3:9).

The question needs to be asked: Is there a manifestation of God's anger that should cause mankind to be concerned? The answer is yes. The word which translates to "anger" also translates as "wrath" in the New Testament. John 3:36 shows us how serious God's wrath is. "He who believes in the Son has everlasting life; and he who does not believe the Son shall not see life, but the wrath of God abides on him." Because every person is a sinner, God's wrath is hovering over him/her.

God himself provided the way to remove his own wrath against us. He sent his Son to become the God/man so he would experience God's wrath on our behalf (1 Thess 1:10; 1 John 4:10). The Lord Jesus willingly suffered the penalty for our sin—the wrath of God. If we receive the Lord Jesus Christ as our substitute, we are removed from God's wrath and given eternal life (John 1:12; 3:36). Do not let anger/wrath ruin you for time or eternity.

7

It's Just a Flag

THE 1936 BERLIN OLYMPICS were the first televised Olympics and proudly featured Adolf Hitler.[1] Many remember that he stormed out of the stadium when the black American track-and-field athlete Jessie Owens won four gold medals. But there was an earlier incident that also upset the Nazi Führer.

During the opening ceremony, every nation was expected to lower their flag as they passed by Hitler and the host country of Germany, as well as give the Olympic salute, which was very similar to the Nazi *sieg heil*. The American athletes refused to follow almost all the other fifty-two nations in lowering their nation's flag. And instead of giving the Olympic salute, they placed their straw hats over their hearts.[2]

It may be just a flag, but its symbolism can be powerful. Planting a flag at a summit can mean something has been conquered whether it is done by the marines at Mount Suribachi, climbers of Mount Everest, or by construction workers when they begin work on the highest floor of a skyscraper. A white flag of truce or surrender is universally recognized. Under international law the Red Cross flag should grant noncombatant protective rights to medical personnel during war.

Flags can also inspire, as was the case of Francis Scott Key, who composed "The Star Spangled Banner" during the battle at Fort McHenry in

1. International Olympic Committee, "XIth Olympic Games—Berlin, 1936," 1–2.
2. Birchall, "100,000 Hail Hitler," 1.

1812. Many churches display the Christian flag with the red cross symbolizing Jesus' blood shed on the cross of Calvary, the blue representing the waters of baptism, and the white representing Jesus' purity.[3]

There are strictly endorsed rules for displaying flags at sea. Pirates would often display a friendly nation's flag until they were within cannon range, and then would hoist the skull and crossbones displayed on black flags known as Jolly Rogers.[4] After a warning shot, if the ship did not immediately surrender, the Jolly Rogers would be replaced with a red flag showing the pirates intended to attack and give no quarter. Since the early seventeenth century, flying certain flags at sea could mean the difference between life and death.

The American flag with thirteen stripes representing the original thirteen colonies was adopted on June 14, 1777. Almost 100 years later, the grandson of Betsy Ross claimed the Philadelphia seamstress designed the first stars and stripes, but without any corroborating evidence. It made a good story and Betsy Ross had a good run, but current historians believe there is much stronger evidence that Francis Hopkinson, a signer of the Declaration of Independence, was the United States flag's designer.[5]

The American flag has been officially modified twenty-six times since 1777.[6] The current design of fifty stars representing the fifty states was designed by a seventeen-year-old high school student for a social studies project. Anticipating Alaska and Hawaii's entry into the union, Robert Heft received just a B-minus for his fifty-star flag design.[7] His friend got an A for picking up five leaves and labeling them in a notebook.

Seeing Heft was upset with his grade, his teacher told him if his design was ever adopted she would change the grade to an A. Heft's dozens of letters and many phone calls to the White House paid off when two years later he received a call from President Eisenhower asking him to attend the official adoption of the new US flag on July 4, 1960. In the end Robert Heft received his A for his flag project and stood with President Eisenhower as the fifty-star flag was raised over the US capital.

Some people treat a flag as just a piece of fabric, but it has proven to be so much more. Flags have represented the highest and lowest

---

3. McTavish, *Theological Miscellany*, 29.
4. Johnson, *Pirates*, 250.
5. Leepson and DeMille, *Flag*, 33.
6. "Evolution of the American Flag."
7. Sielicki, "Robert G. Heft."

ideals of mankind. Flags have stood for tyranny and oppression, but they have also inspired pride and hope and brought tears to the eyes of the strongest and bravest.

Biblical Insight: The Winning Side

by Seth Grotzke

History has demonstrated the communicative power of a flag. Life and death have hung in the balance, determined by a piece of fabric flying in the wind. The invested meaning in the symbols we carry is enormous and capable of defining our path.

But what if the flag we fly, or the symbols we embrace, associates us with the losing or unpopular party? We all want to be on the winning side. We don't want to be known as the coward, or the weakling, or the loser. We want to be part of the popular group. We want our flag to be recognized. Who in their right mind would march under a symbol of weakness or defeat? There is a reason why the losing team's merchandise is marked at bargain prices after their loss. We don't want to be associated with the losers.

Paul, in his first letter to the church of Corinth, expressed this succinctly. "We preach Christ crucified, a stumbling block to Jews and folly to Gentiles" (1 Cor 1:23 ESV). He was admitting the fact that the central Christian message, the cross of Christ, was impossible for the Jews to believe and ridiculous for everyone else. The cross as your banner? Your king's death as your rallying cry? Who would ever plant that flag?

But this flag is the one which Paul flew before governors, military leaders, kings, and the emperor. He raised it high through his words and his actions. He would not lower it no matter what earthly power raged or complained because he believed the cross was the emblem of victory. He did so, not because he was mistaken, but because he realized what the cross of Christ meant for him and for all humanity.

The Roman soldiers crucified Jesus at the insistence of the Jewish leaders. He died there in full view of the masses and was placed in a borrowed tomb. Yet, three days later, beneath the vigil of the Roman guards and the religious leadership, he rose from the dead and appeared to women at the tomb, his disciples, and groups ranging from 200 to 500 individuals (1 Cor 15). He was not dead!

It was at his resurrection that the symbol of the cross moved from being the sign of defeat to the sign of victory (Acts 2:24, 32). When God raised him up it confirmed the promises (Matt 16:21). Jesus' sacrifice on our behalf was effective and sufficient. He had taken our sins and given his righteousness in return (2 Cor 5:21). The cross, once the reminder of a gruesome death, was now the megaphone for the hope we have in Christ. Not only are our sins forgiven and our relationship restored with God, but death's hold on humanity has been broken (2 Tim 1:10). There is no one in Christ who can stay dead, for death no longer has any dominion over him (Rom 6).

While the world considers the fact that Jesus was crucified to be proof of his weakness, we recognize it as the demonstration of his victory. Ironically, a symbol of death is a joke to the ones dying, but to those who are truly living it is a declaration of power. It is beneath this flag that believers around the world are able to stand against the tirades of despotic rulers, the threats of religious leaders, the abuses of oppressive governments. This cross unites us with our brothers and sisters around the world. All who gather beneath this flag gather as a blood-bought family (Gal 3:25–29).

The flags of the nations, associations, or groups reveal the identity, and often the objectives, of those they symbolize. Raising that piece of fabric over a ship, a building, or a hill taken in battle declares ownership and allegiance. Jesus has been victorious over our sin and death. The decisive blow, the death stroke, came upon the cross. And so we proudly bear it as our banner. It is our rallying cry. The cross of Christ is a symbol for our new life.

8

Lewis and Clark Expedition
The Importance of Being Prepared

FRENCH EMPEROR NAPOLEON BONAPARTE faced a new war with England. Short on funding for the war, he was forced to sell the French territory of Louisiana to the United States in 1803. The Louisiana Purchase nearly doubled the size of America and covered land from fifteen of today's fifty states.[1] President Jefferson quickly organized a mission led by Meriwether Lewis to explore and map the exotic new territory before other European countries could lay claim.

It was imperative on such a dangerous venture into the unknown for Lewis and Clark to see around corners and anticipate as much as possible. In preparation, Lewis spent time consulting maps and books from Thomas Jefferson's Monticello library, which was the world's largest on the subject of North American geography.[2] Lewis studied medicinal cures from the esteemed physician Benjamin Rush and navigation from the astronomer Andrew Ellicott.[3] Indian Peace Medals were prepared by the US mints, which were distributed to the indigenous nations they met. Still, nothing could fully prepare them for all the challenges they would encounter.

The Lewis and Clark Expedition, or Corps of Discovery, as it was known, began in St. Louis, Missouri, in May of 1804, with the goal of finding a practical route from the Mississippi River to the Pacific Ocean. The expedition's secondary goals were scientific and economic, studying plant

---

1. Bredhoff, *American Originals*, 26.
2. Jackson, *Thomas Jefferson & the Stony Mountains*, 86–87.
3. Ambrose, *Undaunted Courage*, 511.

and animal life and establishing trade with the Native American tribes they encountered. Over the next two and a half years, Captain Meriwether Lewis and his close friend, Second Lieutenant William Clark, led about four dozen men nearly 8,000 miles across the Western United States.

The Corps of Discovery brought medical supplies, mathematical instruments, presents for the Indians, camp supplies and clothing, advanced firearms and ammunition, and a traveling library. Corps members were bitten by wolves and rattlesnakes, attacked by grizzles, faced starvation, injuries, and disease. The fact that only one of the explorers died on the expedition, and that from a ruptured appendix, is a testament to the fact that they were extremely well-prepared.[4]

Jefferson and many others were mistakenly convinced the explorers might find long-extinct herds of woolly mammoths and giant lions 25 percent larger than modern lions. Lewis was asked by President Jefferson to search for mountains of valuable salt and even a race of European Welsh-speaking Indians, both nonexistent.[5]

What Lewis and Clark did encounter were over seventy Native American tribes and hundreds of plants and animals, many of which are greatly diminished or extinct today.[6] Prairie dogs, wolverines, moose, and bighorn sheep interested them, but it was the grizzly bear that left them in shock and awe. In one encounter it took ten shots, including five to the lungs, to kill the bear. Lewis and Clark witnessed a world we can only imagine today.

The Corps of Discovery documented the American Bison population, then estimated at over 60 million. Bison numbers were staggeringly reduced to just 541 by 1889.[7,8] They saw passenger pigeons before they became extinct. Passenger pigeons may have been the most numerous birds on Earth, as they often blackened the sky. One flock was described as 310 miles long and took 14 hours to pass with an estimated 3.5 billion birds.[9]

Spain felt America was encroaching on their North American territory and sent over fifty soldiers to imprison the entire Lewis and Clark expedition. Arriving in what is now central Nebraska, the Spaniards were

---

4. Peters, *Seven Trail West*, 16.
5. Andrews, "10 Little-Known Facts," 1–5.
6. Uldrich, *Into the Unknown*, 37.
7. "American Bison," paras. 1 & 12.
8. Milner, *Oxford History of the American West*, 245–49.
9. Sullivan, *Passenger Pigeon*, 210–13.

just days late from intercepting the Corps of Discovery, and Spain soon abandoned the mission.[10]

Seven months into their journey, while wintering at Fort Mandan, the captains met Toussant Charbonneau, a French-Canadian fur trapper, and his two Shoshone wives, Sacagawea and Little Otter. Charbonneau had bought the fifteen-year-old, six-months pregnant Sacagawea from the tribe that had kidnaped her as a young girl. On February 11, 1805, Sacagawea gave birth to a son. Charbonneau and Sacagawea, with her three-month-old son, joined the Corps of Discovery when the expedition resumed in April. Although much of what has been written about Sacagawea has been embellished or is fiction, she did aid the expedition as an interpreter and negotiator with indigenous leaders.[11]

Another legendary traveler with the Corps of Discovery expedition was York, Captain Clark's personal slave. He was a skilled hunter and was key to the success of the mission. On November 20, 1805, Lewis and Clark reached the Pacific Ocean and a vote was soon taken where to spend the winter. York, a black slave, and Sacagawea, a woman, were also allowed to vote. Sixty-five years would pass before the 15th Amendment to the US Constitution allowed black men to vote. One hundred fifteen years later, the 19th Amendment granted women the right to vote.

The Lewis and Clark expedition did not meet their objective of finding a continuous waterway to the Pacific Ocean. They did, however, successfully map a route that led from the upper end of the Missouri River to the Columbia River which ran to the Pacific Ocean. Lewis and Clark were the first Americans to cross the Continental Divide, and the first Americans to see Yellowstone and enter into Montana.[12] Lewis and Clark documented over 178 plants and 122 animals previously unknown to science. They established diplomatic relations and trade with at least two dozen indigenous nations from whom they learned and recorded their language and customs. Because of the Corps of Discovery's great leadership, immensely capable members, and their extensive preparation, the Lewis and Clark expedition has gone down in history as a truly remarkable feat in the face of seemingly impossible odds.

---

10. Woodger, *Lewis and Clark Expedition*, 438.
11. Clark and Edmonds, *Sacagawea*, 184.
12. Ambrose, *Undaunted Courage*, 402.

Biblical Insight: Paul's World-Impacting Expeditions

by Ernest Schmidt

It is interesting to compare the expedition of Lewis and Clark with Paul's missionary journeys. Both were well prepared, yet experienced extreme hardships. The Corps of Discovery Expedition did not fulfill its primary goal, but resulted in significant secondary benefits to America. Paul's journeys achieved his primary goals and secondary benefits for the Lord.

Paul's plans began with his conversion. At that moment he asked, "Lord, what do you want me to do?" (Acts 9:6). Three days later, the Lord summarized his future: "Go, for he is a chosen vessel of mine to bear My name before Gentiles, kings, and the children of Israel" (Acts 9:15). This was followed by a period of Paul witnessing for Christ and private instruction from the Lord.

The Holy Spirit motivated the Jews and gentiles from the church at Antioch to send Paul and Barnabas to evangelize "the utmost part of the earth" (Acts 1:8). This ultimately resulted in three missionary journeys for Paul. The Lord had informed Paul his journey would involve opposition: "For I will show him how many things he must suffer for My name's sake" (Acts 9:16).

The beginning of Paul's heartbreaking experiences during these trips occurred when John Mark, who was one of the team, left the ministry expedition at Perga (Acts 13:13). Then Paul was rejected by the Jews in both Antioch of Pisidia (Acts 13:43–46) and Iconium (Acts 14:1–2). He was stoned and left for dead in Lystra (Acts 14:19). His hardships continued in Phillipi (Acts 16:22–24) when he was beaten and put in maximum security with his feet in stocks. In Thessalonica and Berea he was met with intense opposition (Acts 17:5–10, 13–14) while in Corinth he was unjustly brought to court (Acts 18:12–16). Ephesus rejected his ministry, slandered the gospel, and a threatening public protest was held against him (Acts 19:8–10, 21–41).

Before discussing the success of Paul's primary purpose for this journey, the secondary results should be noted. To the advantage of most of the world's population, Gentiles became the focus of the spread of the gospel (Acts 13:46–48; 15:6). This in time resulted in clarification that personal application of the gospel was by grace through faith, not through ritual and law keeping (Acts 15:1–35).

Some secondary results illustrate the mighty power of the gospel. The enemies of the gospel admitted Paul's ministry had a major impact by stating, "These who have turned the world upside down have come here too" (Acts 17:6). In Ephesus, two results honor the impact of lives changed by the gospel. Believers publically burned occult books valued at 50,000 pieces of silver currency (Acts 19:18–19). The gospel was so effective that those who made idol souvenirs for the goddess Diana staged a major protest because they realized their business and the worship of Diana was in jeopardy (Acts 19:23–40).

Paul's primary goals were to see individuals converted to Christ and to start new churches. In these priority areas the journeys were a great success. Wherever Paul ministered he left behind a group of new believers. In Cyprus, Paul was instrumental in the conversion of a Roman civic leader (Acts 13:12), and in Antioch of Pisidia, many Jews, proselytes, and gentiles were also converted (Acts 13:38, 43). A multitude of Jews and Greeks were saved in Iconium (Acts 14:1), and disciples were established in Derbe (Acts 14:21).

Paul won the souls of a businesswoman and jailor in Phillipi (Acts 16:14–15, 31–34), and a multitude of Greeks and many leading women in Thessalonica (Acts 17:4). His work in Berea brought about the conversion of many Jews, and more Greeks and prominent women (Acts 17:12).

In Athens, a city official and a woman named Damaris (Acts 17:34) were saved. Many souls were won in Corinth, including the ruler of the synagogue (Acts 18:8–10). And from his time in Ephesus, the entire southwest corner of Turkey was exposed to the gospel (Acts 19:10). These conversions resulted in new churches springing up and fulfilling his goal (Acts 14:21–26; 16:1–5; 18:23; 1 Cor 1:2; 2 Cor 1:1; Gal 1:2).

You may not travel the great distances of Lewis and Clark, or encounter the endless perils that Paul encountered on his journeys, but on your personal spiritual journey you can make a major difference by sharing the gospel in the sphere of your influence.

9

The Adams Family

CONSIDERING THE INFLUENCE OF the Adams family on American history, it is remarkable that there is no monument to any of the Adams in Washington DC. In fact few schools or cities or anything else are named in their honor. Perhaps it is because the Adamses made powerful political enemies and were involved in some of the most highly contentious presidential campaigns in American history. But their legacy as patriots and their long, distinguished, and honorable career in public service is undeniable and deserves greater recognition.

The Adams family is one of four families to have had two members serve as a United States President; the others were the Harrison, Roosevelt, and Bush families. John Adams, one of America's Founding Fathers, became America's second president. His son, John Quincy Adams, was elected the sixth American president twenty-four years later. Samuel Adams was a second cousin to John and thirteen years his elder. John and Samuel Adams were instrumental in winning American independence and both signed the Declaration of Independence.

Abigail Adams was the closest advisor and wife of John Adams, as well as the mother of John Quincy Adams. John and Abigail wrote over 1,000 letters to each other in which they often discussed political matters.[1] These letters reveal that Abigail's opinions influenced her husband's decisions during the American Revolution and throughout his vice

---

1. History.com editors, "Abigail Adams Urges Husband."

presidency and presidency. She became one of the most erudite women ever to serve as First Lady.[2] Abigail Adams is now designated as the first Second Lady and second First Lady of the United States.

John Adams entered Harvard College in 1751 at the age of sixteen and soon determined he would pursue the legal profession and politics over the objections of his father who expected him to be a minister.[3] Even though John joined the Sons of Liberty during the American Revolution, he still volunteered to legally represent the nine British soldiers charged with manslaughter after the killing of five colonists in the March 1770 Boston Massacre.[4] In a surprising verdict, seven of the British soldiers were acquitted and two others avoided prison sentences.

In 1870, John Adams drafted the Massachusetts constitution, which served as a model for the United States Constitutions and Bill of Rights, itemizing individual liberties such as freedom of the press and worship.[5] This document remains the oldest written constitution still in use in the world today.[6]

The Adams cousins were greatly divided on the central issue of Federalism, which advocated a strong nationalized or federal government. John Adams was a Federalist like James Madison, Alexander Hamilton, George Washington, and John Jay. Samuel Adams feared the concentration of power and succeeded in adding amendments to the Constitution which helped lay the groundwork for the Bill of Rights. Samuel Adams advocated for states' rights and was an anti-Federalist like Thomas Jefferson and Patrick Henry.[7]

When John Adams was appointed Commissioner to France in 1778, he and his ten-year-old son, John Quincy, set sail for France on the American frigate *Boston*. During the treacherous voyage, his ship was pursued and exchanged fire with British vessels, resulting in one death and the injury of five crew members. Later, a lighting storm killed one soldier and injured nineteen others.[8]

2. Withey, *Dearest Friend*, 1–12.
3. McCullough, *John Adams*, 35.
4. McCullough, *John Adams*, 65–66.
5. McCullough, *John Adams*, 220–225.
6. Levy, *Seasoned Judgments*, 307.
7. Benton, "Samuel Adams." 1–2.
8. McCullough, *John Adams*, 186.

While in France, Adams often disagreed with fellow American diplomat Benjamin Franklin and French government officials. By April 19, 1782, the Dutch Republic formally recognized American independence and acknowledged Adams as ambassador. Three years later, Adams was appointed the first American ambassador to Great Britain.[9]

John Adams arrived back in Massachusetts with an already-impressive resume in service to his fledgling country and was ready to retire from public life. But the nation was ready to hold its first presidential election in 1788 and many supported John Adams's candidacy. At this time in American history, two votes were cast by each state's presidential electors to select the President of the United States. Until the 12th amendment to the United States Constitution was ratified in 1804, the candidate with the most electoral votes became president, while the second-place finisher became vice president.[10] Under this system, George Washington became the nation's first president on February 4, 1789, and John Adams became its first vice president. John Adams fulfilled one of the few jobs of the vice president by casting a near-all-time record twenty-nine tie-breaking votes in the US Senate, including a nay vote to keep the capital in New York.[11]

Adams felt the president should be addressed as "His Highness" or "His Majesty," which would be more dignified than the title "President" which was used by local clubs and organizations. This was not well received by the American public who had just recently rid themselves of a monarch.[12]

When George Washington announced he would not be a candidate for a third term, John Adams entered the deeply partisan struggle between the new political parties for the presidency. Like the previous two presidential elections, there was no popular election of candidates for voters to choose between in 1796.[13] The Constitution provided for the selection of electors who would then choose a president. In seven states, voters chose the presidential electors. In the remaining nine states, they were chosen by the state's legislature.[14]

9. McCullough, *John Adams*, 270–27.
10. Levinson, "Twelfth Amendment."
11. Hatfield et al., "Vice Presidents of the United States," 3.
12. Klein, "10 Things about John Adams."
13. McCullough, *John Adams*, 471.
14. Taylor, "John Adams."

John Adams the Federalist edged out Thomas Jefferson the Democratic Republican by just three electoral votes and became the second US president, making Jefferson, his political rival, his vice president. This is the only election in American history in which the president and vice president were from opposing political parties.

Adams ran and lost in a presidential bid for a second term. He returned home to his Quincy, Massachusetts home farm and was heartbroken when Abigail died of typhoid on October 28, 1818. On the 4th of July, 1826, the 50th anniversary of the signing of the Declaration of Independence, John Adams died.

John Adams lived to see his son, John Quincy Adams, become ambassador to the Netherlands, Portugal, Prussia, Russia, and England, as well as a United States senator and Secretary of State to President James Monroe.[15] John Quincy's accomplishments included acquiring Florida from Spain and drafting what became known as the Monroe Doctrine of 1823. John Quincy Adams spoke six languages and is considered one of the greatest diplomats in American history. Before his diplomatic duties, Adams would wake up at 5 a.m., go for a swim followed by a six-mile walk, then return to breakfast where he read a few chapters from his German-language Bible.

When there was no clear winner in the presidential election of 1824, John Adams saw his son chosen by the House of Representatives to become America's sixth president. After leaving the White House, John Quincy Adams served nine terms in the House of Representatives, where he campaigned against further extension of slavery. After serving seventeen years in Congress he died in the Capitol Building in 1848.[16]

The legacy of the Adams family is almost unparalleled in American history even though many of their accomplishments are not remembered or celebrated today. Their service to their country was not for personal gain or glory but a deep abiding love in the concepts of freedom and for the democratic republic they served.

---

15. U.S. Deptartment of State, "Biographies."
16. Traub, *John Quincy Adams*, 527–29.

Biblical Insight: Uncelebrated Legacy

by Ernest Schmidt

The unrecognized legacy of the Adams family is regrettable. Fortunately, it does not remove the legacy. Uncelebrated legacy is almost the norm in Christian history. While a number of believers have been recognized whom the Lord has uniquely used to impact the world, we need to honor the many behind-the-scenes believers who contributed to the success of biblical ministry. Without them church history would look much different.

Two examples are Aquila and Priscilla. Just a few verses relate their ministry, but enough is given to show a significant legacy. They are introduced in Acts 18:2–3. Paul met them after their expulsion from Rome as he served in Corinth. Providentially, they were of the same trade, resulting in Paul staying with them. Their hospitality led to a lifelong friendship and ministry partnership.

Paul mentored them by instruction and example. They observed Paul evangelize under stressful conditions (Acts 18:9–17) and saw the Lord use him in the conversion of very unlikely people (1 Cor 6:9–11).

When Paul concluded his ministry in Corinth, they accompanied him to Ephesus, where he left them to minister (Acts 18:8–21). First Corinthians 16:19 informs us the church established in Ephesus met in their house. While there they made a significant impact on Apollos. Apollos was from Alexandria, Egypt, a cultured and educational center of the Mediterranean world. He was a dynamic orator and well versed in the Hebrew Scriptures (Acts 18:24–25), but his understanding of the gospel of Christ or God's program was limited. Through the help of Aquila and Priscilla, he was able to gain more insight into God's word (Acts 18:26). Their teaching enabled him to increase in his effectiveness in ministry (Acts 18:27–28).

Romans 16:3–5 indicated the political situation changed, allowing Aquila and Priscilla to return to Rome. Again, here they opened their home as the meeting place for the church. When Paul wrote to the church in Rome, he provided insight into their maturing service for the Lord. Though they were of the same trade, Paul emphasized their work for the Lord (v. 3). They made a living by tent-making, but they lived to serve the Lord.

While the details are not given, Paul refers to Aquila and Priscilla's Christian courage (v. 4) and how they risked their lives for Paul. They followed Paul's example related in Acts 20:24, "But none of these things move me; nor do I count my life dear to myself, so that I may finish my race with joy, and the ministry which I received from the Lord Jesus, to testify to the gospel of the grace of God." Their risk created great thanksgiving from Paul and all the churches that benefited from Paul's ministry. Their act of bravery for Paul reveals how spiritually impactful a single act of service can be.

The final time we read about this godly couple is in the concluding verses of Paul's last letter recorded in Scripture (2 Tim 4:19). As Paul finishes his ministry, one of his last remembrances is of Aquila and Priscilla.

This behind-the-scenes couple left an amazing legacy. Aquila and Priscilla's expulsion from Rome led to a lifelong fellowship and shared ministry with Paul. Their home was open for the Lord's workers and a meeting place for churches. Their flexibility in the Lord's work and frequent moves were used to open new avenues of ministry. When they were called upon to risk their lives for the Lord's servant; they did so and were a blessing to Paul and a multitude of gentile believers. They are an example to all who serve without fanfare. "For God is not unjust to forget your work and labor of love which you have shown toward His name, in that you have ministered to the saints, and do minister" (Heb 6:10).

10

Go West, Young Man

THE ECONOMIC PANIC OF 1837 left many in Eastern cities unemployed, hungry, and penniless. Crime was a rapidly growing concern.[1] There was a constant danger of contracting cholera, typhoid fever, dysentery, and even smallpox. Living in large cities in the 1800s brought other challenges. Donald Miller writes in his book, *City of the Century,* that Chicago dealt with mountains of horse manure covered with billions of flies as over 10,000 dead horses a year were removed from Chicago's gutters.[2] The great Chicago fire of October 8, 1871 destroyed 17,450 buildings leaving almost 100,000 persons homeless.[3]

The West promised personal freedom and opportunities with gold to mine, plentiful land to ranch, and rich soil to farm. *New York Tribune* newspaper editor Horace Greeley wrote, or at least popularized, the mantra for America's Manifest Destiny: "Go West, young man, go West, and grow up with the country."[4] John O'Sullivan, in 1845, coined the phrase "Manifest Destiny" to state that it was God's will and the United States's fate to "overspread the continent... for the free development of our multiplying millions."[5]

1. Sides, *Blood and Thunder,* 32–33.
2. Miller, *City of the Century,* 267.
3. "Great Chicago Fire Begins," para. 1.
4. Greeley, quoted in Stephanson, *Manifest Destiny,* xi.
5. Hietala, *Manifest Design,* 255.

In 1803, during Thomas Jefferson's presidency, the Louisiana Territory was purchased from the French government, doubling the size of the United States. In 1848, a war with Mexico ended with the treaty of Guadalupe Hidalgo adding another million square miles to the United States. Five years later, parts of Arizona and New Mexico were purchased from Mexico for an additional $10 million. The current states of Oregon, Idaho, Washington, and parts of Montana and Wyoming were added to the United States when the Oregon territory was established in 1848.[6] It is no wonder that Americans looked West to what they viewed as a new promised land.

In 1832, the Monroe Doctrine was written, stating that the Western Hemisphere was closed to European countries, leading many Americans to view the Great American Plains and the West as unoccupied areas for them to freely settle. But that was far from the case. England, Spain, France, Russia, Mexico, and hundreds of Native American Indian tribes all occupied portions of this American promised land, making conflict inevitable as pioneers moved to these territories.

The peak years of western migration were 1840–75 as miners, ranchers, farmers, business owners, and their families ventured across the country to the new promised land. The majority of settlers set off from Missouri on the four-month, 2000-mile trek along the Oregon Trail and its many diverting routes.[7]

Settlers often underestimated the hardship and depravation of the arduous trip across the Great American Plains. Choosing a quicker route or less experienced leaders to guide them sometimes led to disaster for those seeking a new life out west. Many settled for a sod home and a lonesome life on the prairie, never reaching their West Coast destination. Others looked for shortcuts, like the Donner Party who in 1846 became stranded in a mountain blizzard.[8] Only forty-five of the original eighty-one people in the Donner party reached California, and some of these resorted to cannibalism to survive.[9] Approximately 10 percent overall would die, migrating west, mostly from accidents and disease.

The pioneers that set out on the Oregon Trail in the 1840s in their Conestoga wagons were tough, determined, and relentless. However

---

6. Corning, *Dictionary of Oregon History*, 110.
7. Donovan, *Terrible Glory*, 184–85.
8. Shi and Tindall, *America*, 576.
9. "Donner Party, Westward Movement."

most were oversold on what they would encounter at the end of their journey. Conflicts arose with Indians who resented the settlers' intrusion into the lands they occupied and their wholesale destruction of buffalo herds the Indians relied on to sustain their culture. Vigilante justice was common in the West, with often no government or neighbors to help in time of need. Homesteaders would soon learn the meaning of rugged individualism as they left behind schools and churches, medical help, and markets to buy food, clothing, and supplies.

The United States government greatly encouraged westward migration in 1862 with the Homestead Act, which parceled out 160 acres to individuals willing to pay a nominal filing fee and make improvements to the land. Under the Homestead Act, the government transferred approximately 270 million acres of public domain land to private citizens.[10] Approximately 10 percent of the United States was settled under the Homestead Act. The Pacific Railway Act was passed the same year, allowing settlers safer, faster travel west, and the transportation of farm products, cattle, and mining deposit back east. On May 10, 1869, the Central Pacific and Union Pacific Railroads joined rails at Promontory Summit, Utah, further uniting the country.[11]

From April 3, 1860 until October 24, 1861, the Pony Express delivered mail to over 100 hundred stations and used approximately 180 riders and 500 horses.[12] The only thing faster than the Pony Express was technology as the horseback delivery system was replaced in 1861 with the transcontinental telegraph.

Gold was discovered at Sutter's Mill in California in January of 1848. Within a year, roughly 90,000 "Forty-niners" crossed the Rockies, seeking gold. By 1855, some 300,000 people had journeyed to California as part of this gold rush.[13]

The journey of the early pioneers to their future paradise, or at least new opportunities and freedom, was not an easy one. The fortunate ones who were successful prepared themselves, chose good guides, followed the right route, and worked incredibly hard to achieve their dreams.

10. Potter and Schamel, "Homestead Act of 1862," 359–64.
11. Cooper, *Riding the Transcontinental Rails*, 11.
12. Corbett, "Pony Express," paras. 1–8.
13. "California Gold Rush."

Biblical Insight: A Mansion over a Hilltop

by David Grotzke

There are many different reasons why people would gather all they owned and head west, but most of them would boil down to the fact that they were looking for something better. This was a goal that would prove to be worth significant risk. To some, the risk would be far greater than the reward. For many, the journey west would end their lives. They had hope that there would be something better out west, and faith they could make it happen. But it was not a sure thing, only a possibility, hence the risk.

In Hebrews 11:8–16, Abraham, an Old Testament personality, was also challenged to go west. It would be a risk, but the rewards would be worth it. His faith would begin with hoping for something better. "Now faith is the substance of things hoped for, the evidence of things not seen" (Heb 11:1).

Faith begins with discontentment of things present. Whether it be the stench of manure in the streets of Chicago, or no place to grow crops. There is hope for something better in the future. A person will never exercise faith in God until he is dissatisfied with his life as it now is. Self-satisfaction will keep you from going "West, young man" and discovering "the better" God has for you.

After Abraham's desire for something better, came his awareness of something else: "The substance of things hoped for." There is land to be claimed or gold to be panned. For Abraham it was "A city which hath foundations whose builder and maker is God" (Heb 11:10).

With Abraham's desire for something better and an awareness of something better came the third element of faith—the assurance of something better: "The evidence of things not seen" (v. 1). He had the conviction that there is something better out there. The early pioneers were looking for something better, heard about the possibilities of the West, and were convinced they could make it all work out for a better future. This is a great picture of biblical Hebrews 11 faith. The difference would be the object of their faith.

Some pioneers probably had faith that their transportation could make it to their destination. Some probably had faith that their abilities would bring success. Some probably had faith in their guides, their preparation, or work ethic. Many had faith in their God to get them through. This certainly was what Abraham was counting on.

By faith, the pioneers left their roots and headed west. By faith, Abraham obeyed God and headed west. He didn't know what he would find, but he knew he needed to start. By faith, you can find a new life with God. Abraham did. He became a son of God. So can you. John 1:12 says, "But as many as received Him, to them gave He the power to become the sons of God, even to them that believe on His name."

Ask God to forgive you of your sin and save you, and he will. Romans 10:13 says, "For whosoever shall call upon the name of the Lord shall be saved." That is why Jesus died on the cross. He died for your sins and mine. When we call out to him to save us, we become a new man in Christ. Abraham was a new man with a new Master. He was called by God and received a new mission, to search for a "city" (Heb 11:10) and to seek a "country" (v. 14).

When you receive Christ as your Savior, you also receive a new mission: to bring glory to God as you search for the city of God. For Abraham it meant becoming a stranger or pilgrim in a land that wasn't his own. It meant becoming a camper, dwelling in tents and moving around. It meant becoming a worshiper of the true God, leaving the false gods of the land of Ur. For Abraham, the new mission meant becoming a forefather, and leading his family line to know and worship his God. This should become every believer's mission as well.

As a new man, with a new Master, and with a new mission, Abraham was given a new vision: a vision of the city of God in a better country (v. 16). We call this place "heaven," "rest," "eternal," "a kingdom," "new Jerusalem," "paradise," and "home." This is a place with no impurities, no disease, and no sin. This is a healthy place with no hospitals, no handicapped parking places, no wheelchairs, and no oxygen tanks. This is a place with no heart troubles, no worries, no regrets, and no tears.

Abraham "desired" that country (Heb 11:16) enough to pack up his family, trust God and head west. Where are you headed? Everything around us is as temporary as the contents of a Conestoga wagon. Don't let things dim your vision of the eternal. Keep humming the old chorus, written by Ira Stanphill, "Mansion Over the Hilltop."

11

Soapy Smith

A Master of Deception

THERE WAS PANIC IN America. Banks were collapsing. Life savings were being instantly wiped out. Farmers and small businesses could not get loans. Mortgages were being called due. Before economic downturns, economists called recessions and even depressions what they were—Panics. There were two devastating panics in the 1890s caused by a shortage of gold.[1]

The eventual three-time presidential candidate William Jennings Bryan eloquently advocated for bimetallism, or backing US currency with both gold and silver, in his "Cross of Gold" speech.[2] Of course today American currency is only backed by the "full faith and credit of the US government."[3] Exchanging Federal Reserve notes for gold ended in 1933, and exchanging silver ended in 1968.[4] Back in the late nineteenth century, paper money could only be printed if it was backed by gold, so a shortage of gold meant a shortage of money.

The Klondike gold rush not only promised to solve the gold shortage, but offered fabulous wealth to those lucky enough to strike it rich. Approximately 100,000 fortune-hunters trekked to northwestern Canada between 1896 and 1899.[5] Many of these would-be prospectors started their land journey in Skagway, the largest city in Alaska at the time.

---

1. Zinn, *People's History of the United States*, 277–81.
2. Kazin, *Godly Hero*, 61.
3. Chen, "Full Faith and Credit," para. 5.
4. Kotlikoff, "Is the United States Bankrupt?," 235–37.
5. History.Com Editors, "Klondike Gold Rush," paras. 1, 19–20.

Soapy Smith

Waiting to meet them was a con man named Soapy Smith and his gang of over 200 roughians. New arrivals were taken in by Smith and his men, who steered them to dishonest hotels, gambling dens, and fake businesses, scamming the new arrivals until they were broke.

Before the Alaskan gold rush, Jefferson Randolph, also known as "Soapy" Smith, was a well-known Texas crime boss and was eventually referred to as the "king of the frontier con men."[6] Crowds would gather on a busy street corner watching Smith carefully wrap bars of soap with different denominations of money. Conspicuously he wrapped one bar with a $100 bill for everyone to see. Then "Soapy" Smith covered all the soap bars with brown paper and inconspicuously removed all the bars wrapped in money without anyone noticing. The gullible grabbed their chance to win big buying the altered bars of soap for $1 each. He used this swindle for twenty years along with other scams to deceive the unsuspecting.[7]

But one of Soapy's most ingenious schemes was to open Skagway's first telegraph office. Homesick and anxious to reassure family members, those heading to the Klondike were charged five dollars to send their heartfelt messages to loved ones. A few days later, they paid another five dollars to receive the reply. The problem was, the telegraph wire ran out of the building and ended in the ground a few feet away. Actual telegraph lines did not reach or leave Skagway for another three years.[8]

In the end, Soapy Smith never did come clean. Just four days after the citizens of Skagway honored Soapy as the marshal of the 4th of July parade, he died in a gunfight with one of the Klondike miners he scammed.[9]

Biblical Insight: A Heartless Deceiver

by Ernest Schmidt

If you were asked to choose a word to describe Soapy Smith, what would it be? Words that come to mind might be "liar," "cruel," "conscienceless," and "merciless." Reading about him makes your blood boil, doesn't it? We immediately identify with the victims and their plight. He struck where

---

6. Robertson and Harris, *Soapy Smith*, 1.
7. Smith, *Alias Soapy Smith*, 38–51.
8. Guttman, "Soapy Smith," paras. 23–26.
9. Berton, *Klondike Fever*, 359–65.

these men were most vulnerable. Perhaps you're thinking, "I am glad something like that has never happened to me."

But someone more heartless than Soapy Smith is out to destroy you. He is much more dangerous than Smith. He has deception down pat. His current activity is often as an angel of light, but he is the Prince of Darkness. Yes, Satan is out to destroy you.

The Bible identifies him as a "murderer," "liar" (John 8:44), deceiver (2 Cor 11:3–14; Rev 12:9; 20:3), and as one who tempts (Mark 4:1–11), blinds (2 Cor 4:4), hinders (1 Thess 2:18), ensnares (2 Tim 2:26), devours (1 Pet 5:8), and slanders (Rev 12:10). He attacks where we are most vulnerable. He knows where we are weak mentally, emotionally, physically, morally, and relationally, or any combination thereof. He goes for the jugular. He promises great fulfillment in sin and disobedience to God, and makes them look legitimate. He offers quick physical and emotional fulfillment of our lusts.

Genesis 3:1–6 gives the prototypical picture of the devil's cruel and heartless deception. He begins by subtly raising doubt in God's word (v. 1), asking a question that magnifies the Lord's one negative command: to not eat from the tree of the knowledge of good and evil. Satan's question could be worded, "Am I right in assuming God will not let you eat anything from the garden?" He is hoping Eve's response will be similar to that of a child who is told he may not do what he wants, "You never let me do anything!"

Satan followed this up with a blunt denial and a tantalizing twisted truth. He claimed, "You will not die!" (Gen 3:4) even after Eve affirmed that death would be the result of eating from the forbidden fruit. To support this outright denial of God's word of warning, he offered Eve the position of having knowledge like God. Of course this was impossible, but the devil's bait was too much for Eve. She was deceived by the cruel tyrant who delighted in his gain at the expense of the soul of mankind. The result of the first deception of Satan is history, but it keeps repeating itself.

Unlike the Klondike miners, the Bible has warned you. Do not be duped by Satan. You do not want to be the victim of his deception, and you do not want to experience his destiny: "the everlasting fire prepared for the devil and his angels" (Matt 25:41).

12

Abraham Lincoln
A Cause Worth Fighting for

AT SIX-FOOT-FOUR INCHES TALL and wearing a two-foot, stove-piped hat, America's tallest president seemed to walk in rarified air above any of his contemporaries. Still today, Abraham Lincoln consistently ranks as either the greatest or second-greatest president by both historians and the general public.[1] Yet, when Lincoln entered the White House his success was far from certain with a country torn apart over slavery and states' rights. He faced the most serious crisis since George Washington seventy-two years earlier.

Two years before becoming president, Lincoln gave his famous House Divided Speech in which he quoted the words of Jesus and said: "A house divided against itself, cannot stand."[2] Lincoln went on to say, "I believe this government cannot endure, permanently, half slave and half free." Abraham Lincoln was the 16th president of the United States from 1861 until his assassination in April 1865 at the age of fifty-six. He is revered and admired because he preserved the Union through the American Civil War, abolished slavery, and strengthened the federal government.

Lincoln was born in a one-room log cabin in Kentucky, the second child of Thomas and Nancy Lincoln. Abraham's illiterate, hardworking pioneer parents were members of a Baptist church which forbade alcohol, dancing, and slavery.[3] When Abraham was seven, the Lincolns moved to

1. Rottinghaus and Vaughn, "New Ranking of U.S. Presidents."
2. Foner, *Fiery Trial*, 99–100.
3. Donald, *Lincoln*, 22–24.

Indiana. Shortly after his mother died of milk sickness his father married Sarah Johnson, a widow with three children of her own.[4] Abraham referred to his stepmother who encouraged him to read, as an "angel mother."[5] Abraham had little more than a year of school but he was an avid reader and read the Bible daily as an adult. As a young man Lincoln split wood for rail fencing and had the moniker later in life as the "Rail Splitter."[6] Young Abe was also known for his wrestling skills and storytelling.

It is not hard to understand why Abraham Lincoln had bouts of depression his whole life. Around the age of nine he was knocked unconscious when a horse kicked him in the head.[7] Around the same time, his mother, aunt, and uncle all died from drinking the milk of cows that had grazed on poisonous white snakeroot.[8] His younger brother had died in infancy, and his older sister died during childbirth. Lincoln's first love died of typhoid fever, and of the four sons that he and Mary Todd Lincoln had, only one lived to adulthood. Lincoln's wife developed emotional issues and was eventually institutionalized after his death.[9] He was clubbed on the head during a robbery in 1828, had malaria at least twice, and contracted smallpox shortly after delivering the Gettysburg Address in November 1863.[10][11] Perhaps all this adversity steeled him for what was to come.

Lincoln lost five separate elections before becoming president. Abe returned to Illinois to again practice law after serving just one term in the House of Representatives. He reentered politics when the United States Supreme Court ruled in 1858 that neither Dred Scott nor any other persons of African ancestry could claim citizenship in the United States. He was angered by this ruling and the Democrats opening up slavery in the northern part of the Louisiana Purchase.[12] He became a leader in the new Republican Party and ran for president in 1860, sweeping the North and winning. However, by the time President Lincoln was inaugurated on

4. Gienapp, *Abraham Lincoln*, 4.
5. Donald, *Lincoln*, 26–27.
6. Martinez, *Coming for to Carry Me Home*, 59.
7. Gienapp, *Abraham Lincoln*, 1–12.
8. Bartelt, *There I Grew Up*, 18, 20.
9. Gienapp, *Abraham Lincoln*, 104, 127.
10. Sotos, *Physical Lincoln Sourcebook*, 385–86.
11. Bryner, "Did Abe Lincoln Have Smallpox?," paras. 1 & 9.
12. Zarefsky, *Lincoln, Douglas, and Slavery*, 69–110.

March 4, 1861, seven southern states out of the thirty-four states in the nation had seceded and formed the new Confederate States of America.

What followed of course was the American Civil War, the deadliest war in US history. From 1861–65, brutal combat left up to 750,000 people dead, more than the number of US military deaths in all other wars combined.[13] By one estimate, the war claimed the lives of 10 percent of all Northern white men between 20 to 45 years old, and 30 percent of all Southern white men between the ages of 18 and 40.[14]

On January 1, 1863, President Lincoln issued the Emancipation Proclamation, declaring that all slaves in any state or part of a state still in rebellion against the United States "shall be then, thenceforward, and forever free."[15] Although the Emancipation Proclamation did not in and of itself free a single slave, the Union armies were now viewed as liberators. The Lincoln administration began recruiting black soldiers and sailors, mostly freed slaves (190,000 in all) by the end of the war.[16]

As the Civil War raged, Lincoln spoke at the Gettysburg battlefield cemetery on November 19, 1863. In just 272 words, and three minutes' time, the President's Address encapsulated the Union cause. Lincoln stated that the United States was "conceived in Liberty, and dedicated to the proposition that all men are created equal." He defined the war as dedicated to the principles of liberty and equality for all. He declared that the deaths of so many brave soldiers would not be in vain, that slavery would end, and the future of democracy would be assured, that "government of the people, by the people, for the people, shall not perish from the earth." The Gettysburg Address has become the most-quoted speech in American history.[17]

Lincoln would live just six days after the war effectively ended April 9, 1865, when General Robert E. Lee surrendered to General Ulysses S. Grant at the Battle of Appomattox Court House. The Confederacy collapsed, slavery was abolished, and 4 million black slaves were freed.

When Abraham Lincoln's son, Robert Todd Lincoln fell from a train station platform he felt a hand reach down and pull him to safety by his collar. His rescuer was Edwin Booth a loyal supporter of the northern

---

13. Binghamton University, "U.S. Civil War," para. 8.
14. Huddleston, *Killing Ground*, 3.
15. Klingaman, *Abraham Lincoln*, 228.
16. McPherson, *Battle Cry of Freedom*, 831–37.
17. History.com Editors, "Gettysburg Address," para. 14.

cause and of Abraham Lincoln.[18] About one year later Edwin's younger brother John Wilkes Booth, a southern sympathizer seeking revenge for the Confederate cause, assassinated the president. Abraham Lincoln was assassinated by John Wilkes Booth while attending a play at Ford's Theatre in Washington DC and died on Good Friday, April 15, 1865.[19]

Lincoln's accomplishments were far reaching. In July 1861, the US issued paper currency for the first time. The currency was known as greenbacks, because it was printed in green on the reverse side. The Revenue Acts of 1861 created the first US income tax. A system of national banks was created and a national currency established during Lincoln's presidency. In 1862, Congress created the Department of Agriculture. Because of President Lincoln's leadership in fighting for a cause he believed in, the world today remembers his greatest accomplishments of ending slavery in America and the preservation of the Union.

Biblical Insight: We Are Not the Light, Just the Reflection if We Stand Close Enough to the Source

by Ronald Ian Phillips

It's astonishing how many times Abraham Lincoln stumbled. His personal tragedies were almost Job-like. Abraham Lincoln is a shining example of persevering and steeling oneself for challenges that lay ahead.

One of the most comforting verses in the Bible is found in Jude 1:24 (NIV): "To Him who is able to keep you from stumbling and to present you before His glorious presence without fault and with great joy." What a relief to be reassured we don't have to go it alone. How uplifting it is to know our well-being is not dependent on us holding on to Christ but having him hold on to us.

There are powerful forces that will cause us to stumble or pull us down. Because we are not perfect and do not live in a sinless world, we are bound to have personal setbacks, failures, and tragedies. The farther we move away from God's will for our lives the more we stumble around in the dark. But as believers there is an all-powerful force that will lift us up and help us to walk in the light. John 8:12 says, "Then Jesus spoke to them again, saying, 'I am the light of the world. He who follows Me shall

---

18. Goff, *Robert Todd Lincoln*, 70–71.
19. Bain, *Empire Express*, 214–18.

not walk in darkness, but have the light of life.'" We are not the light, just the reflection if we stand close enough to the Source.

Unlike Abraham Lincoln, most of us will live our lives in the shadows. We may not be called upon to save the nation or emancipate those in bondage. But as faithful servants to God's purpose and mission, God can keep us from stumbling and he will direct our paths. Proverbs 3:6 tells us, "In all your ways acknowledge Him, and He shall direct your paths."

Matthew 5:44 teaches that it takes courage and conviction to stand close enough to the Savior, who is the source of light, and to be his witness: "But I say to you, love your enemies, bless those who curse you, do good to those who hate you, and pray for those who spitefully use you and persecute you." Romans 12:14 also tells us to "Bless those who persecute you; bless and do not curse." As believers we can have hope even in the darkest of times, knowing our God is with us and he is in control. "Keep yourselves in God's love as you wait for the mercy of our Lord Jesus Christ to bring you to eternal life" (Jude 1:21).

The war ended with the surrender at the Appomattox Court House, Virginia. In the aftermath of the American Civil War, peace was eventually restored and the nation healed. As we face seemingly endless strife and division in our personal lives and as a country, it would be good to surrender to God's will and move closer to the light for a brighter future. John Adams, the second President of the United States, said, "Our Constitution was made only for a moral and religious People. It is wholly inadequate to the government of any other."[20]

First John 1:7 plainly states God's plan: "But if we walk in the light as He is in the light, we have fellowship with one another, and the blood of Jesus Christ His Son cleanses us from all sin." Imagine standing in the presence of God in all His glory—faultless, blameless, and free of sin. What great joy awaits believers!

---

20. Palumbo, *Authentic Constitution*, 10.

13

The High Price of Freedom

WASIOJA, MINNESOTA WAS A bustling five-year-old town with a hotel, flour mill, and many stores when the American Civil War changed everything. The town of about 1,000 also had a seminary. Dedicated in 1858, the Wasioja Free Will Baptist Seminary had an enrollment of over 300 just prior to the Civil War.[1] The future looked bright.

But in February 1861, seven states formed the Confederate States of America by declaring their secession from the United States.[2] Then in April of that year, they attacked Fort Sumter and war began. President Abraham Lincoln called for men to enlist and support the Union cause. The seminary students and faculty in the prairie town of Wasioja heard the call and became some of the first to join. Minnesota was the first state to offer and send troops to aid the Union cause.[3]

But what would compel young men studying for the ministry to quit seminary and go off to join a war a thousand miles away? They easily could have avoided service. There was no draft at the beginning of the war and even when Union conscription began in 1863, young men could avoid service by paying a commutation fee of $300, or hiring a substitute.[4]

Yet, from the small town of Wasioja, a half a continent away from the conflict, the most unlikely of young men would join the cause. Like

1. "Seminary Park," paras. 1–3.
2. "South Secedes," 1–4.
3. Moe, *Last Full Measure*, 8.
4. Meier, "Civil War Draft Records," para. 4.

so many from across the United States, they were patriots who believed in the preservation of the Union. These were fathers, sons, and husbands who saw the inhumanity of slavery and were willing to put their lives on the line to end it.

Did they realize what a terrible price they and their loved ones would pay? They would serve in Company C with the 2nd Minnesota Regiment Volunteer Infantry and be involved in many bloody battles. Only a dozen of the original sixty-eight Wasioja Seminary young men would be alive or uninjured at the end of the war and just one of these survivors returned to Wasioja.[5] For a while the seminary continued to operate, although its enrollment had been cut in half. The school soon closed after the war ended, and the town never recovered from the great loss.

Historians describe the American Civil War as brother against brother or a house divided that, in four years of brutal combat, left over 640,000 soldiers dead.[6] This War between the States established that states' rights were in some matters to be subordinate to the national government and ended bondage for the 4 million slaves in America. The United States of America was preserved as one nation.

The young Wasioja seminary men made a sacrifice all Americans should remember, and never forget that the freedoms and strength of this great country we enjoy today came at a great price.

Biblical Insight: Freedom is not Free

by Ernest Schmidt

Other than life itself, nothing is more crucial than freedom. Those who have been enslaved would probably say that without freedom, life is hardly worth living. Though activity is restricted, the mind and will cry out for the privilege to have choice and to express their individual longings.

Our first thought concerning freedom should be thanksgiving. Usually we think of thanksgiving as an expression of gratefulness for material blessings. That is appropriate, but the greatest blessings are immaterial and spiritual.

Do not take your freedom for granted; many men and women have given time, well-being, and their lives for our freedom. The town of

---

5. Eckers, *Boys of Wasioja*, 110–30.
6. "Civil War Casualties," para. 1.

Wasioja, the seminary, and former students all paid the price for the freedom of others. Though their sufferings were especially dramatic, I doubt many of them regretted their costly sacrifice. They had the satisfaction of knowing their sacrifice led to others' freedom. I do not know of any special expression of thanks they received. I do hope you will take it upon yourself to thank those who serve or have served in the military. When I see someone with military gear or a retirement cap, I say, "Thank you for serving our country." This is met with gratitude and at times leads to conversation which can provide a brief opportunity to witness for Christ.

There is bondage worse than physical slavery. All men are slaves to sin (John 8:31–36; Rom 6:16–21) and the fear of death (Heb 2:14–15). Temporal slavery ends at death, but spiritual slavery will last for eternity. In fact, this slavery and its result intensify after death. While it is not specifically revealed, it seems one's passions and addictions will not cease. In Luke 16:24, the man in Hades still retained the desire for his thirst to be quenched. This is part of the physical (no doubt accompanied by the mental) condition there. The experience is graphically described by repeatedly using the word "torment" four times.

The price that was paid to free us from this eternal bondage is beyond earthly comprehension. In fact, when the apostle Paul refers to it he says, "Thanks be to God for his indescribable gift!" (2 Cor 9:15). The Second Person of the Trinity became the God/man. He lived a perfect life, demonstrated God's love through word and deed, and suffered horribly to set us free from sin and its penalty.

The word "redemption" in Scripture specifically describes being set free from the enslavement of sin. Mark 10:45 informs us Jesus has paid the ransom. First Peter 1:18–19 states the price was the blood of Christ shed upon the cross. Since "life of the flesh is in the blood" (Lev 17:11), we are forcefully reminded the Lord Jesus Christ gave his very life for us to be set free from sin and its eternal penalty. Have you received him as your eternal liberator? If so, when was the last time you thanked him?

14

Failure Is Not an Option

HIRAM, A SMALL, TIMID boy, was born in 1822 to hard-working and pious parents from Ohio. He disliked being called by his initials—HUG—so he went by his middle name, Ulysses. His quiet nature was mistaken by children at his school for ignorance, so they began calling him "Useless."[1]

As the oldest son, Ulysses was expected to work in his father's tannery which processed leather from animal hides. The awful smell and bloody process made Ulysses sick and he developed a lifelong aversion to seeing animals harmed or killed.[2]

At the age of sixteen, Ulysses was nominated to the United States Military Academy at West Point, but his congressman inadvertently wrote Ulysses's name with a new middle initial of "S." Other cadets called him by a new nickname of "Sam" because his new initials were now US, as in Uncle Sam.[3]

After graduating from West Point, Ulysses married, had four children, and was often separated from his family for long periods of time while on military assignment. He began drinking and after one riotous night was given the choice by his commanding officer to resign or be

---

1. Waugh, "Ulysses S. Grant," paras. 1 & 2.
2. Brands, *Man Who Saved the Union*, 8.
3. White, *American Ulysses*, 30.

court-martialed.[4] Ulysses resigned and spent the next seven years in one failed business venture after another.[5]

With nowhere else to go, Ulysses rejoined the army which needed experienced officers for the Union cause in the American Civil War. A lifetime of failure had taught him perseverance and tenacity. Ulysses S. Grant was quickly noticed and eventually promoted by President Abraham Lincoln, who was looking for a general willing to fight and win battles. One of General Grant's famous quotes was, "In every battle there comes a time when both sides consider themselves beaten; then he who continues the attack wins."[6]

After a stunning victory and the surrender of 15,000 Confederates at Fort Donelson in 1862, he was given a new nickname of "Unconditional Surrender" Grant.[7] Subsequent victories and General Lee's surrender at Appomattox, Virginia made U.S. Grant a national hero, eventually propelling him to the presidency and the White House.

Elected president for two terms, Grant's administration is sadly remembered for its many scandals and a devastating economic depression. Some historians attribute this corruption and failed economic system to a larger, national moral decline.[8] The collapse of local and state governments and economies after the war and the vast fortunes accumulated at the beginning of the Industrial Revolution, sometimes by unscrupulous means, led to this moral decay.

Grant gave new meaning to the spoil system and nepotism by appointing an estimated forty relatives to various government jobs. President Grant surrounded himself with former military friends and family who betrayed his trust in them.[9] Although Grant himself was honest, these scandals tarnished his reputation.

Failing to receive the Republican presidential nomination for a third term in 1880, Grant attempted another business venture that failed and left him destitute. True to form, however, U.S. Grant persevered even though he was dying of throat cancer, and, with the help of Mark Twain, the former president wrote his memoirs. Finishing the book just days

---

4. Chernow, *Grant*, 84–85.
5. Smith, *Grant*, 82–97.
6. Kohler, *Gettysburg*, ch. 6.
7. Brands, *Man Who Saved the Union*, 164–65.
8. Nevins, *Emergence of Modern America*, 178–202.
9. "Grant Administration Scandals."

before dying, it became a bestseller and provided his family with much-needed financial security.

Some remember Ulysses S. Grant as a first-rate general and a third-rate politician,[10] but all should remember how he conquered adversity and failure with exceptional courage, tenacity, and perseverance.

Biblical Insight: Perseverance through Failure and Great Responsibilities

by Seth Grotzke

Ulysses S. Grant is one of many leaders throughout the history of mankind to conquer in the midst of adversity. The beginning of the book of Joshua details the transition of leadership between two of history's most successful and influential leaders. Moses had stood before the most powerful man of his time and had walked away the victor. Moses had stood on the mountain of God and received the law. Moses had spoken with the Creator.

But now Moses was dead and a new man was needed to lead. Joshua, the man who had watched the mighty hand of God rest upon Moses, would now be responsible for the entire nation. It is only when we recognize the crushing weight of leadership about to be placed on Moses' successor that the wording in the first chapter of Joshua hits us with its full force. Four times it is written, "be strong and courageous." The same commandment is given three times from the mouth of the Lord himself (Josh 1:6–9) and then once from the tribes of Israel (Josh 1:18).

Joshua was about to command a massive group of people who had been wandering in the desert for forty years. This group was not a military nation but a disheveled pack of former slaves prone to murmur and complain, ready to sacrifice their leader for fresh water and a different menu. Yet these were God's people through whom he would reveal himself to the nations, and Joshua was the man God had chosen to lead them.

As we read the Lord's words to Joshua, we can imagine how Joshua was taking the news of his new responsibility. "Be strong and courageous . . . be strong and very courageous . . . be strong and courageous." The God who knows men's hearts obviously had seen Joshua's and knew

---

10. Wallace, *Character*, 171.

what Joshua was lacking. But where would this strength and courage come from? How would God give what he had commanded?

Three key phrases highlight how God would give this new leader the strength and courage necessary to fulfill his divinely given role. First, the Lord reminded Joshua he would fulfill his promises (Josh 1:3). Second, the Lord would make their way prosperous and successful as they followed his word (Josh 1:8). And third, the Lord would always be with him (Josh 1:5-9).

Joshua needed each of these assurances because he not only recognized the greatness of the task, but also his frailty. All he needed to do to remind himself of his desperate plight was to look back upon the life of Israel's national hero, Moses. Although Moses had stood before Pharaoh, he had also fled from Egypt as a convict (Exod 2). Although he had received the law, he had broken it by dishonoring the Lord (Num 20). Although Moses had spoken with the Creator, he had also doubted him (Exod 3). Yet the Lord was with Moses. God had never left him nor forsaken him, regardless of how many times Moses had failed (Josh 1:5). This same God would be with Joshua.

Our lives often look and feel like the lives of Joshua, Moses, and Ulysses S. Grant—full of resounding defeats and failures with staccato bursts of growth and victory. Physically, emotionally, and spiritually we can sympathize with a man who failed in many, many areas, for that is where we often find ourselves. However, Scripture speaks of the just man who falls seven times and rises again (Prov 24:16). In our culture we often attribute the ability to rise again to an individual's own strength and determination. However as we reflect on our personal inabilities, we see that the courage to confront adversity and the ability to rise again is a gift from God.

At times we will fail in our pursuits. At times we will fail our friends and family. At times we will fail our God. Yet while we are sure to see failure, our heavenly Father will never fail us. He is present with us. It is this assurance and his great grace which encourages and enables us to rise again.

15

The Gilded Age
Exceptionally Good, Exceptionally Bad

A BEAUTIFUL BIRD INSIDE a gold-painted or gilded cage might look amazing from the outside, but for the bird, it's still a prison. America's Gilded Age was a period of economic growth, new inventions, and industrialization from after the Civil War until 1900. But the wealth, privilege, and opulent lifestyle of the few was often overshadowed by the huddled masses living in grinding poverty of this time.

Economic growth in the United States during the Gilded Age was astounding as the economy nearly doubled in size.[1] The Second Industrial Revolution was in full swing during the Gilded Age. Americans saw skyscrapers for the first time, or electric lights in their homes, or the assembly-line production at work. It was an exciting time of inventions like the telephone, automobile, phonograph, Kodak camera, and the record player.

Some revered affluent industrialists and financiers like John D. Rockefeller, J. P. Morgan, Cornelius Vanderbilt, and Andrew Carnegie. These men, who built the core of the American industrial revolution, flourished in unregulated laissez-faire capitalism. Admirers called them "Captains of Industry."[2] Their acts of philanthropy were impressive. Andrew Carnegie donated over 90 percent of his wealth; much of it going to

---

1. Census Bulletin, "Census of Population and Housing, 1890."
2. Perry and Smith, *Gilded Age & Progressive Era*, 308.

public libraries.³ The wealthiest man ever in American history, John D. Rockefeller, donated over half of his entire net worth.⁴

Beneath the glittery and gilded surface, Americans witnessed the corruption of government officials while they experienced exploitation at work and felt hopeless despair daily. Critics labeled these industrial giants as "robber barons"[5] as they watched them make their fortunes by often unscrupulous business tactics at the expense of the working class.

During the Gilded Age there was an unequal distribution of wealth. The wealthiest 2 percent of Americans owned more than a third of the nation's wealth, and the wealthiest 1 percent owned 51 percent of property.[6] Some justified this stratification of the wealthy and poor by agreeing with Herbert Spencer's idea of social Darwinism and "the survival of the fittest." But most Americans rejected this belief and protested for a better society.

The vast majority of the 12 million immigrants who arrived in the United States between 1870 and 1900 lived in urban areas.[7] The sheer number of new immigrants, along with Americans moving from rural farms to the city, resulted in easily replaced, cheap labor, and overcrowded conditions in the tenements.

Working 10 to 12 hours a day, six days a week, in hazardous conditions, with low pay, led many workers to support and join labor unions. American industry had the highest rate of accidents in the world.[8] In 1889, railroads employed 704,000 men, of whom 20,000 were injured and 1,972 were killed on the job.[9] Historian Howard Zinn argues that the precarious working and living conditions for the labor class prompted the rise of populist, anarchist, and socialist movements.[10]

An example of this clash between labor and management is the Chicago Haymarket Square Riot in 1886. What began as a peaceful rally in support of workers striking for an eight-hour work day soon turned violent. An anarchist threw a bomb at policemen dispersing the protesters, resulting in the death of seven police officers. Historian Paul Avrich

---

3. Harris, "Gilded Age Revisited," 545–66.
4. Gordon, "John D. Rockefeller Sr.," paras. 1 & 18.
5. Josephson, *Robber Baron*, 1.
6. Fraser, *Age of Acquiescence*, 66.
7. "Immigration to the United States, 1851–1900," para. 1.
8. Shi and Tindall, *America*, 590.
9. Licht, *Working for the Railroad*, 190–91.
10. Zinn, *People's History of the United States*, 258.

maintains that the police fired on the fleeing demonstrators, reloaded, and then fired again, killing four and wounding as many as seventy people.[11] Eight protesters were eventually convicted of conspiracy and four were hanged.

The shortcomings of the Gilded Age that denied the American dream of upward mobility through hard work, education, and sacrifice saw improvement during the Progressive Era (1896–1916). During this new period of civic reform, the problems caused by industrialization, urbanization, immigration, and political corruption were addressed.

Biblical Insight: Almost Persuaded

by Ronald Ian Phillips

If someone took a cursory glance at the Gilded Age, it would be understandable why they would long for these "good old days." But these good old days were only good for a privileged few. Humans often look back with nostalgia, only seeing the glitz and glamour of another place and time. When the present seems hopeless and the future seems bleak, it's natural to long for the past.

Charles Spurgeon, perhaps the most popular preacher during America's Gilded Age, preached on this subject. He is known today as the "Prince of Preachers."[12] At 15, he walked into a church and heard a message from Isaiah 45:22 (NIV), "Turn to me and be saved, all you ends of the earth; for I am God, and there is no other." The preacher looked to him and said, "Young man you look very miserable, you need to look to Jesus Christ."[13] Within four years of his conversion and baptism, Spurgeon was a full-time minister, frequently preaching to audiences numbering more than 10,000. One of his favorite verses to preach from was 2 Corinthians 6:2, which says: "In an acceptable time I have heard you, and in the day of salvation I have helped you. Behold, now is the accepted time; behold, now is the day of salvation."

In his message entitled "Now," Charles Spurgeon stressed the importance of not living in the past or future but living in the here and now. Spurgeon said;

---

11. Avrich, *Haymarket Tragedy*, 20.
12. Ray, *Marvelous Ministry*, 4 & 5.
13. "Charles H. Spurgeon," para. 6.

> I can do nothing with the days that are past, I can do nothing with the days future—yet I reach out towards them—but I cannot improve them. For practical purposes, the only time I have is that which is just now passing. Time present is the only time I may ever have. As far as I know, this day may be the end of my life's career. However much we may speculate upon the past or the future, the present moment is the only time we have, may have, or ever can have. You have a sister unsaved, pray for her now; you have a brother unconverted, write to him if you cannot speak to him, and do it now. Do you feel you have a talent? Use it now . . . we have the wisdom of Solomon on our side.[14]

The wisdom of King Solomon is legendary, as are his words on longing for days gone by. He wrote in Ecclesiastes 7:10 (NIV), "Do not say, 'Why were the old days better than these?' For it is not wise to ask such questions." Maybe Solomon was thinking about the Israelites who were in the wilderness, looking backward, as they headed to the promised land.

The Israelites were enslaved in Egypt for over 400 years. Yet when Moses led them to freedom with the providence of God, Numbers 11:4–6 (NIV) tells us they wanted to return to the good old days: "The rabble with them began to crave other food, and again the Israelites started wailing and said, if only we had meat to eat! We remember the fish we ate in Egypt at no cost—also the cucumbers, melons, leeks, onions and garlic. But now we have lost our appetite; we never see anything but this manna!"

Exodus 16:2–3 continues to show the Israelites' longing for the past:

> The whole congregation of the children of Israel murmured against Moses and Aaron in the wilderness: And the children of Israel said unto them, "Would to God we had died by the hand of the Lord in the land of Egypt, when we sat by the flesh pots, and when we did eat bread to the full; for ye have brought us forth into this wilderness, to kill this whole assembly with hunger."

The Israelites forgot their purpose on earth, which wise King Solomon made plain in Ecclesiastes 12:13: "Let us hear the conclusion of the whole matter: Fear God, and keep his commandments, for this is the whole duty of man."

Philip Paul Bliss was an American composer, conductor, and writer of hymns during the Gilded Age. He wrote many well-known hymns, including "Wonderful Words of Life" (1875); "Almost Persuaded" (1871); and the music for "It Is Well with My Soul" (1876). Bliss wrote the lyrics

---

14. Spurgeon, "Now," paras. 1–3.

to "I Will Sing of My Redeemer," one of the first songs recorded by Thomas Alva Edison.

Long after Philip Bliss died trying to extricate his wife from a burning train wreck, his haunting hymn "Almost Persuaded" continues to plead that now is the time:

> Almost persuaded now to believe;
> Almost persuaded Christ to receive;
> Seems now some soul to say, Go, Spirit, go Thy way,
> Some more convenient day on Thee I'll call.
> Oh, be persuaded! Christ never fails—
> Oh, be persuaded! His blood avails—
> Can save from every sin; Cleanse you without, within—
> Will you not let Him in? Open the door!
> Almost persuaded, harvest is past!
> Almost persuaded, doom comes at last;
> Sad, sad that bitter wail—Almost—but lost!

God is the same now as he has been in eternity past. He is as loving, as just, as merciful, as ready to save, and as ready to call you one of his children with all the countless special blessings and privileges. Jesus said, "There is joy in the presence of the angels of God over one sinner that repenteth" (Luke 15:10). Behold, now is the accepted time; behold, now is the day of salvation.

16

Thomas Nast's Sharp Pencil

THOMAS NAST DREW NASTY cartoons. At least that's what the corrupt politicians running New York City thought in the late 1870s. They feared his political cartoons so much that they offered him $100,000 to leave the country.[1] Playing along, he had them increase the bribe to $500,000 before he declined, saying he had made a promise to himself to see these cronies go to jail.

Emigrating from Germany to the United States as a six-year-old boy in 1846, Thomas Nast developed his craft at a young age. As an adult he created the Republican Party symbol of the elephant and popularized the Democratic donkey. He also drew the modern version of Santa Claus and Uncle Sam.[2] Many of his caricatures and political cartoons were published from the 1850s through the 1880s in *Harper's Weekly*.

During the American Civil War, Nast defended the preservation of the Union and showed the evils of slavery in his *Harper's Weekly* sketches. President Abraham Lincoln called Nast "our best recruiting sergeant" for his drawings of the heroic sacrifices made by Union fighting men on the Southern battlefields.[3] His patriotic illustrations enthusiastically supporting the Union cause were seen by millions. Adding a career as a book illustrator to his work at *Harper's Weekly*, Nast's popularity continued to

---

1. Paine, *Thomas Nast*, 181.
2. Ritchie, *American Journalists*, 117.
3. Paine, *Thomas Nast*, 69.

soar after the American Civil War ended. Over the course of his career, he illustrated more than 110 books.[4]

New York City Hall was known as Tammany Hall and the "Boss" that controlled the mayor and finances of the city was William Tweed. The Tammany Hall Democratic political machine swindled millions of dollars by falsifying what they had paid on city construction projects. They bribed judges and government officials and rigged elections.[5] Newly arrived immigrants were low-hanging fruit for Boss Tweed and his corrupt political friends. Trapped in a large city with no job or housing, immigrants became easy prey for shysters who offered them a tenement house and a sweatshop job on the condition that they voted as they were told.

Although illiteracy was common, people recognized their political leaders in Thomas Nast's cartoons, which eventually brought about their downfall. One drawing portrayed Tweed as a vulture feeding on the bones of New York. At the height of his influence, Tweed was the third-largest landowner in New York City.[6] Boss Tweed realized he was soon to be indicted on fraud and larceny charges and fled to Spain. But cartoons are an international language. Spanish officials recognized Tweed from a Nast cartoon and extradited him back to America where he was sentenced to prison. When Tweed died in New York City's Ludlow Street Jail in 1878, every one of Nast's cartoons attacking him was found among his effects.[7]

Thomas Nast's political cartoons were instrumental in helping a number of candidates win the US presidency, including Abraham Lincoln, Ulysses S. Grant, Rutherford B. Hayes, and Grover Cleveland. Upon assuming the presidency, General Grant attributed his election to the "sword of Sheridan and the pencil of Thomas Nast."[8] Nast's drawings that ridiculed the Democrat candidate Horace Greeley helped Ulysses Grant win the presidency in 1868 and 1872. He became a close friend of President Grant, and the two families shared regular dinners until Grant's death.

Nast became nationally recognized and was in great demand as a lecturer. Unfortunately, the considerable wealth he accumulated was all lost through a series of bad investments, and by 1884 he was destitute. In 1902, Theodore Roosevelt appointed him United States Consul General

4. Caulkins, "Nast on Broadway," para. 2.
5. Hill and Adler, *Doomed by Cartoon*, 1–3.
6. Ackerman, *Boss Tweed*, 2.
7. St. Hill, "Life and Death of Thomas Nast," para. 20.
8. St. Hill, "Life and Death of Thomas Nast," para. 21.

to Ecuador. Less than one year later, at the age of sixty-two, Nast contracted yellow fever in South America and died.

Thomas Nast is considered to be the "Father of the American Cartoon"[9] because he vividly illustrated many iconic American caricatures. He did not fight in the Civil War but was instrumental to the Union's success. Nast not only believed in the American dream of personal gain through hard work but was a crusading civil reformer who improved the lives of many people. He never ran for political office but swayed presidential elections and brought corrupt politicians to justice. Nast used the talents he had to positively change the lives of his fellow citizens.

Biblical Insight: Well Done, Good and Faithful Servant

by Ronald Ian Phillips

Who would have thought a cartoonist using his talents could make such a difference in fighting corruption and injustice? What a tribute to Thomas Nast, who used his skills to sway presidential elections and influencing the outcome of the Civil War!

Discovering and wisely using our God-given talents is a common theme in the Bible. We should not underestimate the impact we can make, using our talents to honor God and to be a blessing to others. First Peter 4:10 says, "As each has received a gift, use it to serve one another, as good stewards of God's varied grace." Nast's sharp pencil was mightier than the sword. With his drawings, he courageously took on formidable enemies and brought them to justice. In doing so, Nast did a great service to his fellow Americans and his country.

Just a few days before his arrest and crucifixion, Jesus gave the parable of the talents, found in Matthew 25:14–30. Describing the kingdom of heaven, this story emphasized the need to remain vigilant and faithful until the Lord's return. Before leaving for a long time on a journey, a master entrusted his property to his servants. According to the abilities of each man, one servant received five talents, the second received two, and the third received only one.

A talent weighing sixty to eighty pounds was a way to measure gold or silver. Biblical scholars estimate a single talent was equivalent to an

---

9. "Thomas Nast," para. 1.

ordinary worker's wages for fifteen years, so even one talent was a substantial amount of money to be entrusted to a servant.

Upon the master's return he asks what they did with the money. The first and second workers doubled their money by investing their talents, and thus received the master's praise. Matthew 25:21 tells us he said, "Well done, thou good and faithful servant: thou hast been faithful over a few things, I will make thee ruler over many things: enter thou into the joy of thy lord." Note that the words were exactly the same in commending both servants. It did not matter if a servant was given five or two talents, what was praised was their faithfulness.

The first two workers realized they were servants, given a valuable gift to be held accountable for when their master returned. They were not boastful or proud of their accomplishments nor did they claim any ownership of the talents entrusted to them but gladly and profitably served their lord until his return.

Sadly this was not the case of the third servant who was given one talent. Matthew 25:24–25 (NIV) tells us he said, "So I was afraid and went out and hid your gold in the ground. See, here is what belongs to you." Worse yet, he saw his master as cruel; not a generous, gracious lord who had entrusted him with a great treasure. He didn't take joy in the promise of the master's return but instead wasted his time, his opportunities, and the master's money. Maybe he buried the money hoping his master would not return and he could claim the talent for himself. He was judged by the master as a wicked, lazy servant and his sentence, as described in Matthew 25:30, was thus: "And cast the unprofitable servant into the outer darkness. There will be weeping and gnashing of teeth."

But this parable is not really about stewardship of money. It is about using the gifts, abilities, and opportunities God entrusts us with for his glory. God highly values the gifts he gives us. First Corinthians 4:1 says, "This, then, is how you ought to regard us: as servants of Christ and as those entrusted with the mysteries God has revealed."

The application of this parable today would be to see these talents as God-given gifts such as time, money, abilities, and authority. No servant's stewardship is insignificant. Our talents are given according to the abilities of each person. We should not feel less self-worth if we lack the skills to be in the bright spotlight of public adulation or be world-class athletes, singers, or speakers. Comforting someone in despair is a service to God. Good stewardship also may be encouraging others by smiling or congratulating others on their accomplishments. Each of us has received something of great value from God, who expects us not to bury or misuse these talents.

After receiving the gift of salvation, servants of God have been entrusted and charged to use their talents in the Lord's service. Salvation is by grace alone. Practicing good stewardship is not about earning eternal life. Ephesians 2:8–9 explains, "For by grace are ye saved through faith; and that not of yourselves: it is the gift of God. Not of works, lest any man should boast." However James 2:18 tells us, "But someone will say, 'You have faith, and I have works.' Show me your faith without your works, and I will show you my faith by my works."

Good works are the consequence of salvation and the evidences of grace within us. Our faithfulness as servants demonstrates that our heart is changed and that we do not serve ourselves, but rather our Lord and Savior. First Corinthians 6:19–20 further explains, "Or do you not know that your body is the temple of the Holy Spirit who is in you, whom you have from God, and you are not your own? For you were bought at a price; therefore glorify God in your body and in your spirit, which are God's."

It does not matter if friends and admirers say flattering words, or detractors have harsh criticism when we use our talents in service for God. It does not matter if our work is unnoticed, unappreciated, or unaccepted. Only the Master's final judgement matters. Colossians 3:23 (NKIV) says, "And whatever you do, do it heartily, as to the Lord and not to men, knowing that from the Lord you will receive the reward of the inheritance; for you serve the Lord Christ." How different it will be from the verdict of our fellow men who are often finding fault, though we do our best, when we hear our Lord say, "Well done, good and faithful servant."

17

Liberty Enlightening the World

MANY COUNTRIES HAVE GIVEN the United States gifts in token of their friendship. In 1916, the Japanese gave America the cherry trees that line the tidal basin in Washington DC. China gave two giant panda bears after President Nixon's trip to China in 1972.[1] But the Statue of Liberty, the grandest of friendship gifts, was presented to the people of the United States from the people of France on July 4, 1884. France financed building the statue and shipping it to the United States for reassembly.[2]

Officially named "Liberty Enlightening the World," Lady Liberty holds a torch with her right arm and a tablet with the inscribed date of the Declaration of Independence, July 4, 1776, in her left arm. Some say the seven spikes on the crown represent the seven continents and the seven oceans of the world, signifying the worldwide concept of liberty while others say they represent the rays of the sun.[3] At her feet is a broken shackle and chains. Just twenty years after the end of slavery and the catastrophic Civil War, this gift from France reminded all Americans that they needed to keep striving to be "One nation under God, indivisible, with liberty and justice for all."

Americans paid for the pedestal and provided the building site in New York Harbor on Bedloe Island, which was renamed Liberty Island

---

1. Keyes, "Top 7 Foreign Gifts to the U.S."
2. Bell and Abrams, *In Search of Liberty*, 37.
3. Hammond, "Statue of Liberty Meaning," para. 12.

in 1956.[4] Lack of funding from wealthy patrons and government sources suspended work on the pedestal before it could be completed. But love of country and the giving spirit of the American people carried the day. Small donations from schoolchildren and other generous but less-fortunate Americans soon flooded in to pay for the pedestal's completion. The Statue of Liberty became an icon of America and the continued sacrifice of her people to lofty democratic ideals.

Only dignitaries were allowed to attend when the 305-foot copper statue was dedicated on October 28, 1886. There was almost no mention of immigrants in their speeches. None of the general public and only two females were invited to the ceremony, although suffragists did charter a boat and circle Liberty Island making speeches to advocate for women's right to vote.[5]

What began as a gift from a longstanding ally and icon of American pride and commitment to high ideals soon became a symbol of immigration around the turn of the century. A poem entitled "The New Colossus" by Emma Lazarus encapsulated America's welcoming spirit. As she wrote, "I lift my lamp beside the golden doors . . ." her words spoke to those willing to work hard to achieve a better life and share in the American dream.[6] In 1903, sixteen years after Lazarus's premature death from Hodgkin's disease at the age of thirty-eight, her sonnet was affixed to the Statue of Liberty.[7]

Gone is the opportunity to ascend to the torch since an explosion set off by World War I German saboteurs in 1916 did minor damage to the Statue of Liberty.[8] Also gone is the original torch, which was removed and replaced in 1984 due to corrosion and water damage.

From young schoolchildren to wealthy philanthropists, Americans from all walks of life who generously contributed to the Statue of Liberty felt ownership of and took pride in the sculpture. Suffragettes adopted her as their symbol. Freed slaves noted the broken chains at her feet.[9] Immigrants found hope in her promise for a new life with limitless possibilities. All this from a gesture of friendship France gave to the American

---

4. Harris, *Statue for America*, 12–13.
5. Little, "Statue of Liberty."
6. Shi and Tindall, *America*, 887.
7. Sladen, *Younger American Poets*, 434.
8. Moreno, *Statue of Liberty Encyclopedia*, 71.
9. National Park Service, "Abolition."

people. Americans still rally around Lady Liberty, who proudly stands today as a visual reminder of freedom and liberty for all.

Biblical Insight: Longing to Belong—Heaven Bound

by Seth Grotzke

"I don't belong."

Those words often come from a crushed spirit. We want to belong. We want to be part of something greater than ourselves. We want to be accepted. All around the world people are fighting for their right to belong. People who have been pushed from their home fight for a place to live. Cultural groups who have been forced to comply fight for the right to live according to their beliefs. Social groups who have been pushed to the side fight for the opportunity to be recognized. Those who accept us become family to us.

But sometimes we still don't belong. Sometimes we still feel marginalized. Overlooked. Ignored. Belittled. At the heart of our desire to belong lies a problem. No one nation, culture, or group can give us the sense of belonging that we crave. The reason is because we were created to find our sense of belonging from our Triune God. Adam and Eve belonged in the garden of Eden with their good God. But they were deceived into believing God had not offered them all they deserved. Since that time humanity has never fully belonged.

The Letter to the Hebrews gives us insight into the story of Abraham and our own desire to belong. In Hebrews 11:9–16 (ESV) we read,

> By faith he went to live in the land of promise, as in a foreign land, living in tents with Isaac and Jacob, heirs with him of the same promise. For he was looking forward to the city that has foundations, whose designer and builder is God . . . These all died in faith, not having received the things promised, but having seen them and greeted them from afar, and having acknowledged that they were strangers and exiles on the earth. For people who speak thus make it clear that they are seeking a homeland. If they had been thinking of that land from which they had gone out, they would have had opportunity to return. But as it is, they desire a better country, that is, a heavenly one. Therefore God is not ashamed to be called their God, for he has prepared for them a city.

Abraham, and the accompanying men and women of faith in chapter 11, were all looking for a home, a country, a city whose Builder and Maker is God. Their hearts' longing would be fulfilled when they entered their heavenly city. There they would belong. There they would rest. There they would be home.

As Lady Liberty stands as an invitation to the poor and oppressed, the displaced and those searching for a home, this great figure points us to a greater city. Though we may love our country, we realize we are no more than strangers and exiles here. We long to belong. The day is coming when we will.

18

Fanny Crosby

"All the Way My Savior Leads Me"

FANNY CROSBY WAS AN unlikely candidate to become one of the most influential women in American history, yet when she died in 1915, she left a remarkable legacy and was a household name. Many may remember that she wrote more than 8,000 hymns[1] with 100 million copies printed, but that is just part of her astonishing story.[2]

Just six weeks old, Fanny Crosby became ill and had mustard bandages applied to her inflamed eyes. The treatment left her permanently blind.[3] When her father died five months later, she was raised by her Christian mother and grandmother. They helped her memorize five chapters of the Bible each week. By the age of fifteen, Fanny had memorized the first five books of the Bible, the four gospels, and many other Scriptures.[4]

At the young age of twenty-three, Crosby lobbied Congress in support of education for the blind. In 1843, she became the first woman to speak to the United States Senate.[5] Later advocating for the blind, Fanny Crosby spoke to the joint houses of Congress and also met with numerous US presidents throughout her lifetime.

1. Osbeck, *Amazing Grace*, 206.
2. Hawkinson, *Character for Life*, 35.
3. Charles, "Westchester Guide," 1.
4. "Fanny Crosby," para. 5.
5. Hall, *Biography of Gospel Song*, 38.

Fanny taught for twenty-three years at the New York Institution for the Blind where she had once attended. When a cholera epidemic broke out in New York City, Crosby stayed at the NYIB to care for the sick rather than leave the city.[6] She lived much of her life with the urban poor and newly arrived immigrants in the poorest areas of New York City. During the last thirty years of her life she rededicated herself to serving the poor, and often said she would rather be remembered for her rescue mission work.

As a member of the Sixth Avenue Bible Baptist Church, Crosby wrote many hymns with her minister Robert Lowry, including "All the Way My Savior Leads Me." One of the greatest evangelists of the nineteenth century, D. L. Moody, gave worldwide recognition to her gospel songs which included: "Pass Me Not, O Gentle Savior," "Blessed Assurance Jesus Is Calling," "Praise Him! Praise Him!," "Rescue the Perishing," and "To God Be the Glory."

Crosby said, "It seemed intended by the blessed providence of God that I should be blind all my life, and I thank him for the dispensation. If perfect earthly sight were offered me tomorrow I would not accept it. I might not have sung hymns to the praise of God if I had been distracted by the beautiful and interesting things about me."[7]

Crosby often heard from those who had been saved through the message of her hymns, but we will never know from this side of Heaven if Crosby reached her goal of winning a million people to Christ.[8]

Fanny received very little compensation for all her wonderful songs and often gave what she did have to the poor. Nearly destitute by the end of her life, a fundraiser was held to help pay for her housing and food.

Crosby once said, "When I get to Heaven, the first face that shall ever gladden my sight will be that of my Savior."[9] She continues to be joined in Heaven by those led to Christ through her songs and remarkable life.

---

6. Blumhofer, *Her Heart Can See*, 198.
7. Christianity.com staff, "Fanny Crosby," para. 11.
8. Morgan, *100 Bible Verses*, 38.
9. Christianity.com staff, "Fanny Crosby," para. 1.

Biblical Insight: Is Blindness Really a Blight?

by Ernest Schmidt

Do you find yourself thinking, "I wish I was blind like Fanny Crosby?" I doubt it. If we were in her shoes, would we accept it and consider blindness an opportunity to serve the Lord? Since we are not Fanny Crosby, what should we learn from her experience?

I met a modern-day Fanny Crosby while discussing his interest in enrolling in seminary. Both he and his wife are blind. They are both content with the Lord's providence in their lives. I have never heard them complain about their lack of sight. He did well in seminary. In fact, he learned the grammar of both Hebrew and Greek, taking a year-long class for one and self-study for another. Since then, he has earned a PhD and is teaching in a well-known university, functioning as salt and light in a secular environment.

So, do we need to be blind to be used by God? No, but we need to have a God-focused attitude toward the negative experiences the Lord brings into our lives. Whether they are financial, physical, or relational, the Lord orchestrates our circumstances for specific purposes. As Romans 8:28 reminds us: "And we know that all things work together for good to those who love God, to those who are called according to His purpose."

The Bible identifies purposes for our problems. James reminds us trials are for our maturity: "My brethren, count it all joy when you fall into various trials, knowing that the testing of your faith produces patience" (Jas 1:2–3). We can rejoice (v. 2) since what we experience is not dumb luck or random chance. We are to confidently endure (v. 3) because endurance in trials has great byproducts (v. 4). Trials properly viewed make us perfect. "Perfect" does not imply perfection, but maturity. We are made complete, meaning well-rounded, spiritually. First Thessalonians 5:23, using the same word, illustrates the idea: "Now may the God of peace Himself sanctify you completely; and may your whole spirit, soul, and body be preserved blameless at the coming of our Lord Jesus Christ." The words "lacking nothing" (Jas 1:4) assure us the Lord designs our challenges to provide us with all that is necessary to live and serve as a fully equipped and balanced Christ-like believer.

So you do not have to dread what would normally be considered tragic or undesirable situations in life. The ideas of why all experiences in our life not only work for good, but for our good, continues in Romans

8:29: "For whom He foreknew, He also predestined to be conformed to the image of His Son." Capitalize on your circumstances and, along with Fanny Crosby, rejoice in how it results in Christlikeness.

19

Alexander Graham Bell
A Problem-Solver

IN LIFE THERE ARE problem-identifiers and problem-solvers. Alexander Graham Bell was an inventor, scientist, and engineer who not only identified problems but spent a lifetime solving them. One of the greatest inventions of the past 150 years is the telephone. Although in 1922 they were not the seemingly human appendages that cell phones are today, people noticed when 60,000 American and Canadian telephone operators silenced 13 million telephones. The moment of silence honored Alexander Graham Bell who had died that year on August 2.[1]

Bell was not trying to invent a means of long-distance communication, but rather a hearing device for his deaf mother and wife.[2] Bell's father and grandfather were already accomplished in phonetics, acoustics, and elocution, information he used in the early attempts to aid the deaf in learning to speak. Working with hearing-impaired students continued throughout his life, eventually inspiring him to open his Boston School of Vocal Physiology and Mechanics of Speech in 1872.[3]

Alexander Graham Bell's hearing-device research led him to invent the first practical telephone, which was patented in 1876.[4] Ironically, the

---

1. Klein, "10 Things about Alexander Graham Bell," 1–4.
2. Bruce, *Alexander Bell and the Conquest of Solitude*, 419.
3. Petrie, *Alexander Graham Bell*, 15.
4. Black, *Canadian Scientists and Inventors*, 18.

inventor did not allow a telephone in his study, as he considered it to be a disturbance to his further scientific work.[5]

Born in Scotland, he eventually moved to and became a citizen of the United States where he met one of his most famous pupils, six-year-old Helen Keller, who lost her sight and hearing at age nineteen months. He eventually referred Helen to her teacher, Anne Sullivan, who had a profound impact on Keller's life. Helen Keller dedicated her autobiography to Bell, one of her lifelong friends.[6]

Another pupil was Mabel Hubbard, who had lost her hearing from a childhood illness at the age of five. Although Mabel was ten years younger than Bell, she was to become his wife and the most important influence in his life.

Although helping his deaf wife learn to speak was the primary motivating factor in his life, attempting to solve other problems led to future, far-more-spectacular inventions by him and others using his research. This was a repeated pattern in Bell's life. A prime example is his work on translating sounds into readable patterns which helped develop computer speech recognition today.

One of the first metal detectors was another of Bell's inventions. He used the device in attempting to locate the bullet after US President James A. Garfield was shot in 1881. Alexander Bell's detector did not find the assassin's bullet, partly because the metal bed frame on which the President was lying gave false readings.[7] If Garfield's surgeons had allowed Bell to move the President to a bed not fitted with metal springs he might have survived.[8]

Tape recorders and hard-disk drives use the basic principle of impressing a magnetic field on a record which Bell researched but was unable to perfect. Two decades before the first voice radio transmission, Bell transmitted a wireless voice telephone message over a tenth of a mile. Bell considered his greatest achievement to be the photophone, which was a forerunner to fiber-optics.[9]

Even with all these remarkable achievements, the invention he is remembered most for is the telephone, and with good reason: there are now more mobile phones than there are people on the planet today!

5. MacLeod, *Alexander Graham Bell*, 19.
6. Klein, "10 Things You May Not Know about Alexander Graham Bell," para. 7.
7. Grosvenor and Morgan, *Alexander Graham Bell*, 107.
8. Bennett, *America*, 439–40.
9. Phillipson and Neilson, "Alexander Graham Bell," para. 24.

Biblical Insight: God Hears and Opens Doors

by David Grotzke

In Acts 15, Paul and Barnabas found the church in Jerusalem trying to close the door that God had opened to the gentiles. They apparently felt all of their resources and personnel should be focused on the Jews. Paul and Barnabas helped them to see that when God closes a door someplace, he still opens doors elsewhere. Alexander Graham Bell certainly recognized this and took full advantage of it.

Paul helped the council at Jerusalem to understand that the door to the gentiles was legitimate. He had to explain to them that the law had been fulfilled by Christ on the cross and that salvation was not by circumcision and keeping the law. They were trying to pour new wine into the old wineskins:

> And He spake also a parable unto them: 'No man putteth a piece of new garment upon an old; if otherwise, then both the new maketh a rent, and the piece that was taken out of the new agreeth not with the old. And no man putteth new wine into old bottles; else the new wine will burst the bottles, and be spilled, and the bottles shall perish. But new wine must be put into new bottles; and both are preserved. No man, having drunk old wine, straightway desireth new: for he saith, "The old is better."' (Luke 5:36–39)

It was as if they were stitching up the veil that was in the temple when Jesus died. "And the sun was darkened, and the veil of the temple was rent in the midst" (Luke 23:45).

God opened the door of salvation to everyone, but the legalists were trying to close it again. They wanted a gentile to become a Jew first, then he could become a Christian. One needed to first obey Moses, then he could follow Christ. One had to be a member of a certain group or religion, and then he could be saved. Paul had to show them the door that had been opened, and prepare them for new doors in the future. When a new door opens, step through it or get out of the way of those who will.

Paul and Barnabas's ministry to the gentiles was not a mistake; it was utilizing God's open door. The legalists or Judaizers in Acts 15 were trying to slam the door, and it confused the new churches. This struggle opened another door that solidified the mission of the church.

Paul had help in this defense (Acts 15:6–19) from Peter and James, the brother of Jesus: "And when there had been much disputing, Peter rose up and said unto them, 'Men and brethren, ye know how that a good while ago God made choice among us, that the gentile by my mouth should hear the Word of the gospel and believe'" (Acts 15:7). Peter spoke of the past when he described how God had opened the door for his venture into the gentile world with the gospel. Although it was not his intention to open this door, as displayed by his response to the unclean animals on the vision sheet, God had other plans. "Peter, step through the door!" (Acts 10:15).

Peter and Barnabas spoke on what was happening in the present. "Then all the multitudes kept silence, and gave audience to Barnabas and Paul, declaring what miracles and wonders God had wrought among the gentiles by them" (Acts 15:12). God was validating their open door with miracles in the presence of the gentiles. Luke calls it the "door of faith unto the gentiles" (Acts 14:27).

James then concluded their defense by focusing on the future. He agreed with Peter and the door opened to him to the gentiles, shocking the Judaizers by calling the saved gentiles "a people for His name" (Acts 15:14). That, for centuries, had been a special title used of the Jews; now this opened door made it applicable to the gentiles as well. Salvation is by grace alone and not through the keeping of the law.

The clarification of this one open door affected the mission of every biblical church from that point on. It nailed down salvation by grace alone and the conduct of each believer. It accomplished the goal of bringing unity to the early churches of that day, both Jewish and gentile congregations. This unity attracted the attention of the unbelievers who were beginning to glance through this open door.

What door has God opened for you today? If he has shut yesterday's door, look around, for he is already beginning to open another one, one that will also bring him glory. Paul discovered that when he left the church of Antioch, he was entering a whole new world of open doors. Don't settle for the comfortable; continue to use old discoveries in new ways. Keep stepping through the open doors.

"When one door closes another one opens; but we so often look so long and so regretfully upon the closed door, that we do not see the ones which open for us."[10] Alexander Graham Bell (1847–1922) Inventor, and Teacher of the Deaf.

---

10. Phillipson, "Alexander Graham Bell," para. 1.

20

P. T. Barnum
The Greatest Showman on Earth

As a young man in the late 1830s, P. T. Barnum displayed reprehensible behavior as he toured the South as a showman. Barnum is widely credited with originally saying "There's a sucker born every minute."[1] He owned and beat his slaves.[2] In 1835, at the age of twenty-five, P. T. Barnum purchased and exploited for profit, Joice Heth, a blind and almost completely paralyzed slave woman hawked as being the 161-year-old former nurse of George Washington. When she died, Barnum shamelessly sold tickets to a public autopsy of Heth which revealed she was no older than eighty years old.[3]

Later in life Barnum acknowledged mistakes made during, and expressed regrets about, his youth. Running for a United States Congressional seat as a Republican in 1867, he confessed with remorse that "I lived [in the South] myself and owned slaves. I whipped my slaves. I ought to have been whipped a thousand times for this myself."[4] As a Connecticut legislator in 1865, Barnum supported the ratification of the 13th Amendment to the United States Constitution, which abolished slavery, saying: "A human soul, 'that God has created and Christ died for,' is not to be trifled with . . . it is still an immortal spirit."[5]

1. Shapiro, *Yale Book of Quotations*, 44.
2. Beach, "Life of Barnum."
3. Reiss, *Showman and the Slave*, 2–3, 139.
4. Mansky, "P.T. Barnum Isn't the Hero," para. 20.
5. Barnum, *Life of P. T. Barnum*, 237.

Phineas Taylor Barnum was an American entrepreneur, politician, author, and showman promoting hoaxes and unusual curiosities. Barnum opened a New York City Museum, and by late 1846 it drew 400,000 visitors annually.[6] Attractions included the "Feejee" mermaid—a contrived creature with the head of a monkey and tail of a fish and the twenty-four-inch dwarf Charles Stratton, called "General Tom Thumb," whom Barnum took on tour through Europe, enjoying royal visits with the United Kingdom's Queen Victoria and Tsar Nicholas I of Russia.

With Barnum's promotional skills, Stratton became a famous and wealthy man. Following Stratton's wedding, where 10,000 guests were in attendance, "General Tom Thumb" and his bride were received by President Abraham Lincoln at the White House. Charles Stratton enjoyed a four-decade career, over which biographer Eric Lehman estimates he played 20,000 shows, performed for 50 million people, and visited two dozen countries.[7] Barnum and Stratton eventually became business partners, and when Stratton died at forty-five years old, 20,000 people attended his funeral.

In 1850, P. T. Barnum signed the European opera singer Jenny Lind and promoted her performances in America. Known as the Swedish Nightingale, Lind was an overnight sensation. From her ninety-three concerts, Barnum netted at least $500,000 (equivalent to $16 million in 2019).[8] Lind donated almost all her $350,000 in earnings to charity, in large part toward free schools in Sweden.

The Siamese Twins, Chang and Eng, already world-famous from their own tours, also appeared at Barnum's Museum in October of 1860. They had become US citizens, spoke English fluently, and voted in United States elections. Chang and Eng Bunkers married sisters and fathered twenty-one children, but toured with Barnum briefly when they needed money for their children's college education.[9]

George Hull, an atheist trying to denounce the literal interpretation of the Bible, hired a stonecutter to carve a ten-foot-tall "petrified" man he called the Cardiff Giant, buried it in a New York farmer's field, and had it unearthed a year later in 1869.[10] Some scientists and biblical schol-

---

6. Kunhardt et al., *P. T. Barnum*, 73.
7. "General Tom Thumb," para. 2.
8. Circus Ring of Fame Editors, "Phineas Taylor Barnum," para 16.
9. Orse, *Lives of Chang & Eng*, 2.
10. Kirby et al., "Cardiff Giant," 1–2.

ars were taken in by this elaborate and profitable hoax. When Barnum's attempts to buy the giant for $50,000 were rejected, he created a replica and claimed his was the real giant.[11] A year later both were revealed as fakes in court.

There were many who believed theaters were dens of sin and railed against what they considered racism and the exploitation of people with physical deformities, as well as the oddities and performances on display in P. T. Barnum's museum. He tried to change this public perception, so when his museum burned down in 1865 and again in 1868, Barnum, at the age of sixty-one, started a circus.

P. T. Barnum's circus was in business from 1871–2017. "The Greatest Show On Earth," later called The Barnum & Bailey Circus, toured the world with Jumbo the African elephant as the main attraction. Barnum claimed Jumbo's shoulder height to be 13.1 feet and his weight to be 13,558 pounds.

In 1883, just one week after the opening ceremony of the Brooklyn Bridge, 20,000 people on the bridge feared it was going to collapse. Barnum's circus animals, weighing hundreds of tons, were soon used to cross the bridge and prove it was safe. Jumbo was one of Barnum's twenty-one elephants that crossed the Brooklyn Bridge.[12]

Lacking paved American highways, Barnum moved his circus by train and it was a freight train that tragically struck and killed Jumbo the elephant. Barnum had given a substantial endowment to Tufts University leading the university to adopt Jumbo the elephant as its mascot. Tufts students are still known today as "Jumbos."

P. T. Barnum died in his sleep on April, 7, 1891. Barnum was possibly the most famous American in the world at the time of his death, and most of his critics praised him for his philanthropy, civic-mindedness, and his amazing entertainment career.[13]

Many believe Barnum's moral character changed for the better in his adult life. As a young man he owned and beat his slaves, and yet as a Connecticut legislator he supported abolishing slavery. Early in his life he exploited people with human oddities for profit, but decades later he worked to create the nation's first theatrical matinées, to encourage family time together and reduce crime. While it's difficult to get a good read

---

11. Rose, "When Giants Roamed the Earth," paras. 13 & 24.
12. Saxena, "130 Years Ago," 1–4.
13. Circus Ring of Fame Editors, "Phineas Taylor Barnum," paras. 3, 19, 25.

on the character of Phineas Taylor Barnum, this might be expected from someone known as the greatest showman on earth.

Biblical Insight: The Center of Attention

by David Grotzke

In the past, there have been great showmen and there have been great men. Seldom have they been the same. Sometimes only God can determine which men are both. In Acts 8 we meet one of these individuals. His name is Simon, but he was often referred to as "The Sorcerer." Acts 8:9–10 (KJV) tells us he "bewitched the people of Samaria, giving out that himself was some great one: to whom they all gave heed, from the least to the greatest, saying, this man is the great power of God." In other words, he was the greatest showmen in his part of earth.

As Philip the evangelist preached in Samaria, many became believers and were baptized, including Simon himself. He then continued with Philip, watching the miracles and signs that were done. When the apostles in Jerusalem heard of all the new converts in Samaria, they sent Peter and John to investigate. Realizing the conversions were legitimate, they prayed these believers would also receive the Holy Ghost. When Simon saw the visible outpouring of the Holy Ghost on these new believers, his old life seemed to have resurfaced. His pride returned and he wanted to be the center of attention, offering to buy into the greatest show in Samaria.

Peter harshly rebuked Simon and demanded he repent. Some scholars believe he repented, while others think Simon was just a showman. When we realize pride seems to be at the root of our sins we can sympathize with Simon. Peter's rebuke can be a warning when our own pride rises up and we want to be the greatest showperson on earth.

Only God knows if Phineas Taylor Barnum and Simon the Sorcerer sincerely repented and became followers of Jesus Christ, but we do know that sincere, eternal change can take place in one who calls on the name of the Lord.

Romans 10:9–10 says, "if thou shalt confess with thy mouth the Lord Jesus, and shalt believe in thy heart that God hath raised him from the dead, thou shalt be saved. For with the heart man believeth unto righteousness: and with the mouth confession is made unto salvation."

The author of the book of Romans, the apostle Paul, could have been "The Greatest Showman on Earth" during his day. He certainly had the attention of the religious world and the fear of the early church. As a young man, Saul, later called Paul, used his standing in the Jewish religion to encourage murdering and imprisoning believers in Christ. Even though Saul's name didn't immediately change to Paul, it was not a gradual change that came upon Saul, but a dramatic event that changed Saul into Paul, the apostle of Jesus Christ. The fallacy of his belief did not just dawn on him, but was illuminated by the glory of God as he traveled to Damascus and saw a light so bright it blinded him for three days. The blindness didn't just wear off; his spiritual eyes needed to be changed. His thinking could not just wear off; it had to be changed, made new, by his encounter with the risen Lord.

Paul knew what he was talking about when he said "If any man be in Christ, he is a new creature. Old things are passed away, behold all things have become new" (2 Cor 5:17). It was not just a change of mind, but a transformed heart, a transformed way of life with transformed relationships, and most importantly, a transformed standing with a holy God. Imagine changing from murderer to martyr so others would embrace the Savior!

This change is not just needed by those who beat slaves or murder Christians, but by all those who would have their sins forgiven. The blood of bulls and goats might temporarily cover a person's sin, but only the blood of Jesus, shed on the cross, can pay the price for our offense against a holy God. "All have sinned and come short of the glory of God" (Rom 3:23). And the wage of that sin is death, but the gift of God is eternal life through Jesus Christ (Rom 6:23).

When Paul met Jesus face to face, he went from the "Chiefest of sinners," the "Greatest Showman on Earth," to the "Greatest Soul-Winner on Earth." Only the Holy Spirit could bring such a change. "And ye shall receive power, after the Holy Spirit comes upon you. And ye shall be witnesses unto me both in Jerusalem, and in all Judea, and in Samaria, and unto the uttermost parts of the earth" (Acts 1:8). If he can change Saul to Paul, he can change us into the "sons of God, even to them that believe on His Name" (John 1:12).

21

The Great Flood of 1889

IN THE WAKE OF cataclysmic events the warning signs seemed hard to miss, and it's hard to understand why people ignored them. Such was the case with the Johnstown Flood, one of the worst natural disasters and greatest losses of life in American history. During a violent thunderstorm on the afternoon of May 31, 1889, following several days of heavy rain, an earthen dam holding back Lake Conemaugh gave way. Fourteen miles away and 450 feet in elevation below the dam was the unsuspecting, quiet mining town of Johnstown, Pennsylvania, with a population of 30,000 that was about to be devastated.[1]

Major structural changes had been made to the abandoned earthen dam when the South Folk Hunting & Fishing Club took possession of the lake and stocked it with expensive game fish. The club lowered the dam by three feet; removed an emergency relief system to reduce the water level when the lake became dangerously high; and when the dam sprang leaks it was patched with mud and straw.[2]

Civic leaders and others, fearing the dam was not safe, had it inspected and realized there were defects, but their warnings were dismissed. So as wealthy Pittsburgh industrialists such as Andrew Carnegie, Henry Frick, and Andrew Mellon enjoyed their private lake and mountain retreat, a calamity was waiting to happen.

1. Hutcheson, "Floods of Johnstown."
2. History.com editors, "Over 2,000 Die."

As the violent storm continued, the club management realized the dam would eventually give way. Frantic messages were sent by telegram to Johnstown but after years of false alarms the warnings were ignored. Around 3 p.m. those around the dam watched in disbelief as the earthen dam collapsed, unleashing the rising waters of a lake two miles long, one mile wide, and sixty feet deep.

A sixty-foot-high wall of water and debris traveling at 40mph, with a flow rate equaling that of the Mississippi River, destroyed everything in its path.[3] The torrent swept up rocks, trees, railroad cars, and barbed wire as it raced downstream. As the water roared down through the valley, it collected homes, barns, animals, and people, dead and alive from four small communities in its path before reaching Johnstown.[4]

Just under one hour after the South Fork Dam collapsed, the flood hit Johnstown. Some residents tried to escape to attics or run for higher ground, but the surging floodwater meant it was already too late for many. It took just ten minutes for the flood to pass through Johnstown, driving debris into the old Stone Bridge. When forty feet of debris piled up at the old Stone Bridge the floodwaters backed up creating a second flood surge. Eighty people died when this debris caught on fire turning it into a raging inferno. The fire burned for three days.[5]

A total of 2,209 died in the disaster, of which one-third were never identified.[6] It was the worst flood experienced in nineteenth-century America. Sixteen hundred homes were demolished and four square miles of downtown Johnstown were completely destroyed. One baby survived on the floor of a house as it floated seventy-five miles from Johnstown.[7]

Clara Barton and others from the American Red Cross arrived just days after the flood, initiating the organization's first major disaster relief endeavor.[8] Many club members contributed to recovery efforts, including Andrew Carnegie who built Johnstown a new library.

---

3. Perkins, "Johnstown Flood."
4. Hutcheson, "Floods of Johnstown."
5. McCullough, *Johnstown Flood*, 185.
6. "Facts about the 1889 Flood," para. 2.
7. History.com editors, "Over 2,000 die."
8. American National Red Cross, "Founder Clara Barton," paras. 1–3.

David McCullough, who wrote one of the best accounts of the Johnstown Flood, said it "was not an act of God or nature. It was brought by human failure, human shortsightedness, and selfishness."[9]

Biblical Insight: Whose Fault?

by Ernest Schmidt

It would be easy to play a blame game and assign guilt to the ones responsible for the Johnstown Flood. Even with the perspective we have over a century later, a case could probably be made for the guilt of specific individuals. But there is a greater responsibility. While not desiring to be calloused, it must be recognized that the greatest tragedy was a lack of response to warnings. Those who perished were warned.

Warnings are all around us, but we become immune to them. We tend to act as if a warning is someone crying wolf. Some warnings are more serious than others. The seriousness is measured by their impact. There are ads that make the lack of owning a product sound devastating. Some warnings are immediate and are very serious. Hopefully when we hear a tornado siren or phone alert, we take immediate action. It is wise to seek medical attention when you have persistent chest pain/heaviness.

The most serious warning you will ever receive is that which concerns your eternal destiny. It is both serious and urgent. You may be tempted to say, "I have heard this for years." The people of Ezekiel's day expressed this attitude. They said, "The vision that he sees is for many days from now, and he prophesies of times far off" (Ezek 12:27). The judgment Ezekiel prophesied did occur within a few years. Their denial did not prevent their doom.

It is popular to view the Lord Jesus as sentimental, excusing all sin in the end. Yes, he is loving, kind, and merciful, but he is also righteous and just. Thus, he must act accordingly toward sin and mankind's rejection of his provision for our forgiveness.

John 3:16 reveals the heart of the matter. We are told God expressed his love for us by sending his Son so that we "would not perish." This does not refer to the loss of our being, but the loss of our well-being. To perish is to be ruined for eternity. Other portions of Scripture refer to it as "torment" and suffering in the "lake of fire" (Luke 16:23–25, 28; Rev

---

9. Begos, "125 Years after Johnstown," para. 10.

20:14–15). The verse makes it obvious God provided the Lord Jesus' death as the way to avoid God's righteous judgment.

Since the Lord is who he is, he must judge sin because of its enormity against a perfect, holy, righteous, infinite God. He would not be God or a just God if he did not punish sin.

So, the issue is not a lack of warning. It is a matter of response. Will you put off heeding the warning, or respond and accept God's provision of deliverance? A church sign says it all: "Eternity is a long time to think about what you should have done!" Heed the Lord's warnings so you will live in joy with the Lord forever, rather than live with eternal regret.

22

Not One of the Idle Rich
John D. Rockefeller

JOHN D. ROCKEFELLER IS widely regarded as the wealthiest American of all-time, and one of the richest people in history.[1] He was America's first billionaire. Estimates of his personal fortune range from 350 to 450 billion in today's money. His company, Standard Oil, was the world's first industrial monopoly. Was he a robber baron to be vilified, and who wrongly crushed small businesses to create a ruthless monopoly? Or was Rockefeller a captain of industry to be venerated, and who paid above-average wages to his 100,000 employees, made kerosene and gasoline affordable to almost all, and became one of the world's greatest humanitarians?

One thing for certain is that John D. Rockefeller did not have an easy upbringing. It's hard to imagine a married couple having more different personalities than John's parents. His father preyed on society while his mother prayed for society. Known as "Devil Bill" by the locals, his father, William Rockefeller, was a con man and a bigamist.[2] Without any medical training, he sold elixirs to supposedly cure cancer. At the age of forty-two he married a seventeen-year-old but remained married to John's mother until her death. Earlier he had abandoned first his wife, his son John, and John's siblings, leaving them penniless.

---

1. Hargreaves, "Richest Americans in History," paras. 1–3.
2. Chernow, *Titan*, 7.

John's mother, Eliza Rockefeller, was left to raise her five children. She was a devout Baptist and impressed upon her children the importance of charity, civic responsibly, and self-control. As the oldest son, John felt the responsibility of helping support his mother and siblings. John was born again in the Erie Street Baptist Mission Church. He made a public confession of his Christian faith by his baptismal immersion and then became a church member. Rockefeller served as a Sunday school teacher and trustee and attended church services two or three times a week his entire life.[3]

Rockefeller dropped out of high school at sixteen years old and worked as an assistant bookkeeper. By the time he was twenty-five, John had entered the emerging oil business and had controlling interest in a Cleveland, Ohio refinery. At first, Rockefeller made a fortune on kerosene until Edison's electric light bulb started to replace the kerosene lamps. About the same time the kerosene market plummeted, the automobile industry skyrocketed. John established the Standard Oil Company in 1870, which within a decade controlled over 90 percent of the refineries and pipelines in America.[4] By the time he retired at fifty-eight, he was the richest person in the country.

Rockefeller was quoted as saying, "It has seemed as if I was favored and got increase because the Lord knew that I was going to turn around and give it back."[5] By the time of his death in 1937, at ninety-seven years old, he had given away some $540 million dollars, making him one of the most generous philanthropists in American history.[6]

When Rockefeller was twenty years old he contributed money to a black man in Cincinnati so he could buy his wife out of slavery. He married Laura Spelman, who shared his lifetime compassion for the African-American community. Mrs. Rockefeller became the founder and namesake of Spelman College, a college for black women in Atlanta, Georgia.[7]

In 1890, the University of Chicago was founded by Rockefeller, with contributions from the American Baptist Education Society. He contributed to medical research to eliminate hookworm, as well as malaria,

---

3. Chernow, *Titan*, 52.
4. Segall, *John D. Rockefeller*, 48–49.
5. Chernow, *Titan*, 67.
6. Gordon, "John Rockefeller Sr," para. 18.
7. Weir, *Class in America*, 713.

scarlet fever, tuberculosis, and typhus.[8] He believed God had given him a talent to make money just as others have artistic or athletic talents. His remarkable generosity toward the betterment of his fellow man is a real testimony of his faith in action.

Biblical Insight: Serving God by Serving Others

by Ronald Ian Phillips

John D. Rockefeller became one of the most respected philanthropists in history. He gave away much of his vast fortune, but also devoted his life in personal service to others. He is a shining example of Christian charity. But those that think Rockefeller was rich and could afford to be generous with his time and money might be more impressed with the wonderful story of the widow from Zarephath, as told from the biblical account in 1 Kings 17.

The story begins in the midst of a famine when the prophet Elijah is instructed by God to go to Zarephath. This is where the wicked queen Jezebel was from. Queen Jezebel and her husband, King Ahab, led the Northern Kingdom of Israel during a time of much evil in the land. They and their subjects worshiped the pagan god Baal and so infuriated God that He caused a three-and-a-half-year drought and famine to punish them. We are told, "Ahab did more to provoke the Lord, the God of Israel, to anger than all the kings of Israel who were before him" (1 Kgs 16:33).

So, Elijah goes to Zarephath and encounters the widow that the Lord had predicted would sustain him. Elijah finds her by the city gates as she gathers sticks so she can bake the last morsel of bread for herself and her son before they die. Elijah asks her to give the food to him instead!

The prophet is a total stranger to her, and they have nothing in common: neither nationality, religion, or culture. The widow was a gentile who referred to God as Elijah's God: "As the Lord thy God liveth . . ." (1 Kgs 17:12). Elijah must have wondered why God didn't send him to someone rich like Rockefeller, but instead used a desperately poor, near-death gentile widow to feed and house the prophet.

She had lost her husband, was starving, and knew within hours she and her son would be dead. She had resigned herself to their coming

---

8. Gordon, "John Rockefeller Sr."

demise and had lost all hope. And now this stranger was asking for everything she had left.

But Elijah told her to make him a small cake and not to fear because the Lord God of Israel said, "The bin of flour shall not be used up, nor shall the jar of oil run dry, until the day the Lord sends rain on the earth. So she went away and did according to the word of Elijah; and she and he and her household ate for many days" (1 Kgs 17:14–15).

But the story isn't over yet. The widow's son suddenly dies while Elijah is living in a room above her home. The prophet prayed and God brought the child back to life as recorded in 1 Kings 17:22–24:

> Then the Lord heard the voice of Elijah; and the soul of the child came back to him, and he revived. And Elijah took the child and brought him down from the upper room into the house, and gave him to his mother. And Elijah said, "See, your son lives!" Then the woman said to Elijah, "Now by this I know that you are a man of God, and that the word of the Lord in your mouth is the truth."

The widow of Zarephath's service and charity to Elijah saved her physically and spiritually. God had chosen this emaciated and broken widow to be part of something that would influence people of faith down through eternity. Jesus referred to this incident in the gospel of Luke 4:26. Her story lives on thousands of years later as a testament and example of our responsibility to help others in their time of need. God uses the charity of the richest and poorest as readily as he will use our talents and resources to benefit others and accomplish his purpose.

Matt 25:35 (NIV) says,

> For I was hungry and you gave me something to eat, I was thirsty and you gave me something to drink, I was a stranger and you invited me in, I needed clothes and you clothed me, I was sick and you looked after me, I was in prison and you came to visit me. Then the righteous will answer him, "Lord, when did we see you hungry and feed you, or thirsty and give you something to drink? When did we see you a stranger and invite you in, or needing clothes and clothe you? When did we see you sick or in prison and go to visit you?" The King will reply, "Truly I tell you, whatever you did for one of the least of these brothers and sisters of mine, you did for me."

23

Their Fate Was Sealed

SWEATSHOPS WERE COMMONPLACE AT the beginning of the twentieth century, where workers toiled nine hours a day, seven days a week for low pay in deplorable conditions. People moving from rural to urban areas and the large surge in immigration made labor cheap. In 1907, New York City saw an average of 10,000 foreigners processed each day, and one time, at its peak, 21,000 immigrants were admitted in a single day looking for housing and work.[1] Droves of people filled New York City's diseased-infested tenement buildings, with many finding jobs in the sweatshops. Muckraking journalists wrote about the sweatshops' deplorable, dangerous working conditions and there were frequent worker strikes, but striking workers were easily replaced by new immigrants.

One of the largest sweatshops in New York was the Triangle Shirtwaist Factory. Five hundred women worked in this ten-story wooden tinderbox, earning $7 a week to make blouses, also known as shirtwaists.[2] Fires had ignited earlier from boxes of scrap fabric workers kept under their tables, but fire safety measures were never taken.

On March 25, 1911, a tragic fire broke out on the top three floors of the factory. The eighteen-inch-wide fire escape was too narrow and collapsed, sending many girls to their death and making that evacuation route impossible. The two freight elevators continued to rescue workers

---

1. McCarthy, "Brief Passage," paras. 22–23.
2. Von Drehle, *Triangle*, 105.

until many attempted to get out of the burning inferno by riding the cables down. So many young women fell to their deaths on top of the elevators the system was soon rendered inoperable.[3]

New York City had one of the best fire departments in the world, but ladders were only six stories tall and were unable to reach the fire-trapped workers on the eighth, ninth, and tenth floors.[4] The partitions that had been constructed to control employee theft, limited exiting the building to one employee at a time. Also, in an effort to prevent theft and unauthorized breaks, the owners locked the doors to the stairwells and exits during factory hours, sealing the fate of those in the burning building.

The fire in the Triangle Shirtwaist Factory lasted only about thirty minutes, but it was the deadliest workplace disaster in New York City's history for the next ninety years. About one-third of the 146 garment workers who died did so as a result of jumping or falling from the eighth and ninth floors.[5] Some waited until they were on fire before they leaped to their death.[6] Firemen tried to save them, but canvas life nets were torn by the impact of the falling women.

Horrified spectators stood powerless. Most of the victims were recent Italian and Jewish immigrant women and girls, between the ages of fourteen and twenty-three.[7] Later these young women who had died from the crushing fall or asphyxiation and burns were identified from "buttons on their shoe, a ring, or stockings" by grieving sweethearts, husbands, and family members.[8]

One of those who helplessly watched from the crowded streets below was Francis Perkins, who later became the first woman cabinet member as President Franklin Roosevelt's Secretary of Labor. At the time of the Triangle Fire she had been working as a building inspector. In the aftermath of the Triangle Shirtwaist Factory fire, Francis Perkins dedicated her life to improving building safety and labor laws.[9] As the longest-serving Secretary of Labor, Perkins helped abolished child labor, set a minimum wage, and guaranteed the right of workers to organize

---

3. Lange, *Triangle Shirtwaist Factory Fire*, 58.
4. "Triangle Shirtwaist Factory Fire."
5. Wagner, "Triangle Shirtwaist Factory."
6. Shi and Tindall, *America*, 1013.
7. Kosak, "Triangle Shirtwaist Fire."
8. Von Drehle, *Triangle*, 274.
9. "Remembering the 1911 Triangle Factory Fire."

and bargain collectively.[10] Through the lessons learned from the tragedy of the Triangle fire and the subsequent work of Francis Perkins and many like her, workplace conditions have steadily improved.

Biblical Insight: Life after Certain Death

by Seth Grotzke

What terror did the people in that burning inferno face that made jumping from a ten-story building their only hope of escape? Fear can drive us beyond the breaking point. What would I have done in that circumstance? Where would I have turned? When we see the extreme measures people will take to escape imminent death, the reality of life presses upon us.

Fire, and the panic caused by fire, has claimed countless lives throughout the millennia, and we are right to fear the flame. But the terror, the panic, the sheer desperation produced by being trapped in a fire is not unique to those imprisoned in burning buildings. Sadly, the desperation produced by a raging fire is being felt in homes all across the country. There are no flames or locked exits but a quiet despair which drives the individual to their breaking point. Life itself is the impetus for terror. For some, the living of life with no meaning or significance is sufficient for desiring death.

When one comes to the conclusion that this whole world is an accident, a product of time and chance, the suffocating weight of meaningless is too much to bear. For some, the only legitimate option is to leap, but for many, many more the rational response is indifference. "I don't care anymore. This life is merely an opportunity to eat, drink, and be merry." It is here that we meet many of our family, friends, neighbors, and coworkers.

However, in contrast to the fire in the Triangle Shirtwaist Factory, the leap into certain physical death is not our last chance. There is hope. What we have in Christ is a hope which grows stronger the closer we stand to our own death. If Jesus is who he says he is, then there is every reason to have hope as we see our own final day approaching. Perhaps one of the best examples of this can be seen in the thieves on the cross:

> One of the criminals who was hanged railed at Him, saying, "Are you not the Christ? Save yourself and us!" But the other rebuked him, saying, "Do you not fear God, since you are under the same

---

10. U.S. Department of Labor, "Chapter 3."

sentence of condemnation? And we indeed justly, for we are receiving the due reward of our deeds; but this man has done nothing wrong." And he said, "Jesus, remember me when you come into your kingdom." And he said to him, "Truly, I say to you, today you will be with me in paradise." (Luke 23:39–43 ESV)

For one criminal, if Jesus was who he said he was then he should come down off the cross and bring his two fellow sufferers with him. This mocking man found nothing better to do than use some of his final words to highlight the irony of a crucified "savior." For him, Jesus was simply a delusional teacher, the object of all the misplaced hopes of the simple-minded. Reality said death was coming, you might as well embrace it.

But the voice from the other side told a different story. For the second criminal, Jesus was not a self-deceived messiah; he was the sinless sacrificial Lamb, the Righteous One punished for the sinner. For him, Jesus was his hope, his future, his King. And his plea was the cry of hope in the midst of the darkened sky, "Jesus, remember me when you come into your kingdom."

When the flames of death close in, there is a hope in the One who hung upon the tree, was buried in the cave, and rose from the dead. "Truly, I say to you, today you will be with me in paradise" (Luke 23:43 ESV).

24

Carry A Nation

CARRIE AMELIA MOORE REALIZED she was pregnant and married to an alcoholic. She had married Dr. Charles Gloyd in November 1867 against her parents' wishes; they had objected to the marriage because he was not a Christian and was known to have a drinking problem.[1] Carrie believed the birth of her very sickly daughter and her husband's death two years after they were married were results of his alcoholism.

It was not uncommon for wives and children to be left hungry, homeless, and abandoned by husbands and fathers who were struggling with alcohol addiction. Carrie's life was profoundly altered when her husband died from alcohol abuse. She became a passionate advocate for the temperance movement and prohibition of liquor.

Facing financial ruin after her husband died, Carrie earned a teaching certificate and taught in a Missouri high school for four years. In 1877, Carrie married a second time to a man named David A. Nation. He was nineteen years older than her and was a newspaper editor, attorney, and minister in Kansas.[2]

David and Carrie Nation moved to Texas and tried a number of different unsuccessful occupations, including farming, opening a law practice, and operating a hotel. In 1889, they moved back to Kansas after David became involved in the Jaybird-Woodpecker War, a racially

---

1. Meyer, *Kansas Myths and Legends,* 106–9.
2. Wilson, "Nation, Carry Moore."

charged feud.[3] At their new home in Medicine Lodge, Kansas, David became the pastor of the Christian Church and Carrie Nation established a local chapter of the Women's Christian Temperance Union.

Believing she was on a divine mission for the prohibition of alcohol, Carrie claimed direct revelations from God to become more militant in her crusade.[4] She began to correct her husband during his sermons and started using the name Carry A. Nation. She claimed she was a "bulldog running along at the feet of Jesus, barking at what He doesn't like."[5]

In 1880, Kansas became the first state in the union to adopt a constitutional amendment prohibiting alcohol, but the law was widely ignored.[6] At six foot tall and weighing 175 pounds, Carry Nation initially stormed into bars and announced "Men, I have come to save you from a drunkard's fate."[7] And then proceeded to destroy bottles of liquor using rocks she called "smashers."[8] The last heavyweight champion of bare-knuckle boxing, John L. Sullivan, reportedly ran and hid when Nation burst into his New York City saloon.[9] She soon turned to using a hatchet and was arrested over thirty times for disorderly conduct. Carry paid her jail fines with the money from her speaking tours and the sales from souvenir hatchets which had the slogan "Death to Rum" engraved on the handles.

With each tavern attack headline, Carry A. Nation became more famous and her cause spread. By the beginning of the twentieth century, prohibition had become a national movement. But Carry Nation died eight years before the 18th Amendment was passed in 1919, banning "intoxicating liquors."

There is good evidence that prohibition worked. According to a study conducted by MIT and Boston University economists in the early 1990s, alcohol consumption actually fell by as much as 70 percent during the early years of prohibition.[10] Cirrhosis death rates for men were 29.5 per 100,000 in 1911 and 10.7 in 1929. Admissions to state mental

3. Lovett, "Jaybird-Woodpecker War."
4. Kansas Historical Society, "Carry A. Nation."
5. American Experience, "Carrie Nation," paras. 2–3.
6. Milner, *Oxford History of the American West,* 196–206.
7. Asbury, *Carry Nation,* 87.
8. Hanson, "Carry Nation Biography," para. 32.
9. Hanson, "Carry Nation Biography," para. 32.
10. Andrews, "10 Things You Should Know," para. 9.

hospitals for alcoholic psychosis declined from 10.1 per 100,000 in 1919 to 4.7 in 1928.[11]

But there is also strong evidence that the national ban on alcohol failed. The noble experiment became difficult to enforce and led to the opening of illegal bars called speakeasies. During the ban upwards of 10,000 deaths can be attributed to alcohol poisoning in large part from the consumption of illegal moonshine.[12] Al Capone and other organized crime gangsters trafficked in alcohol and vice, allowing them to build powerful illegal syndicates. Overall, crime rose 24 percent during prohibition, including increases in assault and battery, theft, and burglary.[13] The national prohibition era ended in 1933 when the 21st Amendment was passed, repealing the ban on alcohol which was negatively impacting society in many ways.

Carry Nation's tactics were extreme and often violent. However, she was an agent of change that significantly impacted American society. The prohibition movement was an integral part of the turn of the twentieth-century progressive movement that ultimately led to the passage and repeal of prohibition, the income tax, and woman's suffrage amendments.

Biblical Insight: Barking at What Jesus Doesn't Like

by Seth Grotzke

Alcohol has had many negative effects upon the people of the United States. Intoxicating beverages are commonly cited as the culprits for incredible damages to life, property, and time. However, alcohol is not alone in presenting a danger to its users. Nearly every good gift that God has given to humanity, such as wine (Ps 104:14–15), can be twisted, abused, over-indulged in, and even used to replace the Giver himself (Jas 4:1–10). Alcohol may be a good example of a vice because of its history and prevalence, but it is by no means unique in its ability to be misused.

The story of Carry Nation presents us with a problem. How do we know when we ought to further a cause in order to relieve perceived or experienced suffering, or instead defer to the personal liberty of the individual? When ought we to stand up and fight or when ought we to sit

---

11. Moore, "Actually, Prohibition Was a Success," para. 6.
12. Blum, "Chemist's War," paras. 2 & 3.
13. Towne, *Rise and Fall of Prohibition*, 159–62.

back and watch? Do we have sufficient strength and resources to deal with every abuse of God's creation? While we must navigate many waters in these ethical dilemmas, we can initially recognize several key principles which will help us orient ourselves. Scripture provides us with the what, the who, and the how.

Our first question when addressing a moral code is: What is required by God? While both creation (Rom 1:19–20) and our conscience (Rom 2:14–16) can tell us the truth about God and ourselves, Scripture is our clear guide (2 Tim 3:16–17). Our experiences, emotions, and dreams are not reliable guides. We turn instead to the revealed will of God as found in his written revelation. As we open the pages of Scripture we must walk through the hermeneutical principles which help us to determine what God is saying to his intended audience. These principles are not as difficult as they might seem, but they do require asking questions and thinking critically. While it may be easier to go out and find some smashers, we may find ourselves going against the very One we are trying to follow, as we will see.

Our second question moves us further. When we encounter a command or manner of living, we ask: Who is required to obey this? Is this command given to an individual (2 Kgs 5:10), a nation (Lev 23:9–14), or humanity as a whole? In certain situations it is clear that followers of Jesus Christ are held to a different moral code than those who would deny him (Eph 5:18–21). And yet in other situations it is clear that all who bear the image of God must obey the laws of God. One is not exempt from the sixth commandment, "You shall not murder" (Exod 20:13), merely because they believe there is no God. Jesus did create a ruckus, overturning tables and scattering crowds, but he did so in his Father's house. He went into the temple and cleansed it (Matt 21:12–17), but we do not read of him entering the soldiers' barracks of the Roman army, or the gentiles' marketplace. When we make the effort to determine what Scripture is saying in its context and application, we will see that God is clear about what he expects from all his creations, and what he expects specifically from his children.

Our final question at this time is: How should this be enforced? Carry A. Nation was not the first to attempt to enforce her law on others. Nor could she ever be the last. In the gospels we have an excellent example of what happens when we attempt to step in front of Jesus and use coercion to enforce a personal moral code. While Jesus prayed in the garden, Judas came with soldiers, officers, chief priests, and Pharisees to arrest him. "Then Simon Peter, having a sword, drew it and struck the high priest's servant and cut off his right ear. (The servant's name was Malchus.) So Jesus said to Peter, 'Put your sword into its sheath; shall I not drink the cup that the Father has given me?'" (John 18:10–11 ESV). In the confrontation, Peter steps forward to "bark at what Jesus doesn't like," and he swings a sword.

Peter had answered our first question correctly, he knew that God forbade murder, and this was obviously the intended and stated plan of the religious leaders. He had answered the second question partially correct, for he also knew this moral code should be upheld regardless of whether he was a Jew or a Roman. But he had erred in neglecting God's specific revelation about the Messiah's death ("the cup that the Father has given me"). Jesus had been consistently teaching that he must die, but Peter had not seen it. The final question, the how, had been missed.

We can applaud Carry for her desire to relieve others from the control of alcohol. We can honor her tenacity and audacity to do what she believed is right. But we also must realize her method did not align with our Savior's. There are times to stand up and fight. There are times to overturn tables and protest. We fight to uphold the moral code God has given to all his image-bearers. And yet we can also say there are times when instead of fighting with swords or smashers we must lay our lives down for others, sacrificing ourselves. And as the application of God's commands narrow, we need to be quick to arms over our own sin, and thoughtful and consistent as we approach the sins of others (Matt 7:1–6). When we remember the prohibition era, the oft-heard maxim still rings true, "God's work, done in God's way, will have God's blessing."

25

Annie Oakley
A Sure Shot

PHOEBE ANN MOSES WAS born into a poor Quaker family and seldom attended school when she was young. Her father, twenty-one years older than her mother, died when Phoebe was just six years old, leaving her mother with nine children to raise.[1] For two years Phoebe was sent to live and work for a family that physically and mentally abused her. Eventually she ran away and returned to her mother but often referred to this cruel family as "the wolves."[2] Phoebe hunted animals and sold the meat to a local grocery store. With the profits she was able to pay off the $200 mortgage on her mother's house.[3]

Then on Thanksgiving Day 1875, Frank Butler, a professional marksman, came to Cincinnati, Ohio and placed a $100 bet that he could win a shooting match with anyone in town. Imagine his surprise when his last opponent was a fifteen-year-old, five-foot-tall girl named Phoebe Ann Moses. Phoebe not only won the contest, but Frank's heart as well, as the two were married just one year later. Mrs. Frank Butler started using the stage name Annie Oakley while she and her husband traveled the country demonstrating their sharpshooter skills.

In 1885, Annie Oakley and her husband joined the Buffalo Bill Wild West Show.[4] The show was immensely popular across the United States

---

1. Riley, *Life and Legacy of Annie Oakley*, 5.
2. Whiting, *What's So Great about Annie Oakley?*, 10–11.
3. Duffy, "Story Behind Wild West Sharpshooter," 1–5.
4. Milner, *Oxford History of the American West*, 780–82.

and Europe and included reenacting Custer's last stand, Indian attacks on wagon trains, and riding the Pony Express. However, sharpshooter Annie Oakley was still the headliner who many came to see, making her one of the show's best-paid performers.

Sharpshooting in the late 1800s was primarily dominated by males, but petite Annie Oakley matched her skills with some of the strongest men in the country. Her feats of marksmanship included splitting the thin edge of a playing card at thirty paces. And as cards were thrown into the air she would put a forty-five bullet hole in them before they hit the ground. When ushers punched a hole in a ticket to indicate a free admittance to circus, theater, or sporting events, the tickets were known as Annie Oakley's because they resembled the cards Annie shot during performances.[5] Sitting Bull, who had defeated George Custer at the 1876 Battle of the Little Big Horn, also joined the Buffalo Bill Wild West Show. He became friends with and an admirer of Oakley, nicknaming her Little Sure Shot.

When the Spanish-American War broke out in 1898, Oakley wrote President William McKinley offering the services of fifty women sharpshooters. Her proposal was rejected.[6] As America prepared to go to war again in 1917 she contacted the United States Secretary of War, asking to be allowed to train women sharpshooters to fight in World War I. There was no response. So, during the war, Annie Oakley volunteered and raised money for charities like the Red Cross and the National War Council of the Young Men's Christian Association. Annie Oakley is believed to have taught more than 15,000 women how to use a gun as a form of exercise and a means to defend themselves.[7]

In 1889, Annie Oakley and her husband, Frank Butler, joined the Buffalo Bill Wild West show in Paris. Approximately 32 million people attended the Paris Exposition, an event commemorating the 100th anniversary of the French Revolution.[8] A widely circulated story at the time claimed that the future German World War I leader, Kaiser Wilhelm II, allowed Oakley to shoot a cigarette from his mouth on this tour. *The New York Times* reported that Annie later realized her mistake. Years later, during World War I, she wrote to the Kaiser asking for a second shot. He did not respond.[9]

5. Klein, "10 Things about Annie Oakley."
6. National Archives, "Letter to President William McKinley."
7. Wills, *DK Biography*, 112.
8. American Experience, "Annie Oakley in Europe,"
9. Blazeski, "Annie Oakley," paras. 1–10.

Annie Oakley was featured in some of the earliest movies, such as Thomas Edison's 1894 film *The Little Sure Shot of the Wild West*. After her death, the long-running 1946 Broadway musical *Annie Get Your Gun* was followed by a successful movie of the same title in 1950.[10]

In 1926, Annie Oakley died from natural causes at sixty-six years of age. After fifty years of marriage, her husband Frank was so grief-struck he stopped eating and died just eighteen days later. Without any consideration of her size, Phoebe Ann Moses stood tall and became one of the true American Western folk heroes. Her talents spoke for themselves, matching the toughest of America's most famous cowboys.

Biblical Insight: Surprising Transformation

by Ernest Schmidt

You can almost hear people say, "Wow, where did Annie Oakley come from?" It would be interesting to see the expression on their faces when they were given her background. She had a very limited education, and poverty at home required her to spend two years in an abusive home. Her start resulted from humiliating a man who was an expert in his field. He lost in marksmanship but gained a wife. This transformed her future.

The Lord loves to transform the most unlikely people in a similar manner. An example is Matthew, a turncoat. He betrayed his people when he hired out to their oppressors. He was employed by the despised government working in their burdensome tax system. In spite of all that disqualified him, he was transformed spiritually in a single day!

Since he lived in Capernaum, Jesus' adopted hometown, he knew of the Lord's life, teaching, and miracles. Matthew (Levi) no doubt knew also of Jesus' love and compassion for people. Because of his choice to serve Rome and its oppression of the Jews, he probably thought he could never be forgiven by the Lord Jesus. To his surprise the opposite was true.

Matthew 9:9 states, "As Jesus passed on from there, He saw a man named Matthew sitting at the tax office. And He said to him, 'Follow Me.'" The Lord did not shun him. He invited Matthew to become one of his followers! Matthew's response was immediate. "He arose and followed Him."

---

10. Bloom, *Broadway Musicals*, 13.

Immediately following his decision, Matthew invited the Lord Jesus as his guest for a great banquet. He intentionally invited his friends, former associates in the tax business, to personally know the One who changed him (Matt 9:10). His motivation certainly appeared to be providing his guests with an opportunity to hear and experience the life-changing compassion the Lord had offered him.

When traditionalist ritualistic religious leaders observed Jesus eating and conversing with tax collectors and sinners, they self-righteously questioned the Lord's disciples about his conduct. They implied he condoned the lifestyle of those who were identified with the oppressing government (Matt 9:11). Instead of a reply from the disciples, Jesus answered. In light of the purpose for the occasion, Matthew could not have been more pleased with the Lord's answer. "When Jesus heard that, He said to them, 'Those who are well have no need of a physician, but those who are sick. But go and learn what this means: I desire mercy and not sacrifice. For I did not come to call the righteous, but sinners to repentance'" (Matt 9:12–13). This is exactly what Matthew wanted his guests to hear! He wanted them to know the Lord came to save sinners.

This initial evidence of his spiritual transformation led to a lifetime of service for the Lord. As a disciple he was trained to serve effectively. "And when He had called His twelve disciples to Him, He gave them power over unclean spirits, to cast them out, and to heal all kinds of sickness and all kinds of disease" (Matt 10:1). As a result of his time with, and service for, the Lord, Matthew was used to write an inspired record of the life and ministry of the Lord Jesus Christ, one that has been used to introduce people to the Lord and edify believers for almost 2,000 years.

In the future he will have a leadership ministry during the Lord's 1,000-year reign on earth. "So Jesus said to them, 'Assuredly I say to you, that in the regeneration, when the Son of Man sits on the throne of His glory, you who have followed Me will also sit on twelve thrones, judging the twelve tribes of Israel'" (Matt 19:28). For eternity his name will be inscribed on the foundation stones of the New Jerusalem. "Now the wall of the city had twelve foundations, and on them were the names of the twelve apostles of the Lamb" (Rev 21:14).

When you think of Matthew's journey from a betrayer of his own people to eternal recognition, it is obvious: the Lord Jesus can take the most unlikely person and transform him/her into a significant servant of God. He desires to do the same for you.

26

Shadow of Death
Theodore Roosevelt

IF THERE EVER WAS one who charged fearlessly into death's long shadow, it was Theodore Roosevelt. Many know of Teddy Roosevelt's triumphs and accomplishments, but few know the extent of his hardships. When you're born rich, well educated, widely traveled, a war hero who becomes President, and the image of your face is carved on Mount Rushmore, people think you have lived a charmed life. Such was not the case for Teddy Roosevelt.

There was no cure and little relief from the life-threatening asthma that made young Teddy feel like he was suffocating. Taking the advice of his father that he needed to endure the drudgery of strengthening his body, he was motivated by this adversity and overcame his physical limitations. Roosevelt challenged himself and later challenged others to stay physically active in what he would term the "strenuous life."[1]

When Theodore was just twenty years old, his father, whom he adored, died prematurely. Teddy used this personal tragedy and his inheritance wisely. Carrying on his father's work as a reformer, Teddy entered politics and got involved with civic reform.

Roosevelt had many mountaintop experiences, and one was the birth of his daughter. Just two days after her birth, he entered the deepest valley of death's shadow when his two greatest loves in life were taken on the same day. He sat with his mother as she died of typhoid fever

---

1. Roosevelt, *Strenuous Life*, 3–22.

in the upstairs room of their New York home on 43rd Street. Later that same day, his wife Alice died in his arms from Bright's disease.[2] It was Valentine's Day, and Teddy would later say it was the day the light went out of his life.[3] Roosevelt spent the next two years at his cattle ranch in Dakota Territory where he transformed himself from a snobbish New York aristocrat into a rugged frontiersman.

After his cattle and half of his ranch investment were wiped out by the severe Dakota winter of 1886, Roosevelt experienced another setback, losing the New York City mayoral race.[4] Motivated to overcome this setback, Roosevelt wrote *The Winning of the West*, which became a bestseller.[5]

Over the objections of the political bosses, Theodore Roosevelt became vice president under President William McKinley in 1898. When an assassin killed McKinley in September 1901, Roosevelt became president and led the United States into a new era as a world power.

Disappointed with his handpicked presidential successor, William Howard Taft, and shunned by the old guard Republicans, Theodore Roosevelt ran as a Progressive third-party candidate in 1912. While giving a campaign speech in Milwaukee, Wisconsin, he was shot in the chest.[6] Stating that it takes more than that to kill a Bull Moose candidate, he finished his ninety-minute speech before going to the hospital. The bullet slowed down by passing though his eyeglass case and a fifty-page speech he carried in his breast pocket.[7] This bullet, lodged in his chest, was never removed. His would-be assassin, John Schrank, was committed to a state hospital in Wisconsin, where he remained until his death in 1943 at age sixty-seven. In more than thirty years of confinement, Schrank never received a visitor or a letter.[8]

Although he had an uncanny ability to use tragedy and setbacks to propel him forward with personal growth, there were two events in Theodore Roosevelt's life he could not overcome. Coming in second to Democrat Woodrow Wilson in the 1912 presidential race drove Roosevelt to embark on the last adventure of his life. While he said it was "his

---

2. History.com editors, "Theodore Roosevelt's Wife and Mother Die."
3. Millard, *River of Doubt*, 17.
4. National Park Service, "Theodore Roosevelt the Rancher."
5. Miller, *Theodore Roosevelt*, 197–200.
6. Remey, et al. *Attempted Assassination*, 1–23.
7. Klein, "When Teddy Roosevelt Was Shot."
8. "Theodore Roosevelt," para. 8.

last chance to be a boy," Roosevelt nearly died on a trip down a dangerous, uncharted Amazon River tributary named The River of Doubt.[9] He wrote, "The Brazilian wilderness stole away ten years of my life," and he would battle recurring malaria until his death.[10]

The final loss Roosevelt never overcame was the death of his youngest son Quentin, an American World War I pilot who was shot down behind enemy lines.[11] Six months later, Roosevelt's remarkable life of triumph over adversity came to an end when he died in his sleep at his home at Sagamore Hills. A poem Theodore Roosevelt wrote after leaving the presidency best epitomized his philosophy on life:

The Man in the Arena

It is not the critic who counts; not the man who points out how the strong man stumbles, or where the doer of deeds could have done them better. The credit belongs to the man who is actually in the arena, whose face is marred by dust and sweat and blood; who strives valiantly; who errs, who comes short again and again, because there is no effort without error and shortcoming; but who does actually strive to do the deeds; who knows great enthusiasms, the great devotions; who spends himself in a worthy cause; who at the best knows in the end the triumph of high achievement, and who at the worst, if he fails, at least fails while daring greatly, so that his place shall never be with those cold and timid souls who neither know victory nor defeat.[12]

Biblical Insight: Perseverance

by Seth Grotzke

There is a strength that comes from resolving to live a life of perseverance amidst difficulty. Teddy Roosevelt demonstrated through his commitment and courage that obstacles of all sizes can be faced and overcome.

---

9. Ornig, *My Last Chance to Be a Boy*, xv.

10. Theodore Roosevelt Center at Dickinson State University, "River of Doubt," para. 4.

11. Millard, *River of Doubt*, 342–43.

12. Theodore Roosevelt Center at Dickinson State University, "Man in the Arena," para. 9.

But as his life and the lives of great men and women from all time have demonstrated, there will always be a challenge too big, too difficult, too consuming for us to complete. At some point in our lives we will be faced with the option of retreat.

Retreat, however, is only one option. There is a second option of which David spoke in the book of Psalms: rest. "The Lord is my shepherd; I shall not want. He makes me lie down in green pastures. He leads me beside still waters. He restores my soul. He leads me in paths of righteousness for his name's sake" (Psalm 23:1–3a ESV).

Even when the Valley of the Shadow of Death threatened his next step, David chose to walk that path. He did so, not in his own strength and ability, but in the security which comes from the Good Shepherd. He, too, lived with commitment and courage, taking on tasks too great for his humble origins and simple training. Yet David did so, knowing his soul could rest in the care of the Lord, his Shepherd. His heart could feast at the banquet table which his God provided, no matter the circumstance which surrounded him.

Great men such as Teddy Roosevelt challenge our natural desire to live lives of comfort and ease, and rightfully so. Their acts of courage and strength motivate us to step up to the looming challenges before us. For each one of us there is a question which ought to prod our souls: Am I persevering in order to be great, or am I persevering because I follow a great God?

If you persevere in order to be great, there is the chance you will be celebrated by men. However if you persevere in the strength which God alone provides, goodness and mercy shall follow you all the days of your life, and you will dwell in the house of the Lord forever.

27

Mary Jane (Blight) Phillips
An Immigrant's Story

MARY JANE BLIGHT WAS born in 1879 in Cornwall, England, and by age nine she had completed the compulsory third-grade public education required for all English children. Although it was not one of the "ragged schools,"[1] funded by charitable donations for the poor that Charles Dickens wrote about, public schools were strict and taught the very basic reading, writing, arithmetic, and Bible studies.[2]

After her formal education had ended, Mary Jane's parents sent her to live with a wealthy family to do general housekeeping. Meagerly fed and clothed as a servant girl, she was often hungry and missed her family, whom she visited on rare occasions and at Christmas. It was common for poverty to play a major role in the exploitation of children during the Victorian Era, often taking away from them their innocence and childhood.[3] Mary Jane said she looked forward to Heaven where maybe she could have both jam and butter on toast, which was a forbidden extravagance in her servant's quarters. Shortly after Mary returned home to the small family farm from her time as a house servant, her father died. So, she continued to work to support the family.

At age twenty-eight, Mary was listed on her marriage certificate as a "spinster" when she married Charles Phillips. They were rising their four young children when Charles volunteered to joined the British cause in

1. "Letter from Charles Dickens on Ragged Schools," paras. 1 & 2.
2. Walvin, *Child's World*, 117–20.
3. Cody, "Child Labor."

WWI. In November of 1917, his Duke of Cornwall light infantry unit suffered a direct hit from German artillery in the battle of Cambria.[4] Mary was notified that he was missing in action. After five years of waiting and hoping her husband would someday return she finally received a letter stating he was most likely killed in action.[5] Mary's daughter, Louisa, had died in her arms a few years earlier from diphtheria, a highly contagious bacterial disease, also called the "Strangling Angel," because of how it kills cells in nose and throat. Mary's sister, Emily, also struggled with life in England. Her husband, Dennis, and three grown sons also served in the military. Emily's husband was shot and gassed in the war and on his return he abandoned his wife and family.

Twice a year, Mary Phillips was required to validate that she and her children were alive so she could continue to receive her meager widow's war veterans' pension in England. Arriving at the office of the nearby Anglican Church with her three boys, Mary was asked if she had a pen by the assistant vicar who was in charge of validating her pension. Of course she did not because pens in those days required a bottle of ink and cost more money than she could afford. The assistant vicar voiced his indignation and disgust that Mary did not have a pen, but Mary made no reply. After his completion and signing of the necessary forms, Mary and her three boys immediately went to a stationery store, bought a pen, and a bottle of ink, using their merger food funds: went back to the assistant vicar's office; placed these items on his desk and said, "This is for the next widow who comes into your office and asks you to witness their signature!"[6]

Feeling there were better opportunities for her boys in the United States, Mary Phillips bravely decided to immigrate to America. Third-class tickets were bought, and Mary, her three boys—Art (13), Jack (7), and Bill (6)—and her sister Emily embarked for America on the *RMS Berengaria* in September of 1922. A few days out to sea, a violent storm tore thirty-six feet of guard railing from the *Berengaria*. The ship was known to be top-heavy and previously had its funnels lowered nine feet and cement added to the hull, but the ship remained unstable.[7] Everyone was seasick when the call went out to report to their muster station

4. History.com editors, "World War I Battles," 1–8.
5. Phillips, *Military History*, 18.
6. Family oral history from author's father, Jack Phillips, referenced in acknowledgments.
7. Grace, "Cruise Ship History," paras. 3–5.

with lifejackets. A boy had washed overboard and Mary feared it was Art since she was unable to locate him. Once on deck, Art was located and they could see the young boy in the water. The captain refused to send a lifeboat or turn the *Berengaria* around to rescue the boy. The crew threw lifejackets to him but he could not reach them and he subsequently drowned.

In third class there was a loud ruckus in the cabin next door. Art was sent to get the purser while Mary told her sister to stay with the other boys and lock the door. Taking a broom, she pounded on the cabin door. When no one answered, she entered the cabin. By the time Art returned with the ship's personnel, they found Mary beating three men over the head as they were trying to push a fourth man out through the porthole. They had been drinking and gambling, got into a fight and the three were trying to shove the fourth out the porthole and into the sea.

The voyage across the Atlantic Ocean took four days longer than normal when a propeller broke. Finally, their traumatic journey ended as the Statue of Liberty came into view and they debarked at Ellis Island in New York Harbor.

Many people like Mary Jane immigrated to the United States and were processed through Ellis Island. Two out of every five Americans today, or approximately 100 million citizens, can trace their ancestry to immigrants who arrived in America through Ellis Island.[8]

In the thirty-five years before Ellis Island opened in 1892, approximately 8 million immigrants arrived in New York City. Twelve million more immigrants were processed through Ellis Island from 1892 until it closed as an immigration gateway in 1954.[9] Before 1880, the majority of immigrants were Northern and Western Europeans from Germany, England, France, and Scandinavian countries. After 1880, immigrants were mainly Southern and Eastern Europeans from Italy, Poland, Hungary, Turkey, and Russia.[10] There were many anti-immigration laws passed in the 1920s in part due to fears that immigrants were bringing with them the ideas of anarchy or communism, or had mental disabilities.

Arriving on Ellis Island, the new immigrants walked a gauntlet under the watchful eyes of United States officials. Art arrived with an injured hand which had been bandaged by the ship's doctor. As he walked

---

8. Timberlane Regional School, "Industrial Revolution," para. 1.
9. Kennedy, "Most Immigrants."
10. Gilbert, *History of the Twentieth Century*, 217, 291.

past one door, an official marked an x on his sleeve. His younger brother looked at him in horror and told him to wipe it off but his mother advised him to leave it. Art was pulled from the line. The family was told to keep moving without him and they became gravely concerned because sick family members were often not allowed to enter the United States and were returned to their homeland. Although Ellis Island became known as "The Island of Tears" for those sent back to their countries of origin, only about 2 percent were actually not admitted due to a contagious disease, criminal background, or insanity.[11]

It was not until the following afternoon that Art's mother found her son was in the hospital, living like a king in beautiful surroundings, with a nice bed, clean sheets, doctors, nurses, and wonderful food. In contrast, the rest of the family was herded like cattle where men, women, children, all slept in one great big room. The beds with thin mattresses were made of steel and stacked four high.

Mary's son, Jack, recalled, "When we entered the sleeping area, there was a black attendant who gave my mother extra blankets and told her to get into bed with the rest of her family and stay there all night. He told us there were so many thieveries going on that one gentleman carrying diamonds swallowed them in order to keep them safe."[12] After a few days on Ellis Island, Mary and her three sons were allowed to continue their journey to Minneapolis, Minnesota, where family members who had arrived earlier awaited them.

As British citizens living in America, there were challenges. Mary's son, Jack, returned from school and proudly told his mother he had received the "citizen of the year award." "You're not a US citizen, Jack," she said. "You will have to return the plaque."[13] School officials graciously made it an honorary award.

In 1936, Jack came home to find the king's picture in the trash can. Mary told her son, "King Edward VIII abdicated the throne to marry the woman he loves. Some may see this as a great love story, but I do not! Your father fought and gave his life for England, and this man won't give up a two-time divorced American woman for his country."[14] Wallis Simpson, having two living ex-husbands, was politically and socially

---

11. Kennedy, "Most Immigrants," para. 13.
12. Family oral history.
13. Family oral history.
14. Family oral history.

unacceptable to the prime ministers and Church of England.[15] Later, as WWII approached, King Edward VIII, Duke of Windsor, met with Adolf Hitler and was accused of holding Nazi sympathies.[16] Many have speculated how different America and the world would be today if Edward VIII had remained as king and kept England out of World War II, perhaps resulting in a Nazi Germany victory.[17]

Eventually all three of Mary's sons would become US citizens and serve in World War II. Jack was a US Army Master Sergeant on Guadalcanal in the Pacific when he learned his mother had died, but he was not permitted to return for her funeral. After completing his service, Jack reunited with his wife. He had four children and is the source of much of his mother Mary Jane's life story.

Mary Jane Phillips exemplifies women of the strongest character and who resolve to overcome adversity and better the lives of all around them. By immigrating to America she neither expected nor received anything for herself and her decedents other than to take part in the greatest land of opportunities.

Biblical Insight: Sacrificial Love

by Seth Grotzke

Loss, pain, deprivation, fear, and loneliness are all around us, and can be felt by each one of us. And if, by grace, we do not experience them in our daily lives, they are in our history. Every family tree holds many scarred and battered branches.

Lives like Mary Jane's clash with what we look for in a happy story. We all want a happily ever after. We want everything to work out in the end. But for Mary Jane there was no prince who rescued her from the cold servants' quarters. There was no unexpected windfall and subsequent feasting. There was no husband who returned home from the battle, against all odds. There was no wealthy patron, inviting mansion, or financial security. There was loss. There was difficulty. There was sacrifice.

But there was also love. Mary Jane loved her boys. The debilitating circumstances and crushing series of events were not able to deprive

---

15. Windsor, *King's Story*, 330–31.
16. Ziegler, *King Edward VIII*, 434.
17. Kline, "Scandalous Romance."

her of that love, but rather strengthened and revealed it. In the midst of her pain, she sought to protect. In the midst of her need, she sought to provide. In the midst of her uncertainty, she sought to remain stable. And she did.

There is a love—a deep, strong, throbbing love—which can only be seen and experienced in the light of personal loss. It is a sacrificial love which moves people to put loved ones before themselves. She gives up her dreams so her boys can be safe. He lays down his desires so his wife can be safe. There is a transfer, uncoerced and extravagant, to the detriment of one for the benefit of another. This voluntary loss is the gift of oneself. There is no other way for this depth of love to be experienced. It has to involve pain. There has to be a sacrifice. My life for yours.

This love runs deep because it is the love which flows from the Creator himself into his creations. The Triune God formed our world from this love and pulled from its dust his own image-bearers so they might experience and rejoice in it (John 17). This love called out humanity in their sin and pursued them through the ages (Exod 34:6–7). This love motivated the gift of the Son by the will of the Father (John 3:16).

This love led Jesus to the cross. Shortly before his death, he told his disciples, "Greater love has no one than this, that someone lay down his life for his friends" (John 15:13 ESV). He was about to walk into the gaping maw of death of his own volition. No one would take his life—he would give it. Spears rattled and soldiers taunted. Crowds screamed and rulers postured. But it was Jesus alone who could lay down his own life. His life for ours.

Every time we see this sacrificial love around us, or in our own personal history, it is another testament to our loving God. Sacrificial love is the divine imprint on the dust of this earth. And those who lay down their lives for those they love stand with their torches to the heavens, pointing the tired, the poor, and the masses to the One from whom all love flows. Jesus told his disciples, "Greater love has no one than this, that someone lay down his life for his friends" (John 15:13 ESV).

28

Sinking of the Lusitania
He Will Direct Your Paths

A MAJOR CAUSE OF the United States' entry into World War I was the sinking of the British passenger ship Lusitania by a German submarine. The Lusitania was the largest vessel crossing the Atlantic after her sister ship, the Titanic, sunk a few years earlier in 1912.[1] When the LMS Lusitania left New York for England on May 1, 1915, most ignored a newspaper ad warning passengers not to board the British ship, as it was sailing into a war zone.[2] The United Kingdom and Germany had been at war for ten months.

As trench warfare on land and naval encounters at sea raged between the Allies and Central Powers in Europe, the United States tried to remain neutral. America's President Woodrow Wilson said, "America was too proud to fight,"[3] but the British naval blockade of Germany resulted in the United States trading almost exclusively with England, caused starvation in Germany, and drew America closer to war.[4]

Captain William Turner assured his passengers the Lusitania was faster than any submarine or U-boat. After all, the Lusitania had already made 222 transatlantic crossings and was designed for not only luxury but speed. And Captain Turner was confident Germany would never attack a passenger liner. Most that boarded that day did not realize German

1. Gilbert, *History of the Twentieth Century,* 371.
2. Washington Times, "German embassy warnings," Front page.
3. Levin, *Edith and Woodrow,* 79.
4. O'Shea, *Back to the Front,* 123–24.

U-boat captains had been given orders to fire without warning. Nor did they know the ship might be carrying contraband munitions.[5]

Tragedy struck when Captain Turner slowed down the Lusitania off the coast of Ireland to make port at high tide and it was attacked and sunk in just eighteen minutes.[6] There were 1,198 passengers and crew that perished, including 128 Americans.[7] Of the forty-six lifeboats, only six were successfully launched.[8]

But there were survivors, including Margaret Gwyer, who less than a month earlier married Reverend Herbert Gwyer. As the British luxury liner quickly sank, Margaret tried to swim away but was pulled into the vortex and sucked into one of the smoke stacks.[9] Margaret briefly lost consciousness. An explosion shot her back out and she splashed down near a lifeboat. The lifeboat survivors lifted the soot-covered Margaret into the boat, and thought she was African. Her husband who had made it into a lifeboat was in anguish thinking he had lost his wife. The last time Mrs. Gwyer had seen her six-foot-four tall husband he was helping others into lifeboats and giving his lifejacket to another passenger. When they were reunited the Reverend didn't immediately recognize his wife in tattered clothes and covered in grime.[10]

Hopes of America staying out of the war went down with the ship. Although it would be two more years before she joined the allies in the "war to end all wars" the sinking of the Lusitania was a direct cause for the United States entering World War I.[11]

Biblical Insight: God Works in Unique Ways

by Ernest Schmidt

Most would say, "Margaret's experience was amazing, but I don't think I would want it." The truth we need to learn is we do not have the privilege

---

5. Brammer, "Sinking of the Lusitania," paras. 1–5.
6. Preston, *Wilful Murder*, 72.
7. Archibald and Ballard, *Lost Ships of Robert Ballad*, 57.
8. Hesselberg, "Remembering Lusitania a Century Later," para. 20.
9. Hoehling and Hoehling, *Last Voyage of the Lusitania*, 169–74.
10. Hoehling and Hoehling, *Last Voyage of the Lusitania*, 181–83.
11. Strachan, *First World War*, 223–32.

of choosing how the Lord works in our lives. One size does not fit all. Each believer is custom-made, so the Lord's work in our lives is unique to us.

Margaret's experience reminds us not to limit the Lord in our thinking. He is all-wise, all-powerful, and all-loving. He expresses these attributes in working through us. Our heavenly Father specializes in the unusual in order to accomplish his purpose. As his children we have a vital role in fulfilling his plan.

Jonah's experience in the great fish is close to Margaret's deliverance, but that will probably not be how the Lord works in your life. The Red Sea will not part for you, nor will the Jordan River stop at flood stage. Your needs will neither be met with manna from heaven nor water from a rock, as in Moses' day. Nor will you have a cloud lead you in the day or a pillar of fire by night. You will not feed a large crowd like how the Lord fed 5,000 with two fish and five loaves.

Bible narratives show us what God did in the past. Though there are crucial truths presented in them, narratives are not given as descriptions of how the Lord always works. Do not expect to walk on water just because Peter did for a short distance! All these wonderful accounts reveal God's great power, love, and concern for his people, but will probably not be duplicated in our lives.

So then, how will the Lord work in your life? His dealings with you are not limited to miracles. He usually works behind the scenes in his providential activity, but this method of God's intervention is no less direct. In fact his quiet intervention at times can involve working in the lives of many people, using conditions or perfect timing in circumstances over vast geographical areas, with you as the center of his coordinated activity.

On January 23, 2019, five women were murdered at a bank in Sebring, Florida. God intervened in unique ways to prevent the killing of additional people. Circumstances prevented at least two people from being at the bank at that time. One individual was on his way to the bank and remembered he had more checks at home that needed to be deposited. He returned home to get the additional checks and missed being there at the time of the shooting. Another individual received a very lengthy phone call, which resulted in her not being at the bank during the time of the tragic event. Both of these individuals viewed their circumstances as a normal interruption in their schedule until they received news of what they escaped as a result of that interruption!

We do not have to have a smokestack experience to witness God's working in our lives. We need to go about our daily activities knowing God is in control. He will providentially do amazing things as we walk with him, whether we realize it or not at the time.

It is enough to know what David states in Ps 37:23 about events in our lives: "The steps of a good man are ordered by the Lord."

29

Unprepared for a Pandemic

WHEN COVID-19, ALSO KNOWN as the Coronavirus Pandemic, began to spread from its origin in Wuhan, China, in December of 2019, much of the world seemed unprepared. Without a vaccine or effective therapeutics, medical facilities lacked the space, ventilators, and PPE (Personal Protective Equipment) to effectively take care of the sick. As of March 2022, more than 441 million cases have been confirmed, with more than 5.9 million deaths attributed to COVID-19.[1] Authorities across the world responded by implementing travel restrictions, social distancing, lockdowns, and facility closures.

The strain put on medical facilities, personnel, and families dealing with COVID-19-related human suffering and deaths have been overwhelming. Mandatory shutdowns resulted in catastrophic losses of small businesses and educational opportunities, and delayed medical treatments from which many never recovered. COVID-19 has caused the largest global recession since the Great Depression, resulting in food shortages and famines which have affected hundreds of millions of people.[2] There is a high price for being unprepared.

Although the current pandemic continues to inflict suffering and death, it is dwarfed by past pandemics. A quick history lesson of past

---

1. https://www.worldometers.info/coronavirus.
2. United Nations, "Global Humanitarian Response Plan,"

pandemics reveals it was just a matter of time before another deadly pandemic began.

Some historians believe the first and one of the deadliest plague pandemics was the Plague of Justinian spread by infected rats and fleas. Although death totals widely vary, it is estimated that over 25 million people died, which was equivalent to almost half of Europe's population at the time.[3] Named after the Roman emperor in Constantinople, the plague's major outbreak was from AD 541 to 549, but persisted for three centuries. Genetic studies suggest the Justinian plague originated in China and was transported to Egypt.[4]

The Justinian plague had a profound impact, economically and militarily, on the Byzantine Empire. Crops could not be planted or harvested, resulting in famines. Massive debt, followed by high taxation, led to inflation, while a sickened and diminished population led to a greatly weakened military.[5]

The Black Death was an even more deadly, global-bubonic plague that originated in China in 1334. It reduced the world population down to possibly 300 million. The plague killed 150 to 200 million, with some estimates claiming that up to 60 percent of Europeans died from the Black Death.[6] Some historians believe society subsequently became more violent as the mass mortality rate cheapened life and thus increased warfare, crime, and popular revolts.[7]

The Spanish flu, or the 1918–1919 flu pandemic, infected 500 million people—about one-third of the world's population at the time.[8] The death toll is estimated to have been anywhere from 50 to 100 million, In the US, about 28 percent of the population of 105 million became infected, and 500,000 to 850,000 died.[9] Massive dosages of Bayer aspirin were recommended as a pharmaceutical treatment for the Spanish influenza. Historians believe many of the deaths from the Spanish flu were either caused or accelerated by aspirin poisoning.[10]

---

3. Rosen, *Justinian's Flea*, 3.
4. Horgan, "Justinian's Plague," paras. 1–2.
5. Wade, "Europe's Plagues Came From China."
6. Austin, *Pest in the Land*, 21.
7. Cohn, "Black Death," 703–38.
8. "1918 Pandemic (H1N1 Virus)," para. 1.
9. "1918 Pandemic, (H1N1 Virus)," para. 2.
10. Infectious Diseases Society of America, "Aspirin Misuse."

Comparatively few people in China were affected by the 1918–19 flu, leading to speculation that the pandemic originated in China, where the population acquired immunity before the virus mutated into a far deadlier strain as it spread worldwide.[11]

The Spanish influenza was particularly deadly because it caused an overreaction of the body's immune system. Young adults between twenty to forty years old were most at risk because of their stronger immune systems. Ninety-nine percent of pandemic influenza deaths in the United States occurred in people under sixty-five.[12] Even the wealthy and famous did not escape the disease, although the many who survived the virus included Woodrow Wilson, Franklin Delano Roosevelt, Greta Garbo, Walt Disney, John J. Pershing, Mahatma Gandhi, Georgia O'Keeffe, and Keiser Wilhelm II.

The Spanish flu of 1918–19, the last similar pandemic to COVID-19, has been labeled by some historians as a "forgotten pandemic."[13] The pandemic was overshadowed by World War I and epidemiologists at the time greatly underestimated the global death toll. With celebrations of the armistice ending WWI and the beginning of the Roaring 20s people wanted to put the pandemic behind them.

With the exception of AIDS, epidemics have tended not to become global pandemics in recent times. SARS in 2003 was confined to Asia; MERS in 2012 was limited to the Middle East; Ebola in 2014 stayed in Africa. But these were all warning signs. Years of underinvestment in public health infrastructure left the world unprepared for the greatest public health crisis in 100 years. Joshua Lederberg, Nobel laureate in Physiology and Medicine, famously said: "The single biggest threat to man's continued dominance on the planet is the virus."[14] Fortunately, pandemics don't happen very often, but with today's increased mobility and a world population of nearly 8 billion people, a highly contagious virus can spread worldwide in a matter of weeks. It is more important than ever today for governments and world leaders to prepare and try to mitigate the next disease outbreak.

---

11. Vergano, "1918 Flu Pandemic," para. 12.
12. Simonsen et al. "Pandemic Versus Epidemic," 53–60.
13. Crosby, *America's Forgotten Pandemic*, 319.
14. Specter, "After Ebola," para. 2.

Biblical Insight: Be Prepared for the Worst

by Ernest Schmidt

You have probably seen the words "Prepare to meet your God" on a billboard or in other public places. The phrase is a quote from Amos 4:12. Amos's use of these words may be somewhat of a shock. In context, his words were akin to telling them to prepare for a pandemic.

Amos's ministry was unenviable. After Solomon's reign, Israel split into Northern and Southern Kingdoms. As a Southerner, God commissioned Amos to deliver messages of judgment to the Northern Kingdom. In chapter four of his book he reminded them of the Lord's providential activity to bring the Northern Kingdom back to a relationship with him.

Amos 4 lists the wake-up calls God sent to get their attention so they would repent and return to him. Following each, Amos writes the spiritually haunting phrase that is repeated five times, "*yet you have not returned to me*, says the Lord."

1. "Also I gave you cleanness of teeth in all your cities, and lack of bread in all your places; *yet you have not returned to me*," says the Lord (v. 6).
2. "I also withheld rain from you . . . *yet you have not returned to me*," says the Lord (v. 8).
3. "I blasted you with blight and mildew." Concerning the crops He also said, "The locusts devoured them. *Yet you have not returned to me*," says the Lord (v. 9).
4. "I sent among you a plague after the manner of Egypt; your young men I killed with a sword, along with your captive horses; I made the stench of your camps come up into your nostrils; *yet you have not returned to me*," says the Lord (v. 10).
5. "I overthrew *some* of you, as God overthrew Sodom and Gomorrah . . . *Yet you have not returned to me*," says the Lord (v. 11).

Israel's sin and lack of repentance prepared them to experience the pandemic of pandemics—meeting God in judgment. "Therefore thus will I do to you, O Israel, because I will do this to you, prepare to meet your God, O Israel!" (v. 12). Israel, who had prepared herself for the worst, faced the eternal, all-powerful God, who had stacks of evidence against them. Human imagination cannot conceive of a more frightful end of life than facing God in judgment.

So what about us? The bad news is we don't have to prepare for God's judgment. We are already an object of God's judgment. "He who believes in Him is not condemned; but he who does not believe is condemned already, because he has not believed in the name of the only begotten Son of God. . . . He who believes in the Son has everlasting life; and he who does not believe the Son shall not see life, but the wrath of God abides on him" (John 3:18, 36). The good news is God has *prepared* a way for us to avoid his condemnation and wrath.

The word "propitiation," used a few times in the New Testament, speaks of that which removes wrath. The pagans used the word when trying to appease their gods, but the New Testament usage is the polar opposite of this. First John 4:10 is the epitome of God's view of propitiation. "In this is love, not that we loved God, but that He loved us and sent His Son to be the propitiation for our sins." Instead of man's effort to appease God, he gave himself a reason for not pouring out his wrath on us. He expended his wrath on the Lord Jesus as our substitute. "For He made Him who knew no sin to be sin for us, that we might become the righteousness of God in Him" (2 Cor 5:21).

This is the reason both John 3:18 and 3:36 state we are to believe in Jesus Christ. This is not just acknowledgment of who he is and what he has done, but trust in him alone for the removal of God's condemnation and wrath. Unlike the unrepentant nation of Israel, we are to admit our sin against God and receive his provision for a right relationship with him. We do not have to prepare for the worst. We can receive what God has prepared for our best.

"For God so loved the world that He gave His only begotten Son, that whoever believes in Him should not perish but have everlasting life" (John 3:16). "But as many as received Him, to them He gave the right to become children of God, to those who believe in His name" (John 1:12).

30

Death-Defying Harry Houdini

How many times do we wish we could talk to family or friends one last time after they die unexpectedly? This was true for many families who lost loved ones in both the Civil War and World War I. Maybe as a result of so many war casualties, the Spiritualist movement became especially popular from the 1860s through the 1920s.

Harry Houdini grieved for months after his mother passed away, and some believe the fraud he encountered while consulting mediums to communicate with her after her death turned him against the fake spiritualists.[1] Mediums preyed upon these grieving individuals, professing that they could contact the spirits of the dead. Even the newly invented radio was claimed by some to be a vehicle for connecting with deceased loved ones. People were led to believe a game board could magically and accurately answer questions about the past, present, and future. Fake spiritualists relentlessly created new methods to take advantage of people desperate to make contact with those beyond the grave.

As fake spiritualists exploited those grieving for their loved ones, a magician/illusionist/stunt performer entered, one who knew every trick these charlatans used and how to expose them. He became the bane of their existence. His name was Harry Weisz. Born in Budapest,

---

1. Schwartz, "Biography of Harry Houdini," para. 33.

Austro-Hungary, he immigrated to the United States in 1878 and took the stage name of Harry Houdini.[2]

For decades he fascinated and entertained much of the world with his escape acts. Houdini never claimed to have supernatural mystical powers and railed against those who used this form of entertainment to scam the unsuspecting and vulnerable who were grieving for departed loved ones. Houdini said they were "vultures who prey on the bereaved."[3]

It seemed nothing could constrain Harry Houdini, as he would extricate himself from straitjackets, chains, or handcuffs while sometimes underwater or dangling high above streets from ropes. His incredible physical abilities and sleight-of-hand showmanship convinced admirers like Sir Conan Doyle, author of the Sherlock Homes books, that Houdini had harnessed a paranormal force. Trying to demonstrate there was nothing supernatural about his acts, Houdini revealed his techniques step by step, but Doyle became antagonistic and remained unconvinced.[4]

In his continued effort to expose spiritualists as scam artists, Houdini offered a $10,000 reward to any fortune-teller who could successfully display supernatural powers. No professed psychic was able to perform such powers, and the prize was never collected. In 1926, he supported a bill in Congress to outlaw fortune-telling for compensation.[5]

In 1917, Harry "Handcuff" Houdini registered for the selective service at the age of forty-four. As a patriot and supporter of America's involvement in World War I, he raised money for the war effort and even held classes to demonstrate escape techniques to the US troops.

Harry Houdini's demise came quickly. A college student asked Houdini if he actually could withstand any punch to the stomach as he earlier proclaimed. Without bracing himself Houdini was struck multiple times in the abdomen. When, racked with fever and excruciating pain, a doctor finally examined Houdini, he was found to have acute appendicitis. Within a few days Houdini was dead at the age of fifty-two. Many believe his death from a ruptured appendix was at least partially caused by the blows to his abdomen.[6]

2. Biography.com Editors. "Harry Houdini Biography."
3. Ptacin, "How Harry Houdini," para. 6.
4. Kalush and Sloman, *Secret Life of Houdini*, 419–20.
5. Felix, "Harry Houdini," para. 1.
6. Mikkelson, "Did Houdini Die?," 1–5.

Harry Houdini believed he was better-suited than anyone else to communicate from the hereafter. Just before Houdini died on Halloween night 1926, he gave his wife, Bess, a secret code. He said he would try to reveal the cypher from beyond the grave. A reward was offered to any medium that could reveal the code. After a decade of unsuccessful séances Bess Houdini said, "Ten years is long enough to wait for any man."[7]

Biblical Insight: Avoiding the Occult

by Ernest Schmidt

The life of Houdini is filled with interest in the other side. Contact with the departed seemed to be an obsession. His own promise to communicate with his wife after his death did not materialize. His fame and legacy invites us to consider what we should think about seeking to contact the other side for information.

The only source for addressing questions concerning the afterlife and the future is the Bible. We need to let God's word inform us about what our approach should be toward that subject. In general the Bible forbids any attempts at consulting any source for such information apart from God. In light of the fact that the subject ultimately involves Satan and demons, we need to note a summary of the Bible's presentation of these enemies of God.

In Genesis 3 we note Satan's use of a snake to deceive Eve. His success led to sin and rebellion against God. All of the devastation of disease, death, and ruined relations are traceable to the devil's activity. Genesis 3:15 informs us there will be constant conflict between the "descendants" of Satan and the righteous. The narratives of the Bible and history illustrate this fact.

Just before the nation of Israel entered the promised land, the Lord forbade any involvement with the occult (Deut 18:9–14). A major cause for Saul's death was consulting a medium. The remainder of the Old Testament reveals the problems Israel had as they forsook God's word and followed idolatry and its satanic error. In fact, Manasseh's sin (which included occult practices) was so great the nation was "doomed" to exile for seventy years (2 Chr 33:6; 34:23–25; Jer 25:11).

---

7. Barretta, *Street Smart*, 10.

In the New Testament, a major rise in demonism confronts us. The maladies the demons caused in Jesus' day should be a warning against any form of dabbling in the occult. Demons hindered speech and sight, created great distress, and contributed to self-destructive behavior.

During the days of the early church Satan and his demons actively opposed the gospel. Satan operates by deception, so Paul warns of his devices, craftiness, wiles, hindrances, and doctrine. Peter states Satan is "like a roaring lion, seeking whom he may devour" (1 Pet 5:8). John warns of his activity as the work of antichrists. The book of Revelation is replete with the hateful activity of Satan seeking to prevent the Lord's preparation for Christ's coming rule on earth.

There is danger in toying with the dark side. In fact Paul says our real conflict is with organized satanic/demonic activity (Eph 6:10–12). So how do we respond? First, we must receive the Lord Jesus Christ as our personal Savior from sin and the power of Satan (Acts 26:17–18). James instructs us to "resist the devil and he will flee from you" (Jas 4:7). Peter explains how one is to resist: "Resist him, *steadfast in the faith* . . ." (1 Pet 5:9). We resist by confidence in the promises of God. Paul states this confidence is a shield that will "quench all the fiery darts of the wicked one" (Eph 6:16). This reflects what Christ did when he resisted Satan. He resisted with truth. Satan "does not stand in the truth . . . for he is a liar and the father of it" (John 8:44). Resist Satan by reminding yourself of the truth. Fortune-tellers and others create curiosity concerning the occult, but God condemns it.

31

Trial by Fire
The Glenn Cunningham Story

IT WASN'T UNCOMMON FOR one-room schoolhouses in America to catch fire at the turn of the century. By 1900, there were an estimated 200,000 of these small buildings nationwide.[1] They were tinderboxes filled with flammable material, and the heating systems were wood or coal-burning stoves. It was an accident waiting to happen.

Teachers usually arrived early to open the school and heat the building before the children arrived. But in Protection, Kansas, Mr. Schroeder allowed students arriving early to enter an unlocked side door of their Rolla Sunflower country school to start the fire in the potbelly stove.

The four Cunningham children arrived early one cold February day in 1916 and entered through the unlocked door. Glenn Cunningham watched as his older thirteen-year-old brother, Floyd, accidentally poured gasoline rather than kerosene on the coals igniting a fire that quickly engulfed the boys.[2]

> "A blinding flash seared my eyes and made my head swim," Glenn Cunningham wrote in his book *Never Quit*. "An awful force, as if from hell itself, hurled me painfully back against the wall. Dimly I heard Floyd scream, 'I'm on fire.'
>
> I tried to open my eyes to see what was happening. I couldn't. Nothing but black-red, stabbing pain raced down the

---

1. Wishart, "One-Room Schoolhouses," para. 2.
2. Hersey, "Cunningham Calls It a Career," paras. 13–14.

throbbing corridors of my mind. Suddenly I realized it. 'I'm burning, too!'"[3]

Somehow, with the help of their brother and sister who were not burned, Floyd and Glenn staggered the two miles back to their home. The doctor said Floyd was too badly burned to survive. For nine days he lingered near death. Although he didn't speak, he would hum the melody of the hymn "God Be with You Till We Meet Again." Then one night Floyd said his first words since the school fire, repeating the words from the chorus: "Till we meet at Jesus' feet, God be with you till we meet again." He pressed his mother's hand to his face, and soon after he was dead.[4]

Glenn's battle for his life had just begun. He lost all the toes on his left foot and much of the flesh and muscle on his legs. Infection spread. The doctor told the Cunningham parents that their seven-year-old son Glenn might live, but if the infection got worse, there would be no choice but to amputate his legs. For certain Glenn would never walk again. But after almost two years of rehabilitation and incredible personal determination, Glenn took his first steps.

Not only did Glenn Cunningham learn to walk again, but he recovered to become one of America's greatest runners. As a high school senior, he set the world high school record in the mile run. Glenn went on to set the national collegiate record and participated in the 1932 and 1936 Olympics.[5] His nickname was the "The Iron Man of Kansas."[6] In 1938, he became the world's fastest miler. Cunningham was voted the outstanding track performer in the 100-year history of Madison Square Garden in 1978, and a year later, he was inducted into the National Track and Field Hall of Fame.[7]

Cunningham decided to end his track career when the 1940 Olympics, which were to be held in Japan, were cancelled. With his wife, Ruth, and their ten children, he operated the Cunningham Youth Ranch for thirty years where over 9,000 needy and homeless children learned biblical teachings and a never-quit attitude.[8] Glenn Cunningham's testimony

---

3. Tanner, "Kansas Track Star," paras. 5–6.
4. "Glenn Cunningham, US, Olympian."
5. OlyMadMen, "Glenn Cunningham," para. 12.
6. Hersey, "Cunningham Calls It a Career," para. 4.
7. D'Ambra, "Glenn Cunningham,"
8. Scannell, "Cunningham Still Running His Race," para. 12.

and personal triumph over so much adversity remains an inspiration to so many even today.

Biblical Insight: Fiery Trials

by Ernest Schmidt

A mark of character is what it takes to stop you. Glenn Cunningham certainly illustrates the positive side of that statement. He did not stop in spite of the worst-case scenario. Perhaps you have already asked yourself, "What would I have done in his circumstances?" Or your questioning went in another direction: "Why would God allow such a tragedy? I know it turned out well, but why did he have to go through that experience?" Of course only the Lord knows all the reasons, but we can see the positive outcome.

The Lord is not done using unexpected and often unwanted challenges to reveal his glory through people, but one size does not fit all. We may not experience horrible challenges like Glenn Cunningham, but we do need to accept and use the negative circumstances God allows or brings into our lives. Whether it is a matter of financial challenges, relationship, conflict, physical illness, or other negative situations, they did not—and do not—catch God by surprise. He is involved, and we need to get involved in what he is doing in our lives.

A unique passage of Scripture gives insight into how the Lord uses extreme experiences to accomplish his purposes through us. In John 9, Jesus and his disciples encountered a blind man. The disciples immediately concluded his condition was a result of sin in the family or foreseen sin in the blind man's life (John 9:1–2). It would have been interesting to have seen the shock on the disciples faces when the Lord answered "Neither."

The Lord Jesus explained the reason for the man's blindness from birth and how God works through undesirable circumstances. Like the friends of Job in the Old Testament, the disciples thought problems were the result of things people have done wrong. But God's plan includes much more than our limited perspective. We only see bits and pieces of the big picture in God's plan. The reason for this man's blindness was "that the works of God should be revealed in him" (John 9:3). Note those last two words. The Lord had a specific plan for showing his power in him. The Lord Jesus healed him. His reception of sight was not only a major physical blessing to him, but an opportunity to expose the hypocrisy of "religious people" (vv. 16–41). Ultimately it led him to an eternal spiritual relationship with the Lord (vv. 35–38).

Whatever you are going through now, God is not surprised. If you are not a believer he is perhaps challenging you to trust the Lord Jesus for eternal life. If you are a believer, he certainly will use whatever you are going through in a positive way. In his unique dealings with you as a believer, you may approach your "fiery trial . . . but rejoice . . . when His glory is revealed" (1 Pet 4:12). No matter what your experience, he wants to reveal his work in you.

32

The Lost Generation in the Roaring 20s

FIVE MONTHS AFTER THE war started on July 28, 1914, the so-called "civilized" Western democracies had fought to a stalemate in atrocious World War I trench warfare conditions. Soldiers longed for an end to the bloodshed but there was none in sight. Then on Christmas day 1914, an estimated 100,000 enemy combatants came out of their trenches to meet in No Man's Land where they sang Christmas carols together and exchanged gifts.[1] The widespread unofficial ceasefires occurred along the Western Front.

Just days earlier these same soldiers were using their latest weapons of tanks, machine guns, poisonous gas, and airplanes to slaughter each other. Many realized in that brief reprieve that they had no personal quarrel with those they fought against. Then a few days after the Christmas truce, they went back to killing each other.[2] By the end of the war, all that human suffering, death, and destruction seemed to be for nothing.

In the aftermath of World War I, President Woodrow Wilson's crusade to make World War I the "War to End All Wars" and "Make the World Safe for Democracy" was a colossal failure. The rise of Communism and Fascism in Europe resulted in practically the same countries fighting over the same territories just twenty years later with the advent of World War II.[3]

1. Vinciguerra, "Truce of Christmas, 1914," para. 2.
2. Winter and Baggett, *Great War,* 96–99.
3. Rather and Sullivan, *Our Times,* 588–89.

The Lost Generation in the Roaring 20s

Just as World War I ended, the Spanish flu pandemic of 1918 infected an estimated 500 million people worldwide—about one-third of the planet's population.[4] This strain of influenza killed at least 50 million people and possibly as many as 100 million, including approximately 675,000 Americans.[5] As a result, young people in the 1920s often had a live-for-today attitude, believing life was short. Flappers bobbed their hair, danced to jazz in speakeasies, and smoked "torches for freedom"—cigarettes. Al Capone and other gangsters reaped enormous profits for a short time from racketeering, prostitution, and selling alcohol during prohibition.[6]

The Great War, or World War I, left many to question their trust in governments, business, or religion. "Here was a new generation," wrote the novelist F. Scott Fitzgerald in 1920 in *This Side of Paradise*, "grown up to find all gods dead, all wars fought, all faiths in man shaken."[7] Many felt disillusioned, alienated, and lost.

This rapidly accelerating, modernizing culture saw a substantial number of Americans move to large, impersonal cities. Left behind were family and friends in small, rural societies with close social bonds and a strong sense of community.

The European economy suffered greatly in the aftermath of the Great War as countries tried to pay off wartime debt and deal with the loss of a whole generation of young men. By entering late in the war and profiting from wartime production, the American economy surged ahead in the Roaring 20s. America's industrial output by the 1920s was greater than that of all the other Great Powers—England, France, Germany, Russia, Italy, and Japan—combined.[8] In a time of almost unprecedented prosperity for America, many became self-assured that these good times would last forever. Buying on credit and installment plans allowed families to spend beyond their current means.

Gertrude Stein is credited with coining the phrase "Lost Generation." She wrote, "You are a lost generation . . . all of you young people who served in the war."[9] It was subsequently popularized by Ernest Hemingway, who used the phrase in his 1926 novel *The Sun Also Rises*.

---

4. "1918 Pandemic (H1N1 Virus)," para. 2.
5. "1918 Pandemic (H1N1 Virus)." para. 1.
6. Bergreen, *Capone*, 409. 606.
7. Piper, "Fitzgerald's Cult of Disillusion," 69–80.
8. Douglas, *Terrible Honesty*, 182–83.
9. Monk, *Writing the Lost Generation*, 1.

The lost generation more specifically referred to the American expatriate authors who lived in Paris in the 1920s. They were disillusioned and cynical about the world. Through their writings, they expressed their resentment toward the materialism and individualism that was pervasive in the Roaring 20s. The United States was a nation awash in materialism and devoid of spiritual vitality. "A wasteland," wrote the poet T.S. Eliot, "inhabited by hollow men."[10] Decadent living for short-term gain and binge-buying on credit were some of the causes of Great Depression that followed the Roaring 20s.

Biblical Insight: Taking the Christian Family Name

by Ronald Ian Phillips

Many Americans who survived World War I and the pandemic that followed developed an attitude of "eat, drink, and be merry for tomorrow we die." Cataclysmic events have caused many in history to be fatalistic and lose their faith in institutions, government, and religion.

In an earlier time, the American poet Henry Wadsworth Longfellow's faith was equally shaken with the profound loss of his wife in an accidental fire and his severely wounded oldest son's return home from the Civil War. The song, "I Heard the Bells on Christmas Day," is based on his 1863 poem in which he wrote: "And in despair I bowed my head/There is no peace on earth I said/For hate is strong/And mocks the song/ Of peace on earth, good-will to men!"[11] Longfellow's final lines from this song provided solace to those experiencing great loss: "Then pealed the bells more loud and deep:/God is not dead, nor doth He sleep;/The Wrong shall fail,/The Right prevail,/With peace on earth, good-will to men."

Living life for pleasure's sake alone unfortunately resulted in many in the Roaring 20s turned away from God. Immediate gratification became an all-consuming lifestyle, but there is always a price to be paid for this self-destructive behavior. Galatians 6:7–8 (NIV) warns, "Do not be deceived: God cannot be mocked. A man reaps what he sows. Whoever sows to please their flesh, from the flesh will reap destruction; whoever sows to please the Spirit, from the Spirit will reap eternal life." First John 2:16–17 adds, "For all that is in the world—the lust of the flesh, the lust

---

10. "Jazz Age," para. 5.
11. Longfellow, "I Heard the Bells on Christmas Day."

of the eyes, and the pride of life—is not of the Father but is of the world. And the world is passing away, and the lust of it; but he who does the will of God abides forever."

The Bible tells us this self-serving narcissism will become even more prevalent the closer we are to Christ's return. According to 2 Timothy 3:1–5,

> This know also, that in the last days perilous times shall come. For men shall be lovers of their own selves, covetous, boasters, proud, blasphemers, disobedient to parents, unthankful, unholy, without natural affection, trucebreakers, false accusers, incontinent, fierce, despisers of those that are good, traitors, heady, high-minded, lovers of pleasures more than lovers of God; having a form of godliness, but denying the power thereof: from such turn away.

Heaven still awaits and heartbreaking losses still happen, but Christians have a loving heavenly Father who is omnipresent (God is always everywhere; Ps 139:7–10), omniscient (God knows everything; 1 John 3:20), omnipotent (God is all powerful; Ps 147:5), and omnificent (God is Creator of all; Gen 1:1). God, who has made us part of his eternal family once we have trusted in Jesus Christ, has not left us powerless to face the challenges, griefs, or adversities of this life.

Living a life of joy and happiness serving the Lord is certainly preferable, possible, and biblical. Fortunately, the benefits of the Christian life do not begin at death. Once we are believers and adopted into the family of God, we become sons and daughters of God. Jesus, then, is our high priest and intercedes for us before the Father. Jesus is praying for us in Heaven. Romans 8:34 (NIV) says, "Who then is the one who condemns? No one. Christ Jesus who died—more than that, who was raised to life—is at the right hand of God and is also interceding for us." First John 2:1 (NKJV) states, "My little children, these things I write to you, so that you may not sin. And if anyone sins, we have an advocate with the Father, Jesus Christ the righteous."

And there is more. The Holy Spirit who indwells all Christians is also our advocate. Romans 8:26 (NKJV) tells us that: "Likewise the Spirit also helps in our weaknesses. For we do not know what we should pray for as we ought, but the Spirit Himself makes intercession for us with groanings which cannot be uttered."

Why would the unbeliever chose not to be adopted into God's family and remain an orphan, a slave to sin of their own passions? As God's children we inherit joy, peace, and purpose on earth. We also receive a pardon from our sin and the free gift of eternal life.

33

The Scopes Monkey Trial

CHARLES DARWIN HAD BECOME an agnostic by the time he wrote *On the Origin of Species* in 1859, espousing the theory of evolution. He and his wife, Emma, had many passionate discussions on religion as she continued to attend church and believe in an afterlife. She expressed her fears that they would be separated for eternity.[1]

For the next sixty-six years the question of human origin was debated by countless others, arguing between divine creation as recorded in the Bible and Darwin's theory of evolution. Finally on a hot summer July day in 1925, people from both sides of the argument assembled for a trial in Dayton, Tennessee, hopefully to bring clarity to this debate once and for all. Over 200 newspapers across the United States and Europe featured front-page coverage of the event while the trial was the first to be broadcasted by radio.[2]

Much of rural America, especially in the South, was incensed by the trial reports of H. L. Mencken, who ridiculed nonurban Americans as "yokels," "morons," and "hill-billies."[3] Evolutionists often viewed creationists who believed in the literal interpretation of the Bible as uneducated and clinging to outdated fundamentalist beliefs contrary to the preponderance of scientific evidence. Creationists were chastised for not being

---

1. Heiligman, *Charles and Emma*, 2.
2. PBS, "Monkey Trial," para. 2.
3. "Scopes Trial, Humor," para. 53.

modernists and progressives, and derided for not accepting indisputable views of expert scientists.

Formally known as *The State of Tennessee v. John Thomas Scopes* this legal case has often been called "The Scopes Monkey Trial" or "The Trial of the Century." It remains a landmark court case in American history. A substitute high school teacher, John Scopes, was charged with violating the Tennessee Butler Act, which made it unlawful to teach human evolution in any state-funded school. Fifteen states had anti-evolution legislation pending in 1925, so with this growing trend the American Civil Liberties Union (ACLU) offered to fund the legal defense of any teacher accused of teaching the theory of evolution.[4]

With the dramatic increase of high school students, rising from 18 percent in 1910 to 73 percent in 1940, came greater scrutiny and demands for local control of the curriculum and textbooks.[5] *Civic Biology*, by George Hunter, was the biology textbook used in Tennessee schools at the time, and it shaped the modern high school biology curriculum across the country. Not only did this science textbook include Darwinian concepts on evolution but it also stated the highest of five races on earth were Caucasians. *Civic Biology* also stated that people deemed eugenically unfit such as those with epilepsy, and "feeble-mindedness" should be sexually segregated and sterilized, and those who "take from society, but they give nothing in return . . . are true parasites."[6] This science textbook went on to say: "If such people were lower animals, we would probably kill them off to prevent them from spreading. Humanity will not allow this."[7] Hunter embraced the idea of eugenics as a social doctrine, as did many other evolutionary biologists until World War II. The case may have been seen as a contest between evolution and creation, but it was also about whether modern science and a progressive education should be taught in schools. Many people saw these as dangerous concepts that they did not want taught to their children.

Local leaders in the small town of Dayton, Tennessee hoped a trial of this magnitude would increase publicity and business for their town. They recruited John Scopes, a twenty-year-old football coach and substitute teacher of the high school biology class, to be charged with teaching

---

4. Linder, "Scopes (Monkey) Trial."
5. Goldin, *Race between Education and Technology*, 195.
6. "Scopes Trial Excerpts," para. 9.
7. Hunter, *Civic Biology*, 394–404.

evolution. Scopes couldn't remember if he actually had taught a lesson on evolution, but he agreed to be the defendant. The case quickly drew national attention when the three-time Democratic presidential nominee and former United States Secretary of State, William Jennings Bryan, joined the prosecuting team. Scopes was represented by the agnostic, Clarence Darrow, who was one of the most brilliant lawyers of the time.

The trial quickly turned into a circus. When approximately 700 people crammed into the stifling-hot county courthouse there were concerns the floor might collapse, so eventually Judge Raulston moved the proceedings outside. Clergy and vendors filled the streets, selling everything from Bibles to stuffed monkeys. "Read Your Bible" banners were displayed and trained chimpanzees performed on the courthouse lawn.[8]

William Jennings Bryan was a staunch fundamentalist and defender of the Bible, but as a theistic evolutionist he admitted he did not believe in a literal six-day creation. Bryan was ill-prepared when he unwisely allowed Darrow to cross-examine him about his personal beliefs. Bryan died just five days after the eight-day trial concluded.[9]

When Judge Raulston ruled that the trial was not to decide the truth of creationism or evolution but simply whether John Scopes violated the Butler Act, the defense asked that their client be found guilty so they could appeal to a higher court. It took the jury just nine minutes to deliberate and reach a guilty verdict. While the jury should have set the fine, the judge chose to impose on Scopes a $100 fine, the smallest amount allowed in this case, allowing a higher court of appeals to set the conviction aside on a technicality.

The debate on the origins of man continues today. A May 2005 Gallup poll revealed that 76 percent of Americans would not be upset "if public schools taught the theory of creationism—that is, the idea that human beings were created by God in their present form and did not evolve from other species of animals."[10] A 2012 Gallup poll also found that 46 percent of Americans believe God created humans in their present form within the last 10,000 years, while only 15 percent say humans evolved without God involved in the process.[11] American views on the origin of

---

8. History.Com Editors, "Scopes Monkey Trial Begins."
9. Kazin, *Godly Hero*, 134.
10. Carlson, "Americans Weigh in on Evolution," para. 4.
11. Newport, "Politics In U.S., 46% Hold Creationist View," para. 1.

humans have remained almost unchanged in the thirty years since Gallup first asked the question.

Do the government or publicly funded educational institutions have the right to restrict or limit constitutional freedoms such as free speech in academia? Do federal, state, or local governments have the right to control public school curriculum and textbooks?

Sharing some of the same concerns as parents during the time of the Scopes Trial, many today are challenging what is taught in public schools. Other parents are opting for home or private schooling where they have greater influence over their children's physical and mental well-being. The homeschool population grew dramatically from 2.5 million in 2019 to 3.7 million in 2021.[12]

Biblical Insight: Teach Your Children Well

by Ronald Ian Phillips

In 2016, the National Center for Science Education stated, "Truth in science, however, is never final and what is accepted as a fact today may be modified or even discarded tomorrow."[13] It may be surprising to some that today's scientific facts can later be found to be untrue in the view of modern science. Certainly we would be hard pressed to find any scientists today that still believe much of what was taught as scientific fact in *Civic Biology*.

On the other hand, many Christians hold a steadfast belief that the Bible is infallible. What Christians deem true today will still be their truth tomorrow; God's word is incapable of error because God cannot lie (Heb 6:18). We, as Christians, know the Bible is inspired by God—the Bible's ultimate author (2 Tim 3:16). His book is inerrant: God used human authors to write exactly what he wanted it to say (2 Pet 1:20–21).

Public schools were first instituted by the puritans in Massachusetts in 1647 to ensure children would be able to read Scripture. When many public schools stopped using the Bible as a textbook, Benjamin Rush, a signer of the Declaration of Independence and colonial educator, proposed that the US government require schools to use Bibles, as well as furnish an American Bible to every family at public expense.

---

12. Ray, "Research Facts on Homeschooling," para. 1.
13. National Academy of Sciences, *Science and Creationism*, 2.

Long before the 1920s there have been those who regarded children as collective property, to be shaped and molded according to the state's needs. Courts and society in general have moved public schools to be more secular so the curriculum adheres to the current laws separating church and state. But what are parents to do when schools deviate from teaching core subjects to teaching children morals, religious beliefs, and civic lessons that contradict their family values? How can these two trains of thought exist together in one academic institute?

Teachers assume an awesome responsibility to educate parents' most precious loved ones. The vast majority of public and private school teachers are dedicated to the extreme in fulfilling this mission. Most educators try to develop the skills and knowledge necessary for students to take advantage of the opportunities this remarkable country provides while preparing them to be responsible citizens, to be self-sufficient, and to contribute to the good of society.

However, the winds of political change can usher in a new paradigm shift in education. Once in power, opposing voices are often silenced. William Wordsworth wrote in a poem, as a tribute to the pirate Rob Roy, that, "They should take who have the power, and they should keep who can."[14] James Madison, known as the "Father of the Constitution" and fourth President of the United States, wrote, "The essence of Government is power; and power, lodged as it must be in human hands, will ever be liable to abuse."[15] Abraham Lincoln warned that "Nearly all men can stand adversity, but if you want to test a man's character, give him power."[16]

Thankfully, in the United States of America, citizens can exercise the often-overlooked petition clause that guarantees, Americans can petition the government to redress their grievances without fear of retribution or punishment. The Bible's book of Daniel provides two good examples of how Christians should respond to government authority when it stands contrary to their beliefs.

In the book of Daniel there is a story of four young men taken captive from Judah and brought to King Nebuchadnezzar's Babylon. Daniel, Shadrach, Meshach, and Abednego were enrolled in the school for future civil servants. Even while receiving a pagan education in a pagan society,

---

14. Wordsworth, "Rob Roy's Grave," lines 39–40.
15. Library of Congress, "On These Walls," para. 15.
16. https://www.forbes.com/quotes/76/.

they were not corrupted; they flourished and rose to the top of their class because of their strong commitment to God.

Daniel 1:17 tells us, "As for these four children, God gave them knowledge and skill in all learning and wisdom: and Daniel had understanding in all visions and dreams." When Daniel interpreted one of the king's dreams, the king promoted Daniel and his three friends to great prominence (Dan 2:49). In time, Nebuchadnezzar decreed that all people must worship his golden image and serve his gods.

When Shadrach, Meshach, and Abednego refused, they were thrown into a fiery furnace so hot that it killed the king's guards who threw them into the fire. To the king's astonishment, he saw not three but "four men loose, walking in the midst of the fire, and they have no hurt; and the form of the fourth is like the Son of God" (Dan 3:25). "And the princes, governors, and captains, and the king's counsellors, being gathered together, saw these men, upon whose bodies the fire had no power, nor was an hair of their head singed, neither were their coats changed, nor the smell of fire had passed on them" (Dan 3:27).

Shadrach, Meshach, and Abednego were respectful to those in authority over them (Dan 3:16). And yet they were true to God and would not compromise or rationalize to justify disobedience (Dan 3:17–18). We are also reminded in this account that God was with them and is always with us. Deut 31:6 (NKJV) says, "Be strong and of good courage, do not fear nor be afraid of them; for the Lord your God, He is the One who goes with you. He will not leave you nor forsake you."

A second example of how to handle civil disobedience came when Daniel was in his eighties. He defied King Darius's decree not to pray to anyone other than the king and continued to pray to God three times a day. Daniel's accusers could find no fault in his life, so they used his religious beliefs to destroy him. Daniel was thrown in the lion's den, and of course the story of how he survived this peril is familiar.

With these two examples we are reminded as believers that Jesus rescued us from the death penalty of sin and is always with us, even when things seem hopeless.

It is as admirable now as in the 1920s for parents to pay attention to what is taught to their children in public schools. Christians have the ability to vote, serve in political positions, and work peaceably to change government policies or actions. As the examples in the book of Daniel demonstrate, Christians should resist a government that commands or compels evil or beliefs that are contrary to God's word.

34

Thomas Midgley Jr.
Just Because You Can, Doesn't Mean You Should

THOSE WHO STRIVE FOR solutions to complex industrial problems cannot be expected to get it right every time, but few have gotten it as wrong as Thomas Midgley Jr. He is universally considered one of the worst inventors because his work has caused catastrophic environmental problems, affecting the health of millions.[1] Americans have 400 times the lead in their bodies today as pre-Industrial humans because of just one of his deadly inventions.[2] The health impacts of lead exposure in children include anemia, behavioral disorders, low IQ, reading and learning disabilities, and nerve damage. In adults, lead exposure is associated with hypertension and cardiovascular disease.[3]

Geochemist Clair Patterson stated, "It seems probable that persons polluted with amounts of lead that are at least 400 times higher than natural levels, and are nearly one-third to one-half that required to induce dysfunction, that their lives are being adversely affected by loss of mental acuity and irrationality. This would apply to most people in the United States."[4]

Midgley was a chemical engineer for General Motors who solved the "pinging" noise in internal combustion engines. The fuel in early vintage automobiles did not burn evenly and ignited too quickly, resulting

1. McNeill, *Something New*, 421.
2. Denworth, *Toxic Truth*, 111.
3. Stolark, "Fact Sheet."
4. Denworth, *Toxic Truth*, 111–12.

in a temporary loss of power that made the engine "knock." After years of research he found that adding lead to the fuel completely eliminated the knocking. This discovery led him to develop a compound called ethylene bromide to use in the fuel and discharge the lead additive out of the exhaust pipe and, unfortunately, into the atmosphere.[5] In 1921, Midgley was awarded the Nichols Medal from the American Chemical Society for this achievement.

One hundred years before Christ it was common knowledge that lead poisoning caused insanity and even death.[6] So, predictably, severe health problems and many deaths of workers were reported as they developed the lead gasoline mixture in a plant in Dayton, Ohio and the DuPont plant in New Jersey. At a press conference held to prove the lead-laced Ethyl gasoline was safe, Midgley poured leaded gasoline over his hands and breathed the fumes for a full minute. Shortly afterward he suffered from lead poisoning, but it did not kill him.[7]

The US Public Health Service warned in 1922 that leaded fuel was dangerous. However, it was not until 1999, after an estimated seven million tons of lead from gasoline were released into the atmosphere in the United States alone, that leaded gasoline was phased out.[8]

Thomas Midgley's next invention may have been even more deadly. Refrigerators and air conditioners in the early 1930s used sulfur dioxide and ammonia, and when damaged, these toxic and flammable compounds were released with deadly results. Midgley discovered that a new compound named Freon solved the problem, and within a very short time Freon was used in almost all refrigerators, air conditioners, and eventually aerosol cans.

But, again, there were unintended consequences. Minuscule amounts of chlorofluorocarbons (CFCs) like Freon have apparently caused irreparable damage to the ozone layer, which protects life on Earth from harmful UV radiation. Millions continue to be diagnosed with skin cancer because of Midgley's Freon solution.[9]

Thomas Midgley Jr. was given numerous awards and honorary degrees for his accomplishments. He was elected chairman for the United

---

5. Stolark, "FactcSheet,"
6. Lewis, "Lead Poisoning," 3–11.
7. Kovarik, "Charles F. Kettering."
8. Kitman, "Secret History of Lead," para. 18.
9. "Why Is 'Freon' Being Phased Out?," paras. 1–2.

States National Academy of Sciences and president of the American Chemical Society. It was yet unrealized the lethal impact his inventions would cause on human health and the environment.

The world's possibly deadliest inventor didn't die from lead poisoning or skin cancer but from the result of yet another of his lethal inventions. In 1940, Midgley contracted polio at the age of fifty-one, so he invented a pulley system to help him get out of bed. At the age of fifty-five he was found strangled to death by this contraption when it entangled itself around his neck.[10]

Midgley was neither the first, and nor will he be the last, to find a solution far worse than the problem identified. But his inventions are almost unparalleled for the harm inflicted on the planet and its inhabitants.

Biblical Insight: Good Stewards of God's Creation

by Seth Grotzke

Since the time of creation, God has given mankind the opportunity and responsibility to steward all that was good (Gen 1:27–28; Exod 20:9; Ps 104:23). Work was a good gift God gave to humanity (Eccl 2:24). We were blessed by being able to put things into order. It was a copy of what the Creator had done. He had taken nothing and made something. He had taken the void and brought beauty. Now, his image-bearers were able to take that good creation and continue to put order to it. It was as though God had made vice-regents to rule over this good world and use their abilities to make even more beauty (Col 3:17; 1 Cor 10:31).

God created and called it good. Adam studied it and began to order it. He gave names. He planted. He tended. He worked the garden and expanded it. At least, that is what he and all those who followed him were supposed to do. But they squandered their opportunity and rejected their responsibility when they decided to do things their own way. Adam and Eve thought God must be holding something back. He wasn't nearly as good as they had originally thought. They had been deceived. At least, that is what they understood after the serpent had enlightened them (Gen 3).

Adam and Eve doubted. They disobeyed. They were cast out of the garden they were meant to keep and expand. Instead of pushing at the

---

10. Bryson, *Short History of Nearly Everything*, 196.

borders from the inside and seeing the garden grow, they were on the outside trying to push the borders to get back in.

Although not completely lost, this God-given image of kingdom ruler and garden keeper was marred. This meant that while they still had the desire and the drive to live in God's image, the final outcome was going to be inevitably frustrated. Adam kept planting, Cain kept farming, Abel kept pastoring, but it was different. There were thorns. There were predators. There were fights (Gen 4).

In our modern-day state we still work. It is a good thing to order creation around us, to look for innovative solutions to perennial frustrations, to find cures for diseases, and relief for the hurting. It is built into us. It is a gift from a good God (Ps 8). But we wear ourselves out with the thorns, the predators, the fights. Sometimes we even make horrible decisions, having no idea of the ultimate outcomes. We take risks and lose. We take shortcuts and harm others. When that happens, the problems only get bigger. History tells us, and current headlines remind us, we are not steadily progressing toward a utopia. We are making a mess of things. We need outside help.

When the Second Adam, Jesus Christ, came, he faced the same problems but had different results. There were still thorns. There were still predators. There were still fights. But he took all those onto himself. He bore the infirmities of the weak (Matt 8:14). He touched the untouchable (Matt 8:1). He wept with the hurting (John 11). He multiplied the food (John 6). He calmed the storms (Mark 4:35). And then he took the thorns. He faced the predators. He laid down his life in the fight (Luke 23). And from his sacrifice there is new life! And this resurrected life gives us hope that as Jesus has healed the foundational problem, the rest of creation will one day follow (Rom 8).

Work is still a gift from God. There is still beauty around us. We can still work at ordering the resources we have been given and are wisely stewarding, but we have to remember two things. First, our principal problem, rebellion against God, is found within ourselves and is not merely a product of our environment. And secondly, the solution to that principal problem is outside of us, namely in the person and work of the Second Adam, Jesus Christ. From those points we are able to thoughtfully move forward in doing our work, ordering this world, and imaging our Creator.

35

Amelia Earhart
A High-Flyer Who Lost Her Way

AVIATION SAW GREAT ADVANCEMENTS in the first few decades of the twentieth century. On December 17, 1903, the Wright Brothers made their first successful flight, travelling 120 feet at a speed of 6.8 mph for twelve seconds, just ten feet off the ground.[1] Two years later, Wilbur Wright flew twenty-four miles for almost forty minutes, and by 1909, Louis Bleriot, a French aviator, flew across the English Channel.

By 1918, World War I pilots called "aces" for shooting down five or more enemy planes became household names. Germany's Manfred von Richthofen, nicknamed "The Red Baron," shot down eighty planes in air-to-air combat. France's René Paul Fonck is credited with seventy-five dogfight victories. Even without the added dangers of war, early aviation was hazardous. Fonck survived a fiery crash on his takeoff attempting to fly from New York to Paris a year before Charles Lindbergh's successful solo transcontinental flight in 1927. Others attempting long-distance flights over the ocean were not so fortunate. In early 1927, as many as twenty-one of the forty pilots who tried this perilous feat died.[2]

A former World War I ace airplane pilot, performing at the Canadian National Flying Exhibition in Toronto, spotted Amelia Earhart and a friend in a clearing below and dove at her. "I am sure he said to himself, 'Watch me make them scamper,'" Earhart said. She stood her ground and

---

1. History.com editors, "First Airplane Flies," paras. 1–5.
2. Shapiro, "Celebrity of Charles Lindbergh," 20–33.

was impressed as the red biplane came close.[3] Ten years earlier, Amelia saw her first aircraft at the Iowa State Fair in 1908, which she described as "a thing of rusty wire and wood and not at all interesting."

After World War I, many American pilots became barnstormers, flying under low bridges and performing other acrobatic stunts as well as taking paying passengers for rides. The woman that would become the most famous female American aviator paid $10 for a ten-minute ride at one of these airshows in 1920. "By the time I had got two or three hundred feet off the ground," Earhart said, "I knew I had to fly."[4]

Within months Earhart took her first lesson from the pioneer female aviator Anita Snook. On October 22, 1922, Earhart flew her bright yellow biplane to an altitude of 14,000 feet, setting a world record for female pilots.[5] In 1928, Earhart won international fame by becoming the first female passenger to cross the Atlantic by airplane. Four years later, she was the first woman to make a nonstop solo transatlantic flight. For this accomplishment Earhart was presented an Air Force Distinguished Flying Cross. Others who also have been recipients of this award are the Wright Brothers, Charles (Lucky Lindy) Lindbergh, and John Glenn.

Eleanor Roosevelt flew countless miles across America as the eyes and ears of her polio-stricken husband, President Franklin D. Roosevelt. After an impromptu flight with Earhart on April 20, 1933, the first lady obtained a student flying permit and the two developed a lifelong friendship.

Amelia Earhart's notoriety allowed her to succeed at a number of business ventures. She sold affordable women's clothing exclusively to Macy's and Marshall Field's that included aviation-inspired details like propeller-shaped buttons. Amelia authored a number of bestselling books and wrote about her flights for *National Geographic*.[6]

Earhart made her first attempt at the 29,000-mile, round-the-world flight on March 17, 1936. Earhart and her crew successfully flew from Oakland, California to Honolulu, Hawaii, where the mission had to be abandoned when the plane was badly damaged on takeoff for the second-leg destination of Howland Island.

Amelia took off on a second flight from California—this time headed in the opposite direction—a few months later. Earhart and her very

---

3. Earhart, *Last Flight*, 3.
4. Earhart, *Last Flight*, 4.
5. Long and Long, *Amelia Earhart*, 36.
6. Lovell, *Sound of Wings*, 152.

experienced navigator, Fred Noonan, made numerous stops in South America, Africa, India, and Southeast Asia, eventually arriving in Lae, New Guinea. With 22,000 miles of the journey completed, the remaining 7,000 miles would be over the Pacific.

Earhart and Noonan left Lae on July 2, 1937, believing they could locate their next stop—the small, mile-long Howland Island—using radio and smoke signals transmitted by the US Coast Guard cutter *Itasca*. Although the aviator and her navigator believed they reached the vicinity of Howland Island, they failed to locate the island and they disappeared without a trace.[7] Despite one of the most intense and costly air and sea searches in history, equaling $72 million in today's money, no physical evidence of Earhart, Noonan, or the plane was found. Most historians believe in the "crash and sink" theory rather than any of several conspiracy theories.

Amelia Earhart's accomplishments in aviation inspired many of the more than 1,000 women pilots of the Women Airforce Service Pilots (WASP) who ferried military aircraft, towed gliders, and served as transport pilots during World War II.[8] Her disappearance remains one of the greatest unsolved mysteries in American history, puzzling and fascinating young and old alike today.

Biblical Insight: God Wants a Safe Arrival for His Children

by Ronald Ian Phillips

Have you ever been so absolutely certain about something and found you were wrong? Most of us have. Amelia Earhart knew her final destination and thought with excellent planning, a good navigator, and personal skill, she would arrive safely. But she lost her way. Are you sure you will arrive safely to your final destination?

The Bible tells us that many will take the wrong path to eternity. Matthew 7:13–14 (NKJV) instructs us to, "Enter by the narrow gate; for wide is the gate and broad is the way that leads to destruction, and there are many who go in by it. Because narrow is the gate and difficult is the way which leads to life, and there are few who find it."

---

7. Rogers, "Amelia Earhart Disappears."
8. Regis, *When Our Mothers Went to War*, 102–5.

Does it really matter what religion we follow, or even if we believe in a higher power? Aren't there many ways to climb the spiritual mountain and successfully reach the hereafter? And isn't it more loving and compassionate to envision a God that can ignore evil? The Bible answers these questions and many more.

We are made in the image of God, according to Genesis 1:27, but ever since creation, man has attempted to create a god in his own image. Many have high expectations for their god but low standards for themselves. We read in Romans 1:23–25 that they "changed the glory of the incorruptible God into an image made like to corruptible man, and to birds, and four footed beasts, and creeping things," and "changed the truth of God into a lie, and worshiped and served the creature more than the Creator." Many create these gods based on finite human logic and understanding. They determine who their god will or will not accept and what their god can or cannot do. Romans 1:21–22 says, "Because that, when they knew God, they glorified him not as God, neither were thankful; but became vain in their imaginations, and their foolish heart was darkened. Professing themselves to be wise, they became fools."

They stand defiant, thinking they will suffer no consequences when they rail against God or ignore his attributes. God's mercy, grace, and love are wonderful. Ezekiel 18:32 tells us, "'For I take no pleasure in the death of anyone,' declares the Sovereign Lord. 'Repent and live!'" However, we cannot ignore his holiness and the penalty for doing evil. John 8:24 quotes Jesus as saying, "Therefore I said to you that you will die in your sins; for if you do not believe that I am He, you will die in your sins."

In recent times it seems increasingly difficult to separate the truth from false narratives. Some half-truths are so convincing. But as in the words of a Yiddish proverb, "A half-truth is a whole lie." If we have zeal and passion in our convictions and worship, but it's not according to the truth of Scripture, we remain lost. When we invent a god in our image, we are no longer talking about the God of the Bible. We are told to study the Bible, God's word, and not leave our eternal destiny up to other people's interpretations (2 Tim 2:15).

We have only to follow God's holy word to learn the truth. John 8:32 (NKJV) explains, "And you shall know the truth, and the truth shall make you free." John 4:23–24 (NKJV) says, "But the hour is coming, and now is, when the true worshipers will worship the Father in spirit and truth; for the Father is seeking such to worship Him. God is Spirit, and those who worship Him must worship in spirit and truth."

Jesus could not have said it more plainly, "I am the way, the truth, and the life. No one comes to the Father except through Me" (John 14:6 NKJV). God has provided only one rescue plan to the hereafter which is free and available to all. Second Peter 3:9 (NKJV) tells us, "The Lord is not slack concerning His promise, as some count slackness, but is long-suffering toward us, not willing that any should perish but that all should come to repentance." God wants his children to arrive safely at their final destination in glory with him.

In Joshua 24:15, we learn each of us has to decide if we will accept God's plan. "And if it seems evil unto you to serve the Lord, choose you this day whom ye will serve; whether the gods which your fathers served that were on the other side of the flood, or the gods of the Amorites, in whose land ye dwell: but as for me and my house, we will serve the Lord." Will you accept and serve the God of creation, or the god whom you have created?

36

Mount Rushmore: Bigger Than Life

The Mount Rushmore Memorial is located thirty miles southwest of Rapid City, near Keystone, in the Black Hills of South Dakota. Each year over 2 million tourists visit this national treasure that symbolizes the ideals of American freedom and democracy.

In 1923, South Dakota state historian Doane Robinson conceived the idea of a sculptured monument to stimulate tourism to the area. Robinson envisioned a monument to honor heroes of the American West such as Lewis and Clark, Red Cloud, Buffalo Bill Cody, and Crazy Horse.[1] Robinson brought in sculptor Gutzon Borglum who eventually created the sculpture's design and oversaw the project's execution from 1927 to 1941, with the help of his son, Lincoln Borglum.[2]

Borglum believed the original plan to make the carvings in the granite pillars known as the Needles were a poor site choice because they were too thin to support sculpting. He chose nearby Mount Rushmore, a more expansive location that enjoyed maximum exposure to the sun. For broader appeal in drawing tourists, Borglum chose four United States Presidents that represent the nation's birth, growth, development, and preservation.

George Washington was chosen because he led the colonists to victory in the American Revolution, gaining independence from Great

---

1. OhRanger.com, "Making Mount Rushmore."
2. Roberts, "Immigrant's Contribution."

Britain.³ As the first President of the United States, Washington is recognized around the world as the paragon of a benevolent national founder. Harry "Light Horse" Lee said George Washington was "First in war, first in peace, and first in the hearts of his countrymen."⁴ Borglum chose Washington to be the most prominent figure on the mountain to represent the birth of the United States.

Thomas Jefferson represents the growth of the United States. In 1803, during his presidency, America purchased the Louisiana Territory from France, effectively doubling the size of the United States. Jefferson, as author of the Declaration of Independence and the third president of the United States, said, "We act not for ourselves but for the whole human race. The event of our experiment is to show whether man can be trusted with self-government."⁵

The third face carved on Mount Rushmore is that of Theodore "Teddy" Roosevelt, the twenty-sixth President of the United States. Borglum chose Roosevelt to represent the development of the country. Roosevelt set aside more federal land for national parks and preserves than all of his predecessors combined. His Square Deal program was enacted to create a fair, honest, and just society where all Americans have equal opportunities. He advocated for equality, not equity or free handouts, and believed in the strenuous life with the boundless prospects of advancement through hard work. President Theodore Roosevelt said, "Here is your country. Cherish these natural wonders, cherish the natural resources, cherish the history and romance as a sacred heritage, for your children and your children's children. Do not let selfish men or greedy interests skin your country of its beauty, its riches, or its romance."⁶

Abraham Lincoln represents the preservation of the United States. Lincoln consistently ranks as either the greatest or second-greatest US president by both historians and the general public. The world today remembers Abraham Lincoln's greatest accomplishments of saving the Union and ending slavery in America. President Lincoln was quoted as saying: "Let every American, every lover of liberty, every well-wisher to his posterity, swear by the blood of the Revolution, never to violate in

---

3. National Park Service, "Why These Four Presidents?"
4. Grizzard, *George Washington*, 110.
5. National Park Service, "Why These Four Presidents?," para. 5.
6. Welch, *Encyclopedia of Your Observations*, 51.

the least particular, the laws of the country; and never to tolerate their violation by others."[7]

Gutzon and Lincoln Borglum, along with 400 workers, sculpted the colossal 60-foot-high carvings of the four United States Presidents from October 4, 1927 to October 31, 1941.[8] Each president was originally to be depicted from head to waist, but lack of funding forced construction to end on October 31, 1941.[9]

It is not possible to add another president to the memorial, because the rock that surrounds the existing faces is not suitable for additional carving, and because if additional sculpting were to be done, it might create instabilities in the existing carvings.[10]

The Mount Rushmore Memorial is sometimes referred to as the "Shrine of Democracy."[11] The four "great faces" of the presidents tower 5,725 feet above sea level and are scaled to men who would stand 465 feet tall.[12] This site is not only a reminder of past Americans who preserved and expanded our American democratic republic; it is also a reminder to the millions of visitors today to follow the examples of past American heroes and defenders who worked so hard and sacrificed so much to establish these freedoms we cherish. As Ben Franklin said on the final day of the Constitutional Convention in 1787, when our Constitution was adopted, "We have a republic, if you can keep it."[13]

Biblical Insight: A Test for Greatness in God's Kingdom

by Ronald Ian Phillips

The four United States founders depicted on Mount Rushmore are some of the greatest heroes and defenders of freedoms in American history. If there was a Mount Rushmore for God's early heroes and defenders of the faith, whom would you include? Abraham? David? Deborah? Daniel? Ruth? Jacob? All would be equally worthy candidates to be the four chosen here.

7. Lincoln, *Collected Works of Abraham Lincoln*, 1:112.
8. National Park Service, "Carving History."
9. PBS, "Mount Rushmore."
10. Lawrence, "Adding Fifth Face to Mount Rushmore."
11. Crawford, "Thousands Celebrate," para. 1.
12. Black Hills & Badlands Tourism Association, "Mount Rushmore National Memorial," para. 3.
13. Beschloss, *Presidential Courage*, 137.

We will start with Adam, the first man, who was created in God's image. Genesis 2:7 (NKJV) tells us, "And the Lord God formed man of the dust of the ground, and breathed into his nostrils the breath of life; and man became a living being." God then put Adam in the garden of Eden to tend it and name all the animals. Adam must have been a mature, extremely intelligent human being with a complex language since he not only named all the birds and animals but spoke with God.

Genesis 2:21–22 is the familiar story of Eve, who was made by God from Adam's rib, and when tempted by the serpent ate of the tree of the knowledge of good and evil with Adam. Genesis 3:22 and 24 (NKJV) says, "Then the Lord God said, 'Behold, the man has become like one of Us, to know good and evil. And now, lest he put out his hand and take also of the tree of life, and eat, and live forever . . . So He drove out the man; and He placed the cherubim at the east of the garden of Eden, and a flaming sword which turned every way, to guard the way to the tree of life."

Did you ever wonder why God put the tree of knowledge of good and evil and the tree of life in the garden of Eden? We are created in the image of God—not as soulless robots but as humans with free will. God yearns that we will choose life and good. In Deuteronomy 30:15, God says, "See, I have set before you today life and good, death and evil." The only negative commandment that God gave to Adam and Eve was that they were not to eat from the tree of good and evil or they would surely die. The sin was disobeying God. Adam was the first to fall, but Romans 3:23 tells us, "All have sinned, and come short of the glory of God."

God's testing is to bring out the best in us, not the worst. Even as Adam and Eve were driven out of the garden of Eden and relegated to lives of hardship and misery, God covered them with garments of skins (Gen 3:21). The shed blood would cover sins until God sent his own Son in the form of a human to redeem and take away the sin of the world and offer eternal life to anyone who believes in him.

Noah makes this list of godly heroes because he found grace in the eyes of the Lord when God was ready to destroy all life on the planet. Genesis 6:5–7 says,

> And God saw that the wickedness of man was great in the earth, and that every imagination of the thoughts of his heart was only evil continually. And it repented the Lord that He had made man on the earth, and it grieved Him at His heart. And the Lord said, "I will destroy man whom I have created from the face of

the earth; both man, and beast, and the creeping thing, and the fowls of the air; for it repenteth Me that I have made them."

But then verse 8 says God did not destroy his creation, because, "Noah found grace in the eyes of the Lord." Noah is numbered as being amongst three of the most righteous men in the book of Ezekiel.

Noah was the tenth-generation descendant of Adam, and Noah's grandfather, Methuselah, was the oldest man recorded in the Bible (Gen 5:27). Methuselah lived to be 969 years old. Noah is most famous for building an ark and surviving a catastrophic, worldwide flood that destroyed all humans and land animals, except for Noah, his wife, their three sons and their wives, and two of every kind of animals kept in the ship.

The evilness of Noah's time is compared with the wickedness in the end times. Matthew 24:37–40 (NIV) tells us,

> As it was in the days of Noah, so it will be at the coming of the Son of Man. For in the days before the flood, people were eating and drinking, marrying and giving in marriage, up to the day Noah entered the ark; and they knew nothing about what would happen until the flood came and took them all away. That is how it will be at the coming of the Son of Man. Two men will be in the field; one will be taken and the other left."

Moses is credited with writing the first five books of the Bible through divine revelation. Genesis through Deuteronomy are also known as the Torah and the Pentateuch—the Hebrew, and Greek names—respectively. The Old Testament mentions Moses 768 times, making him one of the most prominent people in the Old Testament. Moses led the Israelites out of Egyptian bondage, through the Red Sea, to Mount Sinai, where Moses received the Ten Commandments.

When Moses didn't return from the mountain for forty days the people made a golden calf god to worship. Exodus 32:4b reads, "'These are your gods, Israel, who brought you up out of Egypt.'" And then they "sat down to eat and drink and got up to indulge in revelry" (Exod 32:6). Because of their great sin, God told Moses he would destroy the Israelites, but Moses was able to secure God's mercy and save them from annihilation. Moses went on to lead the Israelites for forty years through the wilderness until they finally entered the promised land.

Elijah is the fourth of our early heroes and defenders of the faith chosen for a spiritual Mount Rushmore. Elijah appeared with Jesus over 800 years after being carried away alive, to Heaven, in a chariot of fire.

Second Kings 2:11 tells us, "Then it happened, as they continued on and talked, that suddenly a chariot of fire appeared with horses of fire, and separated the two of them; and Elijah went up by a whirlwind into Heaven." Describing Christ's transfiguration, Matthew 17:2–3 says, "He was transfigured before them. His face shone like the sun, and His clothes became as white as the light. And behold, Moses and Elijah appeared to them, talking with Him."

As a prophet, Elijah turned people away from following false gods and toward the one true God. His admonition is still relevant today when he asked, "How long will you falter between two opinions? If the Lord is God, follow Him; but if Baal, follow him" (1 Kgs 18:21 NKJV).

What is the ultimate test of greatness? Jesus gave us the answer in Matthew 18:1–5:

> At the same time came the disciples unto Jesus, saying, "Who is the greatest in the kingdom of heaven?" And Jesus called a little child unto Him, and set him in the midst of them, and said, "Verily I say unto you, except ye be converted, and become as little children, ye shall not enter into the kingdom of heaven. Whosoever therefore shall humble himself as this little child, the same is greatest in the kingdom of heaven."

The early heroes and defenders of the faith chosen above were four of many humble servants of God in the Old Testament. Who would you choose?

37

Compassion for the Forgotten

SEEKING A SECOND TERM in 1936, Franklin Delano Roosevelt ran his campaign by greeting large crowds, exclaiming, "You look happier than you did four years ago!" And when he defeated Alf Landon by a landslide, 523 to 8 in the Electoral College, it was the largest margin of victory in over a century.[1] But the Great Depression was far from over. By the time of President Roosevelt's second inauguration in 1937, he was more concerned than ever for the "forgotten man."[2]

In a 1932 radio fireside chat, Roosevelt coined the phrase "forgotten man" to describe the common man, or those Americans he felt needed the help of social and governmental services. Now, four years later, FDR's promise of a New Deal for all Americans remained in jeopardy. Hopes of a full recovery quickly faded as the American economy went into a thirteen-month tailspin in the middle of 1937.

Banks failed, wiping out the life savings of many. Farms, homes, and businesses were foreclosed, leaving people destitute. Less than 10 percent of those who kept their farms had flush toilets, and only 25 percent had electricity.[3] There seemed to be no relief from the quiet desperation felt by countless Americans who had all but given up. This was a nationwide—in fact a worldwide—depression from which there seemed to be no escape or hope of things getting better.

1. "Franklin D. Roosevelt," paras. 1 & 2.
2. Kennedy, *Freedom from Fear*, 136–37.
3. Walbert, "Depression for Farmers," para. 8.

Accepting government welfare was looked upon as a disgrace, making it a last resort for most people. In many parts of the country those on the dole, or welfare, gave up their right to vote and their names were published in newspapers.[4] Personal pride and public shame prevented many from accepting the help they so desperately needed.

On January 20, 1937, Franklin D. Roosevelt was inaugurated for his second term, and the weather on that cold inaugural day was as dismal as the economy. At noon, the temperature was 33°F. This presidential inauguration would go down as the wettest in history. The 200,000 rain-soaked FDR supporters who came to Washington DC quickly scattered at the end of his speech. Trying to make the best of the day, FDR rode back to the White House after the ceremony in an open, presidential convertible, with a half inch of water on the floor![5]

America's problems during The Great Depression were not easily or quickly remedied. By the late 1930s, FDR's New Deal had lost much of its momentum and war clouds were on the horizon.

But President Roosevelt's inauguration speech inspired the American people to remain resilient, with the hope that their dreams for a better life were just deferred, not denied. And ultimately the mobilization of millions of soldiers and civilians for World War II turned around the failing economy and washed away The Great Depression. But it was not until the prosperity of the postwar 1950s that many of the "forgotten" would have their dreams for a better life realized.

It should be remembered though that through his words, President Roosevelt gave the seemingly forgotten in America the message that there was hope and better days lay ahead. President Roosevelt may have felt like Abraham Lincoln after the Gettysburg Address, discouraged that his speech had been poorly received and a failure, yet his words that day not only inspired many people of his time but would speak to generations to come.

President Franklin D. Roosevelt said:

> Many voices are heard as we face a great decision. Comfort says, 'Tarry a while.' Opportunism says, 'This is a good spot.' Timidity asks, 'How difficult is the road ahead?' Shall we pause now and turn our back upon the road that lies ahead? Shall we call this

---

4. Morain, "Great Depression Hits Farms."
5. NWS Editors, "Inauguration Weather," para. 3.

the promised land? Or, shall we continue on our way? For each age is a dream that is dying or one that is coming to birth.[6]

Biblical Insight: Hope in the Midst of Silence

by Seth Grotzke

President Roosevelt challenged those rain-soaked supporters to push through when there was little hope. So, too, we read of a challenge to push forward when we are tempted to slide into despair. In the life of every believer there will be times of seemingly hopeless circumstances, little growth, and the prospect of complete failure. We will be tempted to question the goodness of our God and the strength of his Spirit.

Times of stagnation may come for a variety of reasons. Sometimes we flounder because we have unconfessed sin in our lives. At other times God may be graciously taking peace from our hearts that we might run to him. At other times we may suffer long periods of the silence of God for reasons we will never know. However, regardless of the purpose of the discouraging circumstances, there is hope. There is hope because this place of the disquieted soul is not our destination. There is a promise of rest.

President Roosevelt brought his hearers to a place where a decision could be made. Would they turn back? Would they remain? Would they push forward? We, too, are given a choice while we wait and wonder. Is following Jesus worth it, or does the world really offer what I am looking for? Should I sit and wait for some clear manifestation of God, or should I continue on in obedience, trusting that the promises are true?

Nearly 2,000 years before this famous, stormy speech, the author of Hebrews gave his hearers a similar choice. He said,

> Therefore, as the Holy Spirit says, "Today, if you hear his voice, do not harden your hearts as in the rebellion, on the day of testing in the wilderness, where your fathers put me to the test and saw my works for forty years. Therefore I was provoked with that generation, and said, 'They always go astray in their heart; they have not known my ways.' As I swore in my wrath, 'They shall not enter my rest.'" Take care, brothers, lest there be in any of you an evil, unbelieving heart, leading you to fall away from the living God. But exhort one another every day, as long as it is called "today," that none of you may be hardened by the

---

6. "'One Third of a Nation,'" paras. 17–18.

deceitfulness of sin. For we have come to share in Christ, if indeed we hold our original confidence firm to the end. As it is said, "Today, if you hear his voice, do not harden your hearts as in the rebellion." (Heb 3:7–15 ESV)

The author of Hebrews sees this time of their testing as an opportunity to turn back, or as a time to pursue Christ and find rest. Looking back at the children of Israel in the wilderness, they, too, faced a choice (Num 13–14). Would they trust God and pursue his promises, or would they turn away from him and go back? They chose to turn their backs and they were never allowed to enter the promised land.

In our times of restlessness we face the same choices. Will we return? Will we remain? Or will we reach forward? There is a promised rest. There is hope in the midst of silence. Let us reach forward with confidence, for God's promises are true.

38

Huey Long

America's Dictator, or a Progressive Populist?

When President Franklin D. Roosevelt called Huey Long "one of the two most dangerous men in America,"[1] many believed the Louisiana senator running for the presidency might become America's first dictator. David Kennedy wrote in his book, *Freedom From Fear*, that Huey Long's quest for power was "the closest thing to a dictatorship that America has ever known."[2] Just a few years earlier, Hitler, Stalin, and Mussolini had consolidated their power to form dictatorships. In the desperate Great Depression era of the 1930s, people began to ask: "Could it happen in America?"

In the early 1930s, John Maynard Keynes, one of the most influential economists of the twentieth century, was asked if there was any precedent for the worldwide Great Depression. He said yes, it was called the Dark Ages, which lasted 400 years.[3] Shortly after his first inaugural address in 1932, FDR said, "The only thing we have to fear is fear itself." A supporter responded, "Mr. President, if your program succeeds, you'll be the greatest president in American history. If it fails, you will be the worst one." "If it fails," FDR replied, "I'll be the last one."[4]

The eleven-year span between when the colonies declared themselves free and independent from British rule in 1776 and when the US

1. Snyder, "Huey Long," 117–43.
2. Kennedy, *Freedom from Fear*, 236.
3. Benko, "Biggest Recession," para. 9.
4. Bardhan-Quallen, *Franklin Delano Roosevelt*, 2.

Constitution was signed in 1787 were also desperate times for America. "What have you given us?" a colonist asked Ben Franklin as he left the Constitutional Convention. He replied, "A republic, madam, if you can keep it." Franklin didn't say a democracy where a majority of 51 percent can crush individual rights and possibly lead to mob rule.[5] He didn't say a monarchy, oligarchy, or dictatorship.

The founders gave us a democratic republic where sovereignty was designed to rest with the people. They echoed the ideals of James Madison and Alexander Hamilton that the few should not oppress the many, and the many should not oppress the few. The US Constitution may be just over 7,000 words, including the twenty-seven amendments, but it has served the United States well. It was designed to be a living document, yet difficult to change without consideration, compromise, and consensus.

So was Huey Long really the dangerous demagogue his political opponents and many historians claim him to be? Others believed he was a progressive populist fighting for the poor and the disenfranchised.

Huey Pierce Long Jr. was born on August 30, 1893, in an impoverished region of the extremely poor state of Louisiana.[6] By all accounts, Huey Long was a bright young man, a skilled debater, and perhaps had an eidetic memory. He convinced his teachers to let him skip seventh grade but soon ran into trouble in high school.

As a student at Winnfield High School, he formed a secret society "to run things, laying down certain rules the students would have to follow."[7] Ignoring a warning from school personal to behave, Huey Long distributed a flyer, criticizing the school for adding the completion of a twelfth grade as a requirement for graduation. When the principal expelled him in 1910, he got revenge by circulating a petition and successfully had the high school principal fired. Huey never graduated from high school.[8] At seventeen years old he became a traveling salesman and part-time auctioneer.

In the fall of 1911, Huey Long enrolled and spent one semester at the Oklahoma Baptist University, with the financial support of his older brother and at the urging of his devout Baptist mother. He decided that law, rather than the ministry, would suit him better, so another semester

---

5. Beschloss, *Presidential Courage*, 137.
6. White, *Kingfish*, 5.
7. White, *Kingfish*, 8.
8. White, *Kingfish*, 8.

was spent at law school, but he found gambling houses more appealing.[9] Two years passed before Long again enrolled in law school, where he successfully petitioned the Louisiana Supreme Court to let him take the bar exam after just one year of studies. In 1922, at the age of just twenty-nine, Huey Long argued and won a case before the United States Supreme Court. Former President of the United States and Chief Justice of the Supreme Court William Howard Taft described Long as one of the best legal minds he had ever encountered.[10]

Huey Long received 96.1 percent of the vote when he ran for the Louisiana governorship in 1928.[11] His nickname became "the Kingfish," with the campaign slogan "Every man a king but no one wears the crown."[12] Approximately 75 percent of the people in Louisiana were illiterate and there were only 300 miles of paved roads and three bridges in the entire state when he took office.[13] By the end of his term, not only did Long provide free textbooks for students and teach 175,000 adults to read, but he directed public funds for hospitals, schools, 9,000 miles of new roads, and over 100 bridges.[14] He also pledged free college education, a 30-hour work week, and a $30 retiree monthly pension.

Huey Long became immensely popular with the poor receiving these benefits but was vilified by industry, banks, and the wealthy. As Long amalgamated his power base, he wheedled legislation that gave him control over the appointment of every public position in the state. He signed a bill allowing all police to make arrests without a warrant and centralized investigative power to himself.[15] Governor Long lambasted the "lying newspapers"[16] and effectively used the new forum of the radio to get his message out.

Still within his first year as governor, the Louisiana House of Representatives voted to impeach him on charges of misuse of state funds, bribery, and blasphemy. After a bloody brawl and fistfights broke out between legislators, the impeachment attempt failed and the legislature

9. White, *Kingfish*, 9.
10. Long, *Every Man a King*, 235.
11. Beggs, "10 Fascinating Facts about Huey Long," para. 5.
12. Beggs, "10 Fascinating Facts about Huey Long," para. 5.
13. Swanson, "Huey Long," 11–12.
14. Beggs, "10 Fascinating Facts about Huey Long," para. 5.
15. History.Com Editors, "Huey Long."
16. Kolbert, "Big Sleazy," para. 24.

soon became a rubber stamp for Huey Long's agenda. Emboldened by these events, Long told reporters, "I used to try to get things done by saying 'please', now I dynamite them out of my path."[17]

Long was elected to the United States Senate in 1932, but often returned to Louisiana to continue consolidating his power. With aspirations for the White House, Long began his 1936 presidential campaign by forming Share Our Wealth Clubs. This redistribution of wealth program would enable every family to have a car, a radio, and a home worth $5,000. It also guaranteed a yearly family income of no less than $2,000 which is equal to $40,000 in 2021. By 1935, there were over 7 million members in 27,000 Share Our Wealth clubs around the country.[18] He was receiving over 60,000 letters a week from supporters and had a radio audience of 25 million.[19] Huey Long defiantly proclaimed that after becoming President of the United States he would abolish the Electoral College and would rule for at least four terms, no longer being limited to just two presidential terms.[20]

Fearing an assassination attempt, Huey Long had surrounded himself with armed bodyguards. But on September 8, 1935, Huey Long was shot at close range at the Louisiana State Capitol by the son-in-law of a judge Long was trying to politically destroy. The assassin, Carl Weiss, was shot more than sixty times by Long's bodyguards.[21] Long was rushed to the hospital but died two days later from internal bleeding at forty-two years of age.

Huey Long was not the first or the last politician who amassed a huge loyal following of desperate people in desperate times. He should be commended for providing much needed aid and reform for the poor during the Depression.

Long's critics, however, may have felt he was no longer a "servant of the people" nor an altruistic representative in America's democratic republic. Critics may also allege that his "Share *Our* Wealth" Robin Hood policies of take from the rich and give to the poor destroyed rugged individualism and capitalism, and his consolidation of power destroyed the balance of power established by the United States Constitution.

17. Parrish, *Anxious Decades*, 164.
18. Snyder, "Huey Long," 123.
19. Snyder, "Huey Long," 123.
20. White, *Kingfish*, 22–24.
21. Rensberger, "Clues From the Grave," .

Biblical Insight: A Failure of Leadership

by David Grotzke

We will never know how much damage to America's democracy Huey Long would have done if he had realized his ambition and become the President of the United States. His track record as the Louisiana governor and senator revealed a failure of leadership often seen in the Bible as well.

It seems all leaders have their critics, even the great ones. The value of a leader is determined by the expectations of those who are asked to follow them and those who are asked to choose them. If we expect the leader to provide freedom from communistic control, they may look different than the one we expect to bring a guaranteed income, health insurance, and free education. Each individual must decide where their priorities lie and then join the process in choosing the leader that best aligns themselves with those priorities.

Many times in their long history, the nation of Israel had to decide what a priority was for them. God had to patiently steer them where they needed to be by using great leaders, judges, prophets, and kings. When Israel turned its back on Jesus, God set Israel aside for a while and began using apostles, evangelists, and preachers to build a new body, the church. God has always used leaders to grow his work.

John C. Maxwell describes a leader this way, "A leader is one who knows the way, goes the way, and shows the way."[22] It has been suggested that the word "good" should be added to that description. There have been many leaders that have not been good leaders, instead misusing and abusing the power they have been given. Some examples that most would agree to would be Herod the Great, who ordered the murder of all baby boys two years old and younger around Bethlehem at the time Jesus was born, as well as Nero, Stalin, and Hitler.

Along with evil kings in Scripture, a few good leaders are inserted to show us that God is still in control. Kings like Josiah, who even though he began to rule at the age of eight, promoted a revival when a copy of the Law was found and read to the nation. The Bible says that Josiah "Did what was right in the eyes of the Lord" (2 Kgs 22:2). Kind David was recognized as a good leader and called, "A man after God's own heart" (Acts 13:22).

---

22. Maxwell, quoted in Cole, "Mark Cole," para. 1.

The greatest good leader found in God's word is Jesus Christ. He had the advantage of being fully God and fully man. He began a ministry that has spread around the world and lasted for 2,000 years. His leadership continues because when he died on the cross to provide a way to deal with man's sin, he also sent the Holy Spirit to earth to do a work in every believer's life. With our sins paid for, the way was opened for us to enter into the presence of God for all eternity. He, by far, is the greatest leader of all time.

So what determines if a leader is good or bad? Who determines if we should follow a leader like Huey Long who may undermine our democratic republic? What should our response be when the leaders of the day do not look so much different than the Ahabs and Omris, or Herods and Hitlers?

God raises up leaders to accomplish his will, for his people, for his time. There are many leaders in the Bible that were raised up for "Such a time as this" (Esth 4:14). The patriarchs, judges, prophets, and kings were all part of God's plan for his people. There are some leaders that might cause us to question whether God had anything to do with their time in power or not. We might wonder about King Ahab and Jezebel, of which the Bible says, "Ahab, son of Omri, did more evil in the eyes of the Lord than any of those before him" (1 Kgs 16:30). The description of his reign may make us ask, "What was God thinking?" In some ways God is in charge of the leadership on earth. Daniel 2:20–23 says,

> Daniel answered and said, "Blessed be the name of God forever and ever, for wisdom and might are His and He changes the times and the seasons; He removes kings and raises up kings; He gives wisdom to the wise and knowledge to those who have understanding. He reveals deep and secret things; He knows what is in the darkness, and light dwells with Him. I thank you and praise you, O God of my fathers; You have given me wisdom and might and have now made known to me what we asked of you, for You have made know to us the king's demand."

Psalm 75:6–7 says, "For exaltation comes neither from the East nor form the West, nor from the South. But God is the judge: He puts down one, and exalts another."

If God raises up a leader, who are we to say that that leader is not good? We can use Scripture to guide us in our judgments of a leader. The Bible describes many of the leaders in early history as either wicked or doing what was right in the eyes of the Lord. We can evaluate a leader by the choices he makes. Do his choices please God or go contrary to God's word? Even godly leaders may make choices that displease God, such as King David. These are warnings for us to be careful of the choices we make.

If you are in a position of leadership (most of us are, either in the workplace or family setting), you should strive to do what is "right in the eyes of the Lord." We have the opportunity to reign with Christ, according to Revelation 20:6. Matthew 25:21–23 says that if we are faithful servants on this earth, we will be "put in charge of many things." Luke 19:12–19 states that some of us could be leaders over cities, in proportion to how we serve on earth. This should motivate all believers to do our best during the few years we live on this earth.

39

Consider Your Ways

RUSSIAN IMMIGRANTS CAME TO America in the 1870s with bushel baskets of winter wheat seed.[1] The wheat grew so well in Kansas and surrounding states, there was an abundant, lucrative surplus to sell Europeans during World War I. Once the Great War was over though, the demand and price for wheat plummeted, so farmers planted even more wheat, trying to compensate for the falling prices.

During the 1920s, gasoline-powered tractors allowed farmers to plow under vast stretches of the deep-rooted prairie grass. Prairie grass seemed indestructible, as it survived fires, buffalo stampedes, and tornados. But the three-inch wheat roots that could not hold the soil created the perfect storm. When the soil became parched it just lifted up, producing massive dirt storms.

At the start of The Great Depression a severe drought began that was to last eight years. The worst area of America's breadbasket that was affected was called the Dust Bowl, which included parts of Texas, Oklahoma, New Mexico, Colorado, and Kansas. This drought, combined with the erosion created by farmers replacing deep-rooted prairie grass with the shallow wheat roots, affected approximately 100 million acres.[2]

Recurring black blizzards in 1935 alone blew away some 850 million tons of topsoil.[3] The worst year was 1937, when 134 "dusters," as they

1. Kansas Historical Society, "Turkey Red Wheat."
2. "North American Tall Grass Prairie," paras. 1–22.
3. Egan, *Worst Hard Time*, 254.

were known, devastated the Great Plains.[4] More than 500,000 Americans were left homeless.[5] More than 350 houses had to be torn down after one storm alone.[6] Grasshoppers, which can eat up to half of their body weight in a single day, blackened the sky and consumed anything edible. When the lungs of people and animals filled with dirt, it was referred to as dust pneumonia, a condition that choked all caught in the path of these Dust Bowl storms. Livestock left unprotected often went blind or perished.

Okies and Arkies saw their farms buried under drifts of dirt. The storms were so electrically charged that the simple act of shaking hands would knock adults to the ground and short-out motorized vehicles. According to historian Timothy Egan, on Black Sunday, April 14, 1935, the day of the worst duster, the storm carried twice as much dirt as was dug out of the earth to create the Panama Canal; the canal took seven years to dig; the storm lasted a single afternoon.[7]

With their once-fertile land now decimated, farmers had no choice but to abandon their farms. They were financially ruined and left with few of life's basic necessities as they migrated by the tens of thousands further west. Little did they realize that California and other states had few jobs or opportunities to offer them, and Dust Bowl families were often turned away at the borders of these states.

Many historians consider this the worst manmade ecological disaster in American history. Maybe the Dust Bowl storms could have been avoided, or at least mitigated if farmers followed modern techniques of soil conservation and agricultural practices. Instead many of their homes and farms turned to dust no matter how hard they worked or persevered.

Today deep-water wells draw from aquifers created by glaciers thousands of years ago. And although they provide a reliable water source, some experts believe these aquifers will be totally depleted in just fifteen years. So the fragile ecosystem in the former Dust Bowl states may soon be in jeopardy again at man's own peril.[8]

---

4. Egan, *Worst Hard Time*, 281.
5. Egan, *Worst Hard Time*, 282.
6. Fleming, "Is There Still Damage?," para. 4.
7. Egan, *Worst Hard Time*, 8.
8. Frankel, "New NASA Data Show."

Biblical Insight: Stewardship of God's Creation

by Seth Grotzke

In the past thousand years humanity has witnessed many poor environmental choices;, many species pushed to the brink of extinction, many earth-altering "advancements." In our culture it is currently in vogue to look back at the ecological choices of the previous generations and shake our heads. "What were they thinking?" we ask ourselves. In some cases there was no way to know the outcome of a certain urban development or farming practice. These choices were often made in ignorance or indifference. Other times their thought was about personal gain and self-advancement, nothing else. It is this second group which receives the wrath of today's environmental movements.

This moral indignation, so often seen on billboards and social media, leads us to ask very important questions: What responsibility do we actually have to this terrestrial globe on which we live? Should we cultivate the earth or slash and burn it? Should we protect animals from extinction, or drive them to it? Should we protect the environment or exploit it?

The answers to these questions depend completely on our understanding of the origins of the universe. If everything came from nothing over a long period of time, and with a little luck, then there is no right or wrong about how we treat this planet, or any other planet for that matter.

If, however, there is a Creator, our entire attitude must change. In Psalm 8 David gives two reasons that help us understand our responsibility in caring for this earth. First, he reminds himself and his readers that God is over all the heavens and the earth. As humans look into the heavens, they see the greatness of God. The moon and the stars point to his eternal power and divine nature while simultaneously revealing our finiteness. The work of God's fingers is beyond man's comprehension. What is mankind that God should even notice them?

Yet, God has noticed and does care for mankind, leading David to his second reference point for proper ecological decisions: there is a divinely structured hierarchy. All living creatures are not equal. Mankind is responsible to steward this earth. This blessing (and responsibility) was given to Adam and Eve in Genesis 1–2, and repeated again to Noah and his family in Genesis 9. What humanity does on and to this earth does matter because God is over man, and man is over the earth.

David's two boundaries keep us from falling into two dangerous ditches, one on either side of the path. First, man is not God. We are here to steward what God has given, but ultimately it is the Creator who controls and keeps this universe in check through his providence. Second, man is not an animal. We cannot live according to primal urges. We cannot merely concern ourselves with food and reproduction. We are God's image-bearers, beneficiaries of all the honors, privileges, and responsibilities bestowed upon that position.

We have been given a responsibility to subdue this earth, but all our efforts, as advanced as they may be, are still made by fallen creatures living on cursed ground. That is why all creation is waiting with eager longing for the restoration of all things. So we keep working while we wait for the Lord to restore the earth (Rom 8).

40

Don't Believe Everything You Hear
War of the Worlds

THE NUMBER OF AMERICANS who owned a radio more than doubled in the 1930s.[1] Many isolated rural areas did not get electricity or a radio until the Rural Electrification Act was passed in 1936. Radio broadcasts back then were a great source of entertainment, with music, soap operas, and comedy shows. Sporting events and local news brought communities closer together, but radio was much more because it was a reliable source of national and international news.

Using the radio, Franklin Roosevelt felt he could counter the political bias of his opponents who controlled most of the print media of his time. Americans listened to President Roosevelt's fireside chats in the depths of The Great Depression as he explained New Deal programs and tried to give people hope. People heard live historical events unfold, such as the Hindenburg disaster and Hitler's rise to power. Newspaper articles could be a week old by the time people read them, while radio was a trusted source of current news.

The evening of October 30, 1938 began much the same for many families as they gathered around the radio, listening to the popular Sunday night *Edgar Bergen—Charlie McCarthy Show*. Shortly after 8 p.m. many changed the channel to enjoy another network broadcast called the *Mercury Theater on the Air*. Tuning in late, some of the 6 million listeners missed the opening statement by Orson Welles, stating

---

1. Marquis, "Written on the Wind, 385–415.

the broadcast that Halloween Eve was a fictional adaptation from *War of the Worlds* by H.G. Wells.[2]

The science-fiction novel was turned into a live news broadcast as horrifying events unfolded. This trusted news source of radio then frantically started describing a Martian invasion that had destroyed much of Europe. Supposedly reporting on the air from Grover's Mill, New Jersey, Carl Phillips is burned to death mid-sentence by a Martian ray gun. The 7,000 National Guardsmen are reported to have been annihilated by the aliens with just 120 known survivors. The Martian marauders would soon be on the doorstep of every American city.

There seemed to be no defense from the Martians that had bodies like gigantic bears, and used ray guns and poisonous gas. An untold number of citizens were instantly frightened by the news of a Martian invasion. One account told of a man finding his wife listening to the broadcast, ready to drink poison rather than face death by a Martian army.[3]

Terrified listeners caused traffic jams on highways trying to escape the Martians and certain death. Churches filled with repentant and scared citizens seeking protection. People pleaded with law enforcement for gas masks to protect them. Many who did not have their radios on now heard from loved ones, or people they trusted, about the false catastrophe awaiting them. This, too, contributed to areas of mass hysteria.

It is widely believed today that such anecdotal accounts of suicides and mass panic perpetuated over the years may have been greatly exaggerated.[4] Yet many were frightened and mass hysteria on some level did take place. A study by the Radio Project discovered that less than one-third of frightened listeners understood the invaders to be aliens; most thought they were listening to reports of a German invasion or of a natural catastrophe.[5] Those who believed the Martian invasion was actually happening were later embarrassed and often angry that they had been so gullible or misled.[6]

Some nineteenth-century scientists and astronomers added credibility to H. G. Wells's book, written in 1898, by speculating that the planet Mars might have once supported life, as evidenced by what was

---

2. Sky History editors, "#ThisDayinHistory 1938,"
3. Emery, "Did the 1938 Radio Broadcast?"
4. Schwartz, *Broadcast Hysteria*, 82–90.
5. Campbell, *Getting It Wrong*, 26–44.
6. Pooley and Socolow, "Myth of the *War of the Worlds* Panic."

believed to be Martian irrigation channels. They added plausibility to the radio broadcast of a Marian invasion forty years later.

H. G. Wells is often considered one of the best science-fiction novelists, with works like *The Time Machine* (1895), *The Island of Doctor Moreau* (1896), and *The War of the Worlds* (1898). He used the latest scientific discoveries and technological advances of his time to write amazingly creative fiction. Science and technology can be used to create a believable false narrative. If the result is science fiction, it is entertaining; but if it is passed on as truth, it can have disastrous consequences, as it did on the night before Halloween in 1938.

Biblical Insight: A False Narrative (Fake News)

by Seth Grotzke

It is easy to view the controlling narrative of a generation ago, with all its accompanying frenzy and hysteria, as foolishness. However, we are often consumed by the same fears and distress when our society speaks of its real or imagined struggles. Yesterday it may have been climate change, and tomorrow it may be the extinction of a species. Next month there could be an asteroid, or next year may bring a tyrannical dictator with weapons of mass destruction. There will always be an apocalyptic wave on the horizon, threatening to sink our small raft.

If we live in a universe of chance where there is no Sovereign Creator, divine plan, and promised future, then there is no security. We are therefore at the mercy of the next big catastrophe. From chaos we have come, to chaos we will go.

Yet our small raft is secure. We can sleep in peace in the bottom of a tossing ship, not because the storm has no force, or because the wind and waves present no real danger, nor because humanity seems to be excellent at surviving. We can be at peace in the midst of the storm because our God is in the boat.

In Mark 4 we read the account of Jesus calming the storm. While the story focuses on Christ, it is the fears of the disciples which provide the backdrop for the demonstration of his greatness. According to Mark's account, they had spent the day listening to the teaching of Jesus and then set out across the lake in the evening. When the windstorm arose, so did the true character of the disciples. Between the gusts of wind and the soaking waves we hear what the disciples believed about Jesus. "Do you not care?" You must not. If you did care about us you would keep us from this storm. "We are perishing!" (Mark 4:35–38). There is no hope, and now you have fallen asleep in our last hours.

These two exclamations stem from a belief which lay under the surface, revealed only in the chaos of the storm: "Jesus is just like us." He should be as frantic as we are. He should be bailing water like we are. He is perishing the same as we are. The disciples express this foundational, yet erroneous, belief through their final statement once the wind had ceased, "Who then is this, that even the wind and the sea obey him?" (Mark 4:41).

We twenty-first-century readers are not amazed. We merely shake our heads at the bumbling disciples. They didn't get it. They were slow to understand. They had watched Jesus cast out demons, heal the sick, and cleanse the leper. Yet they were still afraid in the boat. We fancy that things would have been different for us had we been in the boat.

Is that true? If I make an honest assessment of the previous storm in my life, or the ten before that, similar words have come from my mouth. The same beliefs were revealed in my heart. Jesus must not care. Jesus must not be able to help. Jesus must be the same as me.

In spite of the disciples' unbelief, Jesus still stood up. In spite of their fear, Jesus still spoke. The wind and the waves heard the voice of their Creator and they could do nothing but obey. "Peace! Be still!" (Mark 4:39–40). The storm was not meant to punish the disciples. It was permitted in order to reveal the disciples' true beliefs. It was silenced in order to provide a reason for faith. The storm was how Jesus demonstrated that he cared and was in control.

There are very real dangers and disasters on every side. Our news sources sell them, our society imbibes them, and our hearts fear them. However, there is a truth that is just as real as, and much more important than, what we fear. Jesus cares, and he is in control.

41

Ashes to Ashes

The 1939–40 New York World's Fair

LIKE THE GREEK MYTHOLOGICAL phoenix that was reborn from the ashes of its predecessor, the 1939–40 New York World's Fair was built on a 1,200-acre municipal ash dump which had long been the bane of the Flushing Meadows neighborhood. At one point, the Brooklyn Ash Removal Company was unloading 110 railroad carloads of garbage a day to be burned, and now the ashes had to be graded, moved, and leveled to build the New York World's Fair.[1]

The world was still struggling to come out of The Great Depression that had taken so many peoples' farms, homes, jobs, and life savings. President Franklin Roosevelt said, "When you get to the end of your rope, tie a knot and hang on."[2] Americans were tired of hanging on and wanted to envision a more optimistic time to come. Here at the World's Fair, the international community dared to dream that science and technological innovation would propel them into a utopian future.

The slogan "Dawn of a New Day" was chosen to compliment the fair's theme of "Building the World of Tomorrow." Sixty-two foreign countries and many corporations competed to build the most elaborate pavilions for the eventual 44 million optimistic and wonder-filled visitors who attended.[3]

---

1. NYC Parks, "Flushing Meadows Corona Park,"
2. Rosenberg, "Franklin D. Roosevelt Quotes," para. 10.
3. Herman, *Freedom's Forge,* 58.

Shining white icons of the fair were the 700-foot-tall Trylon and the 200-foot-in-diameter Perisphere, which displayed a city of tomorrow inside the sphere. GM's futuristic scale model of a 1960s city was the most popular attraction. Ridding cities of slums and creating industrial and residential zones where highways provided transportation routes from urban areas to suburbs and farms were all part of this futuristic vision.

One of the stranger displays was the seven-foot-tall robot Elektro the Motoman that could see, talk, smell, sing, and count with his fingers.[4] Visitors were fascinated with other more practical items like color television, electric refrigerators, Plexiglas, asbestos, and electric typewriters.

Burying a time capsule fifty feet deep at the fair site seemed like a good idea to Westinghouse, so they filled it with thirty-five small, everyday items to be opened in 5,000 years.[5]

But it all was to return to ashes. Promising scientific and technological advances to build a better future soon focused on weapons of destruction. In September of 1939, Germany invaded Poland, which began the Second World War that was to cost 50 million lives.[6]

When the New York World's Fair closed in October of 1940 the earlier optimism it created had faded. Ending in bankruptcy, many of the exhibitions built by the sixty-two participating nations were torn down and used as scrap metal for World War II.

Biblical Insight: We Have a Bright Future

by Ernest Schmidt

The longing for utopia is universal. Every election includes more empty campaign promises for a better life. As with the dashing of the optimism of the 1939–40 World's Fair, all hopes that human effort will produce the perfect future are doomed to failure. That is obviously a bleak assessment, but do not give up: there is a bright future for earth.

Our longing for the best of futures is a God-implanted longing he will fulfill. Throughout Scripture there is a theme of hope for earth's history. It will be the result of the Lord Jesus Christ reigning on earth. Isaiah 9:6 summarizes the character of his reign: "Government will be upon His

---

4. Kalan, "Original Futurama,"
5. Jinwoochong, "Buried Under Flushing Meadows,"
6. CNN Editorial Research, "World War II Fast Facts."

shoulder." Isaiah 33:22 further promises the Lord will perfectly fulfill all three areas of government: "For the Lord is our Judge (judicial); the Lord is our Lawgiver (legislative); the Lord is our King (executive). He will save us."

There will be perfect balance in his authority. Strong righteous leadership will be coupled with tender compassion: "The Lord God shall come with a strong hand . . . He will feed His flock like a shepherd; He will gather the lambs with His arm, and carry them in His bosom, and gently lead those who are with young" (Isa 40:10–11). War will cease and there will be real peace during His reign: "They shall beat their swords into plowshares, and their spears into pruning hooks; nation shall not lift up sword against nation, neither shall they learn war anymore" (Isa 2:4).

Other conditions during the Lord's rule on earth are what you would expect from his presence. There will be economic equity: "They shall build houses and inhabit them; they shall plant vineyards and eat their fruit. They shall not build and another inhabit; they shall not plant and another eat . . . they shall enjoy the work of their hands" (Isa 65:21–22). The matter of health care will be resolved: "Then the eyes of the blind shall be opened, and the ears of the deaf shall be unstopped. Then the lame shall leap like a deer, and the tongue of the dumb sing" (Isa 35:5–6).

The environment will be so balanced that it will allow continuous farming. One preparing a crop will ask the harvester to make room for a new crop (Amos 9:13)! Wild life will become tame life. Children can play with formerly poisonous snakes: "The nursing child shall play by the cobra's hole" (Isa 11:8).

The spiritual condition of people during his kingdom will be life based on the new covenant. Jeremiah 31:31–37 describes the covenant and guarantees its fulfillment. Here is a summary: . . . I will put My law in their minds, and write it on their hearts; and I will be their God, and they shall be My people. . . . For I will forgive their iniquity, and their sin I will remember no more" (Jer 31:33–34). Such a lifestyle will create a great worldwide neighborhood.

That which is described above is not just a fantasy or humanistic hope for the future. It is the future of believers guaranteed by God. Believers, we have a bright future!

42

General Douglas MacArthur
The Right Leader for the Right Time?

In 1946, the American Institute of Public Opinion asked Americans to name the greatest living person. General Douglas MacArthur, the Pacific War hero of World War II, topped the list.[1] MacArthur had graduated first in his class from the US Military Academy and holds the third-best record in West Point history, just behind Robert E. Lee and one other graduate.[2] Douglas and his father, Arthur MacArthur, a Union Civil War hero, both received the Medal of Honor, which is the United States's highest military decoration.[3]

During World War II, Douglas MacArthur became Supreme Commander of the Southwest Pacific Area. He officially accepted the surrender of Japan on September 2, 1945 aboard the USS Missouri, and he oversaw the occupation of Japan from 1945–51.[4]

Five years after WWII, the Korean War began as part of a larger Cold War between democratic and communistic countries. The war began on June 25, 1950, when North Korea invaded South Korea. America once again turned to Douglas MacArthur for military leadership. To his admirers he was a brilliant five-star general and a charismatic leader in the fight against Communism, which seemed to be spreading like wild fire across the globe.

1. Brands, *General vs. the President*, 37.
2. James, *Years of MacArthur*, 77.
3. Weintraub, *15 Stars*, 256.
4. Van der Vat, *Pacific Campaign*, 399.

General MacArthur advocated pushing back and occupying the invading Communist North Korea, insisting that Communist China would not side with North Korea and enter the war. MacArthur predicted the Korean conflict would be over by Christmas of 1950.[5] He was proven wrong when a million Chinese charged across the frozen Yalu River, pushing the US-backed UN forces almost into the Sea of Japan at Pusan. A bold and strategically brilliant invasion at Inchon saved the day, but the hopes for a quick end to a limited war vanished.

MacArthur now felt Washington politicians were making the US and other UN troops fight with one hand tied behind their back, and America should be willing to wage total war to achieve total victory.[6] President Truman and other allies, however, were attempting to keep the Korean conflict as a limited war, pursuing a global policy to contain Communism.[7]

MacArthur's critics asserted that he was arrogant, had no respect for civilian government, and was recklessly drawing America into a Third World War. General MacArthur began openly criticizing US civilian authority, which ultimately led to a showdown with President Harry S. Truman. The President was not alone in his assessment that MacArthur was insubordinate and brashly setting foreign policy that might lead to a nuclear war.[8] In April of 1951, President Truman and the Joint Chiefs of Staff had enough, and MacArthur was relieved of command.[9]

The end of MacArthur's military carrier was as remarkable as his earlier achievements. MacArthur returned to the United States after being gone for twelve years to a hero's welcome and ticker-tape parade in downtown Manhattan.[10] After serving his county in the military for fifty-two years, he spoke before Congress in April of 1951 and gave his famous "Old soldiers never die, they just fade away" speech.[11]

A 1952 Gallup poll showed Truman's US presidential approval rating fell to an all-time low of 22 percent, an unenviable record that still

---

5. BBC News, "Home by Christmas."
6. James, *Years of MacArthur,* 590.
7. Nash, *American People,* 825.
8. Weintraub, *15 Stars,* 454–61.
9. Matray, "Truman's Plan for Victory."
10. Ambrose, *Americans at War,* 108.
11. Torricelli and Carroll, *In Our Own Words,* 187.

stands today.[12] Clearly most Americans disapproved of the decision to relieve General MacArthur.

With widespread adulation from Congress and the American people and speculation that he was making a run for the US presidency, MacArthur went on a speaking tour from 1951–52. But it was not to be. Another five-star general by the name of Dwight D. Eisenhower won the Republican nomination and eventually the presidency in 1952. The American people were tired of war and economic hard times and chose a leader whom they thought would restore peace and bring economic prosperity.

Every four years since 1788 Americans are asked to consider what qualifications are needed for a person to serve as the United States President. Choosing the right leader for the right time can challenge the most civic-minded citizens. This is not only one of the great privileges of living in a democratic republic but one of the greatest responsibilities.

Biblical Insight: Godly Leadership

by David Grotzke

Like General McArthur, Moses was also the right leader for the right time. He too would face impossible situations and not handle all of them correctly. The book of Exodus is the life story of Moses and shows the hand of God on his life from birth until death. His life is a great picture of God's plan versus man's plan and contains lessons we can learn from ignoring God's plan or following it.

In Acts 7, Stephen divides Moses' life in three, forty-year segments. The first forty years were spent in Egypt. The second forty years he spent as a shepherd in a foreign country. And the last forty years he led the Israelites through their desert wanderings. There are lessons for us in all three of these divisions. We will see that Moses was not a natural-born leader when God called him to lead several million Israelites out of Egypt, through a wilderness, to the edge of the promised land. God had to teach him many lessons in order to make him the right leader for the right time. Maybe these same lessons will help prepare us to serve God in our best way.

Moses should have been killed at birth because of Pharaoh's extermination edict (Exod 1:22), but God had other plans. God was in control,

---

12. Jones, "Who Had the Lowest Gallup?," paras. 1 & 2.

not Pharaoh. Pharaoh's plan was to have every newborn Hebrew male cast into the Nile River, which Moses' mother, Jochebed, did, but with one addition: God's plan included a waterproof basket. Pharaoh's plan was to exterminate Moses. God's plan was to educate Moses using the finest teachers Egypt could provide, so he grew up with his mother as his nurse, and Pharaoh as his benefactor. This was God's plan.

Pharaoh's daughter's plan was to call this baby Moses, which means "to draw out." God's plan was to empower him to live up to his name and "draw out" Israel from Egypt.

At the time of Moses' birth, his parents probably thought it was the worst time to have a child, but in God's plan it was right on time. Maybe you wish you would have been born at another time, or to different parents, or under better circumstances, or a different nationality, but God has a plan for you, and it is just right. He wants to use you for his glory.

Pharaoh's plan was to raise Moses to become a powerful ruler in Egypt. God's plan was to use Moses to reveal to Pharaoh and all of Egypt the most powerful ruler in the universe. But Moses was not yet ready to accomplish this after forty years in Pharaoh's courts. God had to get him alone, in the desert, to prepare him for the job God had for him. Murdering an Egyptian was the catalyst that sent him into obscurity for the next forty years.

You might feel that you have done something so bad that God could never use you in his service. Was it worse than murder? Then ask God to show you what he wants you to do, and listen and look for his answer. God is developing leaders and you might be one of them.

Moses learned some lessons in the wilderness that prepared him for the time he would get there with the Israelites. Though he was groomed to be a pharaoh, he learned to be a servant (Exod 2:19). Though he was in a prominent position in Pharaoh's court, he learned to be an obscure shepherd in God's house (Exod 3:1). Though he knew his people were being mistreated in Egypt, he learned to trust God and wait on him to deliver his people.

Because of our impatience, we often run ahead of God and get into trouble. We should use these times to draw closer to the Forgiver and Healer. It may take some time in the wilderness to reach the place where God can use you. Don't quit.

You might begin your time in the desert thinking, "I don't deserve this." That would be something your pride would say. Then you might reach the place where you would say, "I'm sick and tired of this." Self-pity might join your pride. Finally, you're ready to say, "I'm willing to accept this." God has gotten your attention and you are willing to trust in a God who wants the best for you. Now you are ready to learn the lessons God wants to teach you.

Graduation day for "The School of the Desert" came the day Moses came upon the burning bush (Exod 3:1–10). It was an ordinary day with a unique visit from a supernatural God. We may not see burning bushes today, but God is still trying to get our attention and get us to respond to his call. Are we watching for those unique visits by God?

Moses had a lot of excuses, but God had all of the answers. Moses saw all of his weaknesses, but God asked him to trust in all of God's strengths. How willing are we to accept the mission God gives to us? If we know it is God's word speaking to us and we are confident in God's power, then we should step out to fulfill God's plan for us.

The third trimester of Moses' life was his forty years leading the Israelites in the wilderness. This came after the power of God was displayed through the plagues against Egypt. He got a great send-off, but still had to learn some difficult leadership skills in his final forty years. Five hazards can be identified in Numbers 1–14.

The first hazard leaders face when working with whiners and complainers is discouragement. In Numbers 11, Moses got so discouraged that he asked God to just kill him. God's plan was to spread out the responsibility of leadership among seventy elders.

This set up the second hazard of jealousy when Joshua thought two of these men were trying to usurp Moses' authority.

The third hazard came when Moses married a Cushite woman and was misunderstood by Aaron and Miriam. They saw this new wife as a threat to their positions of leadership. God dealt with this misunderstanding by letting Aaron and Miriam know that God was okay with this marriage. He made it obvious by giving Miriam leprosy for seven days. Miriam learned not to allow jealousy to challenge God, and Moses learned that sometimes a leader just has to let God deal with a misunderstanding.

The fourth hazard for Moses was having his leadership ignored or vocally rejected. When the twelve spies came back from checking out the land that God gave them, only two agreed to follow Moses' plan. The others incited the nation to reject their leadership even to the point of wanting to stone the current leadership and appoint a new leader to take them back to Egypt.

Only a godly leader could be treated like this and still avoid the fifth hazard of retaliation. It would be so easy to grow resentful and seek revenge, but instead he begged God to spare them so the other nations would not think Israel's God had failed to fulfill his promises. God did promise a consequence for this rebellion, and that was death to the rebellious in the wilderness.

Godly leadership today is never easy, as leaders face discouragement, jealousy, misunderstandings, being ignored, or outright rebellion. This was certainly the case for Moses, and probably the truth for all those who accept a leadership role from their Savior. "Lord, help me to learn these lessons from Moses."

43

The G.I. Bill
When Government Got It Right

WORLD WAR I VETERANS returning home in 1918 were promised a bonus for their service, but it was not payable until 1945. Over 17,000 of these American doughboys and family members, known as the Bonus Army, set up camp in Washington DC, in the summer of 1932 to demand early payment. The Great Depression left many of these veterans unemployed, homeless, and starving.

The federal government's response was to send in the army with tanks, drive out these families, and burn their tents and belongings. Two veterans were shot and killed in the melee.[1] This sad chapter in American history was not to be repeated after WWII. Congress learned from past mistakes and, with guidance from the American Legion, passed the Serviceman's Readjustment Act of 1944, better known as the G.I. Bill.

Economists predicted another economic depression after World War II.[2] Sixteen million soldiers returned home looking for jobs and housing, lacking the training or resources to acquire either. Women had often taken the jobs traditionally held by men who had gone off to war. Most manufacturing plants were retooled to support the war effort and it would take time to convert back to a peacetime economy. For example, between early 1942 and late 1945, no automobiles or commercial trucks were made in the United States.[3]

1. Time Editors, "Heroes," para. 9.
2. Tassava, "American Economy."
3. Heitmann, *Automobile and American Life*, 119.

To almost everyone's surprise and relief the economy did not collapse, and in fact there was a postwar boom in large part because of the G.I. Bill. Rather than a welfare check, the G.I. Bill of Rights provided funding for education, homes, and training so veterans could transition back into society. Instead of the anticipated few hundred thousand veterans signing up, over 8 million, or 51 percent, of all WWII veterans took advantage of these benefits.[4]

There were those in higher education that thought the often blue-collar veterans with no family history of college education would degrade the integrity and rigor of academia.[5] The G.I. Bill recipients not only proved them wrong with their great success in the classroom, but doubled the number of college and university degrees between 1945–50.

Among those helped by the G.I. Bill are many famous people, including Presidents Gerald Ford and George H. W. Bush; Supreme Court Justices William Rehnquist, John Paul Stevens, and Byron White; and US Senators Bob Dole, John Glenn, George Mitchell, and Daniel Patrick Moynihan. Civil Rights activists Medgar Evers and Hosea Williams also used the G.I. Bill, as did legendary entertainers Harry Belafonte, Johnny Cash, Clint Eastwood, Paul Newman, and Walter Matthau.[6]

Another tremendous benefit of the G.I. Bill, which three out of every ten veterans took advantage of, was low-interest mortgages to purchase homes or businesses. Within ten years after the program began, a third of all housing starts were backed by the Veterans Administration.[7] Suburbs like Levittown, New York allowed these families to leave large cities and move into residential, single-family homes. From the 1950s through the 1970s, 83 percent of the nation's growth was to take place in the suburbs.[8] Mass-produced modest homes that sold for $8,000 were reduced to only $400 of upfront costs for some veterans under the G.I. Bill.

Some noted that home ownership increased patriotism and lessened political strife. "Socialism and communism do not take root in the ranks of those who have their feet firmly embedded in the sod of America through home ownership."[9] William Levitt was quoted as saying, "Own-

---

4. Mettler, "How the GI Bill Built the Middle Class," paras. 1–3.
5. Hammond and Morrison, *Stuff Americans Are Made of,* 289–90.
6. Mettler, "Bring the State Back,"
7. Mettler, "How the GI Bill Built the Middle Class," paras. 1–3.
8. Halberstam, *Fifties,* 142.
9. Humes, *Over Here,* 93–94.

ership of homes is the best guarantee against communism and socialism and the various bad 'isms' of life. I do not say that it is an infallible guarantee, but I do say that owners of homes usually are more interested in the safeguarding of our national history than are renters and tenants."[10]

The G.I. Bill was an exemplary example of bipartisan legislation which provided opportunities for millions of Americans to become self-sufficient and civic minded to the benefit of all society.

Biblical Insight: Benefit Others by Benefiting Yourself

by Ernest Schmidt

The educational, economic, and social consequences of men taking advantage of the G.I. Bill are phenomenal. It sounds self-serving to state that we should take advantage of a benefit to help others, but it is a truth of Scripture. This sounds contrary to Scripture, but God does offer us a benefit that in turn will help other people.

Accepting this benefit will allow us to introduce others to the Lord Jesus Christ so they can have their sins forgiven and have a personal relationship with him. This will result in a destiny change from Hell to Heaven. They will be able to live a balanced and exemplary life that positively impacts those around them.

Receiving this benefit gives us the opportunity to introduce others to the privilege of prayer. The ones we influence will have the experience of speaking to the great God of the universe. He knows the solution to every problem we face. He knows the future, so he can guide us in each decision we make. Since he is the Creator and in control, he has the power to intervene in all our dilemmas. In fact, he wants us to bring everything to him in prayer, because he wants to answer every prayer in a manner that is always best for us. "Be anxious for nothing, but in everything, by prayer and supplication, with thanksgiving, let your requests be made known to God; and the peace of God, which surpasses all understanding, will guard your hearts and minds through Christ Jesus" (Phil 4:6–7).

We can assure others that their lives do not need to be plagued with fear and worry. Life is not out of control for believers. They do not live in a world of jumbled, random circumstances. Their relationship to the Lord guarantees God has a unique plan and purpose for each

---

10. Kelly, *Expanding the American Dream*, 48.

believer. "And we know that *all things* work together for good to those who love God, to those who are the called according to His purpose" (Rom 8:28). In the midst of "all things" the Lord provides peace through the blessing of prayer.

Again, if we accept the benefit God offers, we will be able to share with others an understanding of who God is and his desire for their lives. The Bible clearly describes God and his will for his people. We can explain the basic truths of Scripture that will enable them to fellowship with God and discern his guidance for them as individuals:

> But you must continue in the things which you have learned and been assured of, knowing from whom you have learned them, and that from childhood you have known the Holy Scriptures, which are able to make you wise for salvation through faith which is in Christ Jesus. All Scripture is given by inspiration of God, and is profitable for doctrine, for reproof, for correction, for instruction in righteousness, that the man of God may be complete, thoroughly equipped for every good work." (2 Tim 3:14–17)

So what is the benefit we need to accept in order to impact others? It involves receiving a free gift. The gift we receive is described in the words of 2 Cor 9:15: "Thanks be to God for His indescribable gift!" When we realize our sinful, judgment-deserving condition and accept God's offer of eternal life in Christ we receive the opportunity to experience real life and share it with others. "For by grace you have been saved through faith, and that not of yourselves; it is the gift of God, not of works, lest anyone should boast" (Eph 2:8–9). "He who did not spare His own Son, but delivered Him up for us all, how shall He not with Him also freely give us all things?" (Rom 8:32). The G.I. bill provided a wonderful, earthly benefit, but God's gift of salvation is a benefit for eternity.

44

Norman Rockwell Paintings of America's Best

NORMAN ROCKWELL SPENT HIS life painting from his heart and emotionally connecting his art with his viewers. Rockwell is best known as an illustrator who, for forty-seven years, painted 321 magazine covers for *The Saturday Evening Post*.[1] His bucolic snap shots of Americana displayed the charm and warmth of small-town America. His paintings made people smile. *The Dugout,* which is one of baseball's most iconic paintings, is a classic example of Rockwell's ability to project humor and human emotions in his illustrations.

Norman Rockwell reflected on his art by saying, "Without thinking too much about it in specific terms, I was showing the America I knew and observed to others who might not have noticed."[2] During some of his most productive years of The Great Depression and World War II, Americans needed to be reminded of the best part of American life. *Walking to Church* portrays a husband and wife with their three children, walking to church along a city street. Rockwell's style went against abstract modernism, the current trend of his time, as his paintings were realistic, reflecting a nostalgic, airbrushed, happier time from which the American public drew hope and encouragement.

---

1. Biography.com editors, "Norman Rockwell Biography," para. 2.
2. "Norman Rockwell," para. 4.

Norman's childhood home was a boarding house in the upper west side of Manhattan, a city filled with derelicts, filth, and crime. It was only during his family's summer vacations to the countryside that he experienced the romanticized view of life he would later paint. Rockwell once said, "Maybe as I grew up and found the world wasn't the perfect place I had thought it to be, I unconsciously decided that if it wasn't an ideal world, it should be, and so painted only the ideal aspects of it."[3]

Many art critics denigrated and dismissed Norman Rockwell as just an illustrator whose work was commercialized into mass reproductions and painted to please his art editor and the public.[4] A fine-art painter, they contended, would paint to just express themselves, without restrictions. But while it is true that much of his work is perhaps overly sentimental, idealistic, and nostalgic, Rockwell raised illustration to a fine art.

From the over 300 *Saturday Evening Post* covers Rockwell painted, readers voted *Saying Grace* their favorite in 1955.[5] *Saying Grace* became the top-selling Rockwell painting when it sold for $46 million in 2013.[6]

Rockwell painted through times of war, economic hardships, and disparities, as well as cultural and racial divides. Wanting to do his patriotic duty, Norman Rockwell tried to enlist in the US Navy but did not meet the minimum weight requirement of 140 pounds for someone six feet tall. After a night of gormandizing on bananas and donuts he was allowed to join the Navy and spent his tour stateside as a military artist.[7]

In his 1941 State of the Union address, President Franklin Roosevelt articulated four fundamental freedoms that people across the world should enjoy. Although this was eleven months before the attack on Pearl Harbor and America's entry into World War II, Norman Rockwell offered to paint posters for the US government's Office of War Information. An official rejected his talents, saying the government planned to use "fine arts men, real artists."[8] Rockwell spent the next seven months illustrating the Four Freedoms—Freedom of Speech, Freedom of Worship, Freedom from Want, and Freedom from Fear. In 1943, they were published on the *Saturday Evening Post* covers in four consecutive issues and became an

---

3. Biography.com Editors. "Norman Rockwell Biography," para. 4.
4. Rockwell, "Norman Rockwell," para. 5.
5. Post Editors, "Rockwell Video Minute,"
6. Chappell, "Norman Rockwell's 'Saying Grace' Sells."
7. Hills, "Norman Rockwell,"
8. Post Editors. "Rockwell Files," para. 7.

instant sensation. The Office of War Information then printed 2.5 million Four Freedom posters which raised over $132 million in war bond sales.[9]

In later life, Rockwell did not shy away from difficult social issues facing America. His first illustration for *Look Magazine*, *The Problem We All Live With*, appeared in 1964. It depicted a racially charged incident where a six-year-old African-American girl is escorted to school by federal marshals. On the fiftieth anniversary of Ruby Bridges's historic walk integrating public schools in New Orleans, the painting was exhibited in the White House. The painting has come to serve as an important symbol of civil rights.[10]

First Lady Nancy Reagan presented Rockwell's *The Golden Rule* painting to the United Nations on its fortieth anniversary. Later, at the age of eighty-three, Rockwell was awarded the highest civilian honor in America, the Presidential Medal of Freedom, by President Gerald Ford.

Norman Rockwell could have depicted the bloodshed and horrors of war, the seedy underside of cities, or the inhumanity of cultural or racial injustice. He didn't turn a blind eye to them, he just chose to illustrate a brighter future than the present by reminding people there is an America worth fighting for and saving.

Biblical Insight: The Artistry of God

by Ronald Ian Phillips

Long ago, artistic masters documented great historical events and were hired as portraitists of potentates. Famous painters were commissioned to create works of art for the church. Rembrandt depicted the dramatic miracle when Jesus intervened to calm a violent storm on the Sea of Galilee. Leonardo da Vinci painted *The Last Supper*, which portrays Jesus with his disciples. Michelangelo painted awe-inspiring scenes on the ceiling of the Sistine Chapel at the Vatican in Rome.

When cameras and photography became more sophisticated, society lost its need to depict history, religion, or society through paintings. Norman Rockwell found great success, however, by keeping alive portrait painting and scenes from everyday life. The feelings and experiences of

---

9. "Rockwell Files."
10. Solomon, *American Mirror*, 378.

the subjects he painted are easily revealed and so they resonated with viewers.

Where do great artists get their talent? Malcom Gladwell, in his bestseller, *Outliers: The Story of Success,* theorized it takes 10,000 hours of practice to be successful in any endeavor. While it's essential to hone one's craft, in a very real sense all talent and creativity comes from God.

In the first chapter of Genesis we are told God created the sun, moon, and the earth. His perfect creation displays his artistry, with snow-capped mountains and beautiful rivers that flow into the oceans. He painted the first sunset and sunrise. In Psalm 19:1 it is written: "The heavens proclaim the glory of God. The skies display his craftsmanship." The complexity and variety of God's creation are seen everywhere we look. Psalm 104:24–25 says, "How many are your works, Lord! In wisdom you made them all; the earth is full of your creatures. There is the sea, vast and spacious, teeming with creatures beyond number—living things both large and small."

God's crowning achievement in creation is found in Genesis 1:27: "So God created man in his own image, in the image of God created he him; male and female created he them." God is the Creator, and he formed us in his image. As God's image-bearers, it should remind us to treat all people with dignity and respect.

God gave each of us talents and creative minds. Exodus 35:31–33 (NIV) says, "And he has filled him with the Spirit of God, with wisdom, with understanding, with knowledge, and with all kinds of skills—to make artistic designs for work in gold, silver, and bronze, to cut and set stones, to work in wood and to engage in all kinds of artistic crafts." All of us have some level of creativity that is unique to us since we are all made in the image of God. Our sense of self-worth and accomplishment are increased when we use these talents to encourage others and to glorify God.

But there are many who do not give God the credit for creation or their individual talents. The Bible says they are blinded to the truth: "The god of this age has blinded the minds of unbelievers, so that they cannot see the light of the gospel that displays the glory of Christ, who is the image of God" (2 Cor 4:4 NIV). We are told to avoid these people in 2 Timothy 3:2–5 NIV:

> People will be lovers of themselves, lovers of money, boastful, proud, abusive, disobedient to their parents, ungrateful, unholy, without love, unforgiving, slanderous, without self-control, brutal, not lovers of the good, treacherous, rash, conceited, lovers of

pleasure rather than lovers of God—having a form of godliness but denying its power. Have nothing to do with such people.

Nothing exists that does not owe its existence to God the Creator. Our every breath on this earth, and our hope and assurance of life in eternity, is dependent on God, who created and sustains this world and the next in all its richness, diversity, and order.

45

Dwight David Eisenhower
A Man of Remarkable Deeds and Character

DWIGHT DAVID EISENHOWER MUST have looked back on all the accomplishments of his life with a great deal of satisfaction. He became a five-star general who was the Supreme Allied Commander of European forces in World War II; Chairman of the Joint Chiefs of Staff; the first NATO commander; President of an Ivy League college; author of a bestselling book; and a United States President for eight years. Accomplishing any one of these achievements in life would be remarkable.

But an accident at the age of thirteen almost denied him that incredible life of service to his country. Dwight, nicknamed Ike, was the third of seven sons born into an impoverished but hard-working and devoutly religious Kansas family. As a freshman in high school, Ike injured his knee and developed a leg infection which progressed to the point that the family doctor wanted to amputate. Dwight refused to allow his leg to be amputated, and made a miraculous recovery.[1]

Eisenhower's family practiced daily Bible reading, prayer, and attended the Brethren in Christ Church, a Mennonite offshoot. Dwight's mother named him after the evangelist Dwight L. Moody, whose most famous quote was "Faith makes all things possible . . . Love makes all things easy."[2] In 1948, Eisenhower described himself as "one of the most deeply religious men I know."[3] At his first presidential inauguration

1. Ambrose, *Eisenhower: Soldier*, 20–27.
2. Halberstam, *Fifties*, 243–47.
3. Time Editors, "Eisenhower," para 12.

in 1953, Ike took his oath of office upon two Bibles—the one used by George Washington in his 1789 inauguration, and the one his mother gave him upon his graduation from West Point. After being sworn in, Ike personally offered the inaugural prayer. As president, he was baptized in a Presbyterian Church in 1953.

Since Ike could not afford college, and tuition was not required at West Point, Ike applied and was accepted at the military academy in 1911. He made the varsity football team and was the starting running back and linebacker in 1912 when he tackled the legendary Jim Thorpe.[4] Dwight Eisenhower graduated in the middle of the class of 1915, which became known as "the class the stars fell on" because fifty-nine classmates eventually became general officers, including Eisenhower and Omar Bradley, who became five-star generals.[5]

General Eisenhower distinguished himself as a military strategist and oversaw the invasions of North Africa and Sicily before supervising the invasions of France and Germany during World War II. As the Supreme Allied Commander in Europe, he oversaw the D-Day Normandy landings on June 6, 1942. After the war, he replaced George C. Marshall as Army Chief of Staff until 1948. During that year, Eisenhower's memoir, *Crusade in Europe,* was published and became a bestseller. From 1948 until 1953 Eisenhower served as president of Columbia University, while also serving as the first Supreme Commander of the North Atlantic Treaty Organization (NATO). Eisenhower thought NATO would become a truly European alliance, with the American and Canadian commitments ending after about ten years.

Having no political party affiliation in 1948, Dwight Eisenhower was urged to run as a Democrat for the United States presidency. Instead Eisenhower ran as a Republican in 1952 and 1956, twice easily defeating the Democrat, Adlai Stevenson II, who had the perceived disadvantages of being divorced and an egghead, or an intellectual.[6]

"I like Ike" was Dwight Eisenhower's campaign slogan, and just two weeks before the election Eisenhower said he would go to Korea to end the war there. With the Soviet Union withdrawing after the death of Joseph Stalin, and the Chinese exhausted from more than two years of this limited and soon forgotten Korean War, an armistice was signed on July

---

4. Halberstam, *Fifties,* 247.
5. Haskew, *West Point,* 207.
6. Halberstam, *Fifties,* 234–35.

27, 1953. Steven Ambrose, in his biography on President Eisenhower, comments: "Eisenhower had the insight to realize that unlimited war in the nuclear age was unthinkable, and limited war unwinnable."[7]

President Eisenhower developed Atoms for Peace, a program which balanced fears of continuing nuclear armament with promises of peaceful use of uranium in future nuclear reactors. When the Soviet Union successfully tested a hydrogen bomb in late November 1955 and then launched Sputnik 1 into earth's orbit on October 4, 1957,[8] Americans realized our Cold War enemy could now easily hit American cities with nuclear weapons. The Truman foreign policy of containing Communism now became a more dangerous one of brinkmanship under Eisenhower as the arms race intensified. In response to Sputnik being launched, Eisenhower created NASA as a civilian space agency in October 1958.[9]

The Federal-Aid Highway Act of 1956 created 41,000 miles of interstate highway.[10] President Eisenhower wanted a way of evacuating cities if the United States was attacked by an atomic bomb. He also supported this largest public works project in the nation's history as vital to our economy, safety, relief of congestion, and defense.

The Eisenhower era of the 1950s was a time of unprecedented economic growth and prosperity. GDP (gross domestic product) grew by an astonishing 150 percent in the period from 1945–60.[11] In the 1950s, with only 5 percent of the world's population, the US economy produced almost half of the world's manufactured products.[12] Americans drove three-quarters of the world's cars and consumed half of the world's energy.[13] Fifty million babies were born during the baby boom in the Eisenhower era.[14] Alaska and Hawaii were admitted to the Union during Eisenhower's presidency.

Eisenhower suffered seven heart attacks from 1955 until his death. After his presidency, Dwight and Mamie, his wife of fifty-three years, retired to a farm adjacent to the battlefield at Gettysburg, Pennsylvania. On

---

7. Ambrose, *Eisenhower: The President*, 106–7.
8. Halberstam, *Fifties*, 624–28.
9. Britton, *Dwight D. Eisenhower*, 26–38.
10. Weingroff, "Federal-Aid Highway Act of 1956," para. 27.
11. Khan Academy, "Eisenhower Era Unit 8," para. 9.
12. U.S. Department of Commerce, *Statistical Abstract*, 232.
13. U.S. Department of Commerce, *Statistical Abstract*, 232.
14. U.S. Department of Commerce, *Statistical Abstract*, 232.

the morning of March 28, 1969, Eisenhower died in Washington DC of congestive heart failure at age seventy-eight.

Eisenhower left a legacy almost unparalleled in American history. He led the allied forces to victory in World War II, ended the Korean War, sponsored and signed the Civil Rights Bill of 1957, and directed the fiscal policies that let to great prosperity in the 1950s. Historians and the American public often rank Dwight David Eisenhower as one of the top ten United States Presidents of all time.[15]

On March 30, 1969, President Richard Nixon, Eisenhower's Vice President of eight years, gave the eulogy at Eisenhower's funeral in which he said:

> It is, I think, a special tribute to Dwight Eisenhower that despite all of his honors, despite all of his great deeds and his triumphs, we find ourselves today thinking, first, not of his deeds but of his character. It was the character of the man, not what he did, but what he was that so captured the trust and faith and affection of his own people and of the people of the world.[16]

Biblical Insight: What Will Be Your Legacy?

by Ronald Ian Phillips

Dwight Eisenhower remained true to his core belief in living his faith, love for his family, and duty to his country his entire life. His positive legacy is remarkable and should be aspirational for all future American generations. Each of us leaves a legacy as our journey through life intertwines with family, gender, race, nation, and faith. But what a different world it would be if every person chose to leave a positive legacy. Have you ever contemplated how your epitaph will read? If you are currently leaving a negative legacy, would you change?

Imagine waking up tomorrow and reading your obituary in the newspaper with the headline "The Merchant of Death is Dead." According to legend, that's exactly what happened to Alfred Nobel in 1888. A journalist mistook his brother's death for Alfred's and wrote a scathing obituary. Alfred, who had invented dynamite and owned nearly 100 factories that made explosives and munitions, was horrified that the

---

15. "Presidential Historians Survey 2017,"
16. U.S. Gov. Printing, *Memorial Services*, xiv.

"Merchant of Death" was to be his legacy. So Alfred created and financed a foundation that would award peace prizes for accomplishments in science, medicine, literature, and advances in world peace. The Nobel Peace Prize is universally accepted today as his legacy.

The radical transformation of Alfred Nobel's legacy is perhaps similar to the onetime, 180-degree turn a person makes from sin to God when becoming a Christian. The Bible tells us that when we become believers and followers of the Savior Jesus Christ, we begin a whole new legacy. In 2 Corinthians 5:17 we read, "Therefore if any man be in Christ, he is a new creature: old things are passed away; behold all things are become new." We have a choice between accepting a pardon for our sins or rejecting God's offer and suffering the consequences. It is unimaginable that anyone hearing of God's grace and forgiveness would not leap at the opportunity to be under his loving care and accept the promise of eternal life in Heaven, yet so many reject this free offer of atonement for their sins.

No one is born a child of God. When we are born again we are adopted and become a child of God. John 1:12 (NKJV) says, "But as many as received Him, to them He gave the right to become children of God, to those who believe in His name." Isaiah 43:1 (NKJV) tells us, "Fear not, for I have redeemed you; I have called you by your name; you are Mine." Second Corinthians 6:18 gives us the promise, "'. . . and will be a Father unto you, and ye shall be my sons, and daughters,' saith the Lord Almighty."

Ultimately no positive legacy will be ours without repentance and redemption. Ecclesiastes 2:11 states, "Then I looked on all the works that my hands had done and on the labor in which I had toiled; and indeed all was vanity and grasping for the wind. There was no profit under the sun." Mark 8:36 says, "For what shall it profit a man, if he shall gain the whole world, and lose his own soul?" The Bible teaches that we must accept what Jesus has done for us, through his perfect life, his death on the cross for our sins, and his resurrection from the dead. We read in Romans 10:9 (NKJV) "that if you confess with your mouth the Lord Jesus and believe in your heart that God has raised Him from the dead, you will be saved."

At the point of conversion people should notice a change from narcissism to being more loving, kind, forgiving, and charitable. We read in Matt 6:20–21 (NKJV), "but lay up for yourselves treasures in Heaven, where neither moth nor rust destroys, and where thieves do not break in and steal. For where your treasure is, there your heart will be also."

One bad choice can destroy a person's reputation. First Peter 5:8 (NKJV) warns us, "Be sober, be vigilant; because your adversary the devil walks about like a roaring lion, seeking whom he may devour." But we have a loving Father that will help us. Romans 8:38 tells us that God will never leave us or forsake us, "For I am convinced that neither death nor life, neither angels nor demons, neither the present nor the future, nor any powers, neither height nor depth, nor anything else in all creation, will be able to separate us from the love of God that is in Christ Jesus our Lord."

Christians are ambassadors for Christ, with the mission to serve God and share the good news of Jesus Christ's saving grace. We can leave no greater legacy than to lead others to Christ. There is joy in Heaven and angels rejoice when one sinner repents (Luke 15:10). Every one of us has the potential to make a difference and leave a rich legacy. It often takes a daily effort to consciously add value to other people's lives. Acts of kindness, positive conversations, treating others as we would like to be treated are just a few actions all Christians can practice every day. Billy Graham is quoted as saying, "The greatest legacy one can pass on to one's children and grandchildren is not money or other material things accumulated in one's life, but rather a legacy of character and faith."[17]

---

17. *American Legends*, introduction.

46

Life in the Suburbs
A Proud Sense of Community

AMERICA WAS USED TO solving seemingly insurmountable problems throughout The Great Depression and World War II but this one was problematic. Sixteen million war-weary G.I.s returned home in the fall of 1945 when World War II ended. They wanted to get on with their lives by getting a job, finding a home, finding a spouse, and raising a family. William Levitt was one of those returning American servicemen who served with the Seabees at Pearl Harbor. Seabees are US naval mobile construction battalions with the motto "We build, we fight." Levitt used his wartime experience of constructing assembly-line, slab-based army houses for his Levittown project idea. He is widely credited as the Father of Modern American Suburbia. In 1998, he was named one of *Time*'s "Time 100 Persons of the Century."[1]

Following The Great Depression and World War II, housing starts in America had fallen from 1 million a year to fewer than 100,000.[2] In 1945, experts estimated a shortage of 5 million homes nationwide. Veterans returned to "no vacancy" signs and high rents. As late as 1947, one-third of veterans were still living with relatives and friends.[3] Some 50,000

---

1. Time Editors, "Time 100 Persons of the Century,"
2. Halberstam, *Fifties*, 234.
3. Halberstam, *Fifties*, 134.

people were reportedly living in Army Quonset huts.[4] In Chicago, it was so bad that 250 old trolley cars were sold and used as homes.[5]

Resulting from affordable housing in the suburbs, annual housing starts leaped upward from 142,000 in 1944 to an average of 1.5 million per year in the 1950s.[6] The first of William Levitt's eventual seven suburban housing developments was located on Long Island, New York, and called Levittown. It included 17,500 homes, built on a former potato field between 1947 and 1951.[7] Suburbs like Levittown allowed these families to leave crime-ridden, crowded, expensive, large cities, and move into residential single-family homes. Levitt assigned a different crew to each of the twenty-seven steps he identified in home construction.[8] Employing nonunion workers, paid by the task not per hour, sped up production to the point where thirty houses could be completed daily.

Levitt's mass-produced, two-bedroom, 800-square-foot homes sold for $8,000, and included washers, dryers, refrigerators, and television sets.[9] Although their homes were modest, veterans and their new young families enjoyed green lawns, barbecue grills, patios, and the standard white picket fences.

Growing up in the suburbs definitely had its upside. After supper, kids rode their bikes through the winding neighborhood streets with playing cards clothespinned to their spokes, while some sported a Davy Crockett coonskin cap. Their only worry was getting lost since all the houses looked the same. They watched the Mouseketeers, *Gunsmoke*, and *I Love Lucy* on black-and-white TVs. In 1949, there were approximately 1 million television sets in American homes and 19 million by 1952.[10] It was the age of party-line telephones, big-fin automobiles, and hula hoops.

But it was not always happy days for 50s-era baby-boom children. Civil defense duck-and-cover drills required kids to practice hiding under their school desk to protect themselves from a possible thermonuclear bomb attack. Chickenpox and measles were common, but it was polio that was the most frightening public health problem. The 1952 US

---

4. Halberstam, *Fifties*, 134.
5. Halberstam, *Fifties*, 134.
6. Knecht, "Historical Progression," para. 7.
7. Halberstam, *Fifties*, 237.
8. Lacayo, "Suburban Legend."
9. Glaeser, *Triumph of the City*, 174–77.
10. Halberstam, *Fifties*, 186, 195.

polio epidemic was the worst outbreak in the nation's history. Of nearly 58,000 cases reported that year, 3,145 people died, and 21,269 were left with mild to disabling paralysis.[11] When Dr. Jonas Salk's polio vaccine was introduced in 1955 it was so successful he was considered a "miracle worker."[12]

Many in large metropolitan areas seemed to have adopted Shakespeare's line in *As You Like It*: "I do desire we may be better strangers."[13] In contrast, neighbors in the suburbs knew each other well and were more than acquaintances. Relationships were built face-to-face, unlike the social media relationships with total strangers that are becoming the norm today. Neighbors celebrated each other's births, baptisms, and birthdays. With financial loss, illness, or even death there was a real support network of community friends in the suburbs.

Robert Frost wrote in his "Mending Wall" poem that "good fences make good neighbors."[14] So maybe the small white picket fences helped since rarely was the sense of community stronger than in the suburbs. Neighbors helped each other raise children and fix up their homes and yards. They joined the school PTA, voiced their concerns to local government, and joined clubs together. In the second half of the 1950s a record number of Americans said they were very happy.

On a typical Sunday morning from 1955–58, almost half of all Americans were attending church; the highest percentage in U.S. history.[15] During the 1950s, nationwide church membership grew at a faster rate than the population, from 57 percent of the US population in 1950 to 63.3 percent in 1960.[16]

Much has been made by detractors and revisionists who characterize life in the suburbs as living in ticky-tack houses, filled with people of the same race and social economic background. They claim bland conformity reigned while suburban families ate the same TV dinners, watched the same four or five TV shows, and surrounded themselves with people that looked, acted, and thought just like them. Still, the success of the early suburbs stands in stark contrast with the immense struggles and costs of

---

11. Pennsylvania Department of Health, "Polio Fact Sheet," para. 1.
12. Hantula, *Jonas Salk*, 37–39.
13. Shakespeare, *As You Like It*, 61 (Act 3, Scene 2).
14. Frost, "Mending Wall," line 27.
15. Tucker, "1950s," para. 10.
16. Tucker, "1950s," para. 10.

government-run programs attempting to deal with the pandemic, homelessness, crime, poverty, and other societal issues today.

Biblical Insight: The Ideal Church

by Ronald Ian Phillips

With the growth of suburbs came new schools, libraries, grocery stores, shopping malls, and a multitude of other service-related businesses. Houses of worship were also high on prospective homeowners' list of priorities. Finding an ideal church was important for Christians, who enjoyed suburban life with caring, like-minded neighbors in a safe, friendly community. That's probably because Christian life isn't just to be practiced on Sunday morning but applied throughout the week in daily lives.

Picture your ideal church. You probably think of a welcoming church where you can study the Bible, serve, have fellowship, and spread the good news of the gospel. Whether it's at home or in church, it's important to have a Christ-centered environment with caring, accepting, forgiving people who share common family values.

Have you ever heard someone say "I'm praying for you," but then also brought you a meal, drove you to a doctor's appointment, watched the kids, or helped with a project around the house? That's a good beginning point for neighbors or church members. God expects us to care for and love one another. John 13:34–35 (NKJV) says, "A new commandment I give to you, that you love one another; as I have loved you, that you also love one another. By this all will know that you are My disciples, if you have love for one another." Church should be a place we can meet loving and caring people.

The distinction should be made between the two different types of God's churches. The invisible or universal church is made up of all the true believers throughout the world (Eph 4:1–16). The second type of church is a physical structure where people gather to worship: it is refered in Hebrews 10:25: "Not forsaking the assembling of ourselves together, as the manner of some is; but exhorting one another: and so much the more, as ye see the day approaching." It's often repeated, the church is not a building, but a body of believers who worship and grow in God's word and evangelize together.

The church is refered to in the Bible as the bride of Christ, people of God, and body of Christ. Many of the New Testament books of the Bible were letters written to churches. The apostle Paul wrote to the churches at Rome (Rom 1:7), Corinth (1 Cor 1:2), Galatia (Gal 1:2), Ephesus (Eph 1:1), Philippi (Phil 1:1), Colossae (Col 1:2), and Thessalonica (1 Thess 1:1; 2 Thess 2:1). In his letters, Paul repeatedly emphasized that the church was God-ordained and important to the spiritual well-being of believers.

Christians experienced persecution and martyrdom for the first 300 years after the death and resurrection of Jesus Christ. The apostle John writes of this persecution in the letters to seven churches mentioned in the last book of the Bible. John was exiled to the island of Patmos, where he wrote the God-inspired book of Revelation. It's commonly believed that John was the only apostle who died of old age. The other apostles were stoned to death, beheaded, crucified, and suffered greatly in martyrdom while establishing churches and spreading the gospel throughout the ancient world.

The seven churches named in the book of Revelation were far from perfect. Each church had serious flaws, so a warning was given with a command to change and a promise of reward if they were obedient. Many of these churches were divisive, taught false doctrine, made moral compromises, or tolerated immorality. Some church members took great pride in their material well-being but were blind to their spiritual poverty. Revelation 3:17 says, "Because thou sayest, I am rich, and increased with goods, and have need of nothing; and knowest not that thou art wretched, and miserable, and poor, and blind, and naked." Most of these churches had fallen short of their mission to love, persevere, and remain faithful.

Much of the New Testament was written to local churches with instructions that we can apply to our ideal or existing churches today. In 1 Timothy 3:15 we read, "But if I am delayed, I write so that you may know how you ought to conduct yourself in the house of God, which is the church of the living God, the pillar and ground of the truth." We should not have any delusions of finding an ideal church, but our goal should be to help our local church be a welcoming place of worship, Bible study, and evangelism. These are all essential elements to a Christ-centered church.

As recorded in the Bible, the church in Philadelphia is often described as the true or obedient church. Revelation 3:8 (NIV) says, "I know your deeds. See, I have placed before you an open door that no one can shut. I know that you have little strength, yet you have kept My word and have not denied My name." God's word encourages churches to have an open door for all to use their talents with Christ's strength in keeping and proclaiming Christ's message.

Revelation 3:20 (NKJV) says, "Behold, I stand at the door and knock. If anyone hears My voice and opens the door, I will come in to him and dine with him, and he with Me." Picture the image of Jesus standing outside a place of worship that is not Christ-centered, asking to come in. If Christ is knocking at the door of your heart or your church—invite him in. Our Lord and Savior Jesus Christ waits expectantly for all to open their hearts to him.

47

A Struggle for Human and Civil Rights

IT IS EASY TO understand why Dexter Avenue in Montgomery, Alabama is nicknamed "the most historical short street in America."[1] Walking along historic Dexter Avenue today is like walking through a time capsule of former slave markets, where one can witness the struggle for civil rights and basic human dignity. On this short street, Alabama voted to secede from the Union on January 7, 1861, and it is where the first Confederate flag was made and unfurled. The street was the final stretch of the fifty-four-mile, Selma-to-Montgomery March that led to the Voting Rights Act of 1965.[2]

Until the passage of the Thirteenth Amendment in 1865, this area was in many ways one of the epicenters of the slave markets in America. During the Reconstruction period that followed, Jim Crow laws enforcing racial segregation continued to be implemented by local and state governments. In 1896, the United States Supreme Court ruled in the *Plessy v. Ferguson* case that racial segregation was constitutional under the "separate but equal" doctrine. Equality was rarely met in practice.[3] Signs reading "Whites only" and "Coloreds only" still mandated segregation of restaurants, restrooms, drinking fountains, public schools, and public transportation.

---

1. Crow, "Journey through American History," para. 2.
2. Alabama Scenic Byways, "Selma to Montgomery,"
3. Zinn, *People's History of the United States*, 205.

African-Americans, as well as poor white people, were discouraged from voting because of the required literacy test. Some states even created a cumulative poll tax requiring men age twenty-one to sixty of any race to pay a sum of money for every year from the time they had turned twenty-one.[4]

In 1954, progress began to be made in civil rights. The Supreme Court ruled in favor of public school desegregation in the case of *Brown v. Board of Education*. The federal government also passed the Civil Rights Act of 1957, designed to provide federal protection for African-American voting rights. However, it was not until the passage of the Civil Rights Acts of 1964 and 1965 that Congress finally banned Jim Crow laws.[5]

Pushback from segregationists and states' rights advocates was strong and immediate. Nowhere was this more evident than when George Wallace declared "segregation now, segregation tomorrow, segregation forever"[6] in his 1963 inaugural address as Governor of Alabama. Wallace's speech from the Alabama State Capitol was from the exact same place that Jefferson Davis had been sworn in as President of the Confederate States of America in 1861.

The year 1955 witnessed a safe Salk polio vaccine, the launching of the first nuclear-powered USS Nautilus submarine, the opening of Disneyland and McDonald's, and TV shows like *The Mickey Mouse Club* and *Gunsmoke*. While much of America basked in the prosperity of the Eisenhower years, the struggle for civil and human rights continued.

In the shadow of the Alabama State Capitol, on this historically rich street, the Dexter Avenue Baptist Church was founded in 1877 on the site of an old slave trader's pen.[7] The church is now world-renowned as arguably ground zero for where the civil rights movement began. It was from the lower level of this church that its young pastor, Dr. Martin Luther King Jr., at age twenty-six, organized the Montgomery bus boycott in 1955.

King's predecessor, the brilliant yet eccentric Pastor Vernon Johns, was already advocating for racial equality and social justice under the law. He had long encouraged his church members to live by the motto, "If you see a good fight . . . get in it."[8] In December of 1955, Rosa Parks

---

4. "Poll Taxes in the United States Explained."
5. Foner and Garraty, *Reader's Companion to American History*, 178–79.
6. BlackPast, "(1963) George Wallace, 'Segregation Now, Segregation Forever.'"
7. The Dexter Avenue King Memorial Baptist Church, "History."
8. Miller, "If You See a Good Fight . . . ,"

did just that by refusing to relinquish her bus seat to a white passenger. Parks had recently attended a center for training activists and was the Montgomery National Association for the Advancement of Colored People (NAACP) secretary.[9] Many others had resisted bus segregation before her, but the NAACP felt she was the best candidate to challenge Alabama's segregation laws.

Buses had "colored" sections in the rear, but black riders were required to relinquish their seats even in these sections if there were no "white-only" seats left, even though Blacks composed more than 75 percent of the ridership.[10] The boycott dragged on for 381 days before the courts finally ruled that segregation on public buses and transportation was against the law.

There was a high price to be paid for this activism. This was a struggle for basic human dignity, to be treated equally before the law, not for special privilege or personal gain or recognition. When the deacons of the Dexter Avenue Baptist Church unexpectedly accepted Pastor Dr. Vernon Johns' resignation after five previous offers to resign, Johns suddenly realized he had nowhere to go. Even after the deacons disconnected the gas, electricity, and water to the parsonage, Johns refused to move out of the parsonage for nearly a year.[11]

Frustrated and perhaps angry that he had not changed the social injustices and indifference of the people, Vernon Johns never pastored a church again. His last years were spent living on an abandoned gasoline station lot, tending a vegetable stand and preaching occasionally.[12] Although sometimes referred to as the "Father of Civil Rights,"[13] he is largely forgotten by history.

Rosa Parks, on the other hand, was widely and posthumously honored in later years. Yet she received death threats long after the Montgomery bus boycott and was fired from her job as a seamstress. Forced to move out of state to find a job, Parks and her husband suffered stomach ulcers for years.

Dr. Martin Luther King Jr., known for his use of nonviolence and civil disobedience, also paid a heavy price for his involvement in civil

---

9. Branch, *Parting the Waters*, 124, 130–37.
10. Garrow, *Bearing the Cross*, 13.
11. Branch, *Parting the Waters*, 109.
12. Branch, *Parting the Waters*, 902.
13. Fink, *Vernon Johns Story*.

and human rights. The Dexter Avenue Baptist Church parsonage was bombed, he was stabbed in the chest in 1958, and was fatally shot at the Lorraine Motel in Memphis, Tennessee, on April 4, 1968.[14]

After completing the Selma-to-Montgomery March on March 25, 1965, Martin Luther King Jr. delivered his famous "Our God Is Marching On!" speech from the steps of the State Capitol in Montgomery, Alabama.[15] The popular name to this speech is "How Long, Not Long," where King states, "The arc of the moral universe is long, but it bends toward justice."[16]

King often quoted excerpts from James Russell Lowell's 1844 poem "The Present Crisis." Lowell, an ardent abolitionist, replaced Henry Wadsworth Longfellow as professor of modern languages and literature at Harvard. The lines often quoted were:

> Once to every man and nation comes the moment to decide,
> In the strife of Truth with Falsehood, for the good or evil side;
> Truth forever on the scaffold, Wrong forever on the throne,
> Yet that scaffold sways the future, and, behind the dim unknown,
> Standeth God within the shadow, keeping watch above his own.[17]

Biblical Insight: Before the Throne

by Seth Grotzke

The history of human and civil rights is a long and sad one. Throughout the ages it has been the standard practice to separate humanity, whether by skin color, ethnicity, language, culture, sex, or age. One group is always able to find a reason to exclude the other. One side always has reasons for claiming superiority over the other. One person can always demonstrate why another is of lesser value. The ever-present vices, pride, and self-deception are alive and well in every individual (Prov 21:24), and they lead us comfortably down the path of racism. Like a two-edged sword, these impulses validate each other: "I am better than they are" and "I'm not bad."

The plight in which we now find ourselves is not new, nor is it simple. It started back when all things were declared good by God, but we didn't believe him. When humanity chose to doubt God's goodness and attempt

---

14. Levine, "If Martin Luther King Had Sneezed."
15. Wallenfeldt, "'We Shall Overcome,'"
16. Mieder, *Making a Way Out*, 212.
17. Lowell, "Present Crisis," lines 21–22, 38–40.

to take over control, great fissures in the universe opened between God and humanity and between each individual (Gen 3). Those gaps continue to grow and expand, distancing ourselves from our Creator and from our fellow creation. With a problem of this depth and history, it is fair to ask: Is there any hope?

Looking around at our community, our city, our country, and our world, we would be hard pressed to find any hope. But we have to look further. We cannot merely look at more of the problem to find the solution; we need to look to the One with the power to save us. We have to look to our God. In Revelation 7 we can see the final result, and it looks nothing like what we see right now.

> After this I looked, and behold, a great multitude that no one could number, from every nation, from all tribes and peoples and languages, standing before the throne and before the Lamb, clothed in white robes, with palm branches in their hands, and crying out with a loud voice, "Salvation belongs to our God who sits on the throne, and to the Lamb!" And all the angels were standing around the throne and around the elders and the four living creatures, and they fell on their faces before the throne and worshiped God, saying, "Amen! Blessing and glory and wisdom and thanksgiving and honor and power and might be to our God forever and ever! Amen." (Rev 7:9–12 ESV)

But how will we ever move from the news of today to the future prophecies of Scripture? What is the path, the greater Selma- to-Montgomery March, which will culminate in a unified humanity? It begins with a recognition of the depth of the problem. Only God is able to bridge the gap between God and humanity. For this reason, the Father sent his Son to be the Savior of the world (1 John 4:14). And Jesus proclaims he is able to fully bridge the gap between each individual, nation, tribe, people, and language. He does this through addressing the very place of mankind which is overlooked in our prejudices: the heart (Matt 15:10–20). Whereas our physical senses immediately categorize people by their skin color, form of speech, or appearance, Jesus concerns himself with the inner man.

Once we are able to see the problem as it is, we are better able to accept our place in it. As part of sinful humanity, we can accept that pride and self-deception are firmly rooted within us. Each of us can say: "I am part of the problem." However, as a follower of Christ, I am also the temple of the Holy Spirit. The Third Person of the Trinity has taken up residence within me, and is doing as Jesus had promised, convicting and comforting, cleansing and healing (Eph 3:14–21). It is God himself who is actively transforming me so that I might see and love my fellow human beings.

And this is when we can move forward. With the assurance that we are loved and sanctified by our good God, we can turn to those around us, regardless of nation, tribe, people, or language and see the image of our Creator stamped on them and share the love which has been showered on us. When individuals with whom we differ make a stand for equality, we can praise God for his work in and through them. When those with whom we align ourselves ignore or encourage segregation through pride and self-deception, we can condemn it. Reconciliation in Christ is possible when we are able to see the problem, accept our place in it, and pursue the solution through the work of the Spirit. We have hope. Our God is marching on.

48

Sandra Day O'Connor
A Day in Court

SANDRA DAY GREW UP in the late 1930s and early 1940s on the largest single ranch in the Western United States. But the Lazy B Cattle Ranch in Arizona did not afford a life of laziness or luxury. It had no electricity or indoor plumbing or schools nearby, so Sandra lived with her grandmother and attended school in El Paso. On the holidays and during the summer she returned to the Lazy B, where she learned the value of self-reliance and hard work to succeed and survive.[1]

Sandra Day went on to graduate with an economics degree from Stanford University and a law degree in 1952 from Stanford Law School, graduating third in her class. Her job search led her to call every phone number on a bulletin board posting law openings, but no one would hire a woman. With seemingly no other prospects, she offered to work for a deputy county attorney, starting with no salary.[2]

As the years went by, Sandra married John O'Connor III, raised three sons, and became the Arizona Assistant Attorney General and a state senator. Then one day in July 1981, the President of the United States called. President Reagan nominated Sandra Day O'Connor as the first woman to serve on the Supreme Court. Confirmed by the US Senate with a 99–0 vote, O'Connor went on to serve as an associate justice for almost a quarter century.

1. Kamen and Williams, "How Sandra Day O'Connor,"
2. NPR Editors, "'Out Of Order.'"

Unrestrained abuses of power can occur in a true democracy where a simple majority of the people may take away the rights of the other 49 percent. To prevent this from happening, the American Constitutional framers showed one of the most brilliant displays of wisdom. They wisely created a democratic republic with authority separated into three branches of government: Legislative, Executive, and Judicial. A democratic republic more often creates rule of law that protects the individual or the minority. It can be argued that the judicial branch including the US Supreme Court is the greatest vanguard defender for our individual unalienable rights.

Article III of the US Constitution established the Supreme Court of the United States. Since John Jay's appointment in 1789 as the first justice, the Supreme Court was an exclusive men's club for 192 years with 101 men serving before O'Connor join the court. Once nominated by the President and confirmed by the Senate, justices have tenure for life unless they retire, resign, or are impeached.

The late 1980s were difficult for O'Connor as she went through breast cancer treatment and then had her appendix removed in 1988.[3] A year later her husband was diagnosed with Alzheimer's disease. Although Justice O'Connor was successfully treated for her health problems she eventually resigned in 2005 to assist her husband who spent twenty years with advancing memory loss and deteriorating health before passing away in 2009.[4]

For good reason, some consider Sandra Day O'Connor the most powerful federal official woman in American history.[5] As a pioneer she continues to be an inspiration to so many who learn about her remarkable legacy. In 2009, her accomplishments were acknowledged when she was awarded the Presidential Medal of Freedom, the highest civilian award in the United States.[6]

---

3. Greenhouse, "O'Connor Has Breast Surgery,"
4. Sullivan, "Sandra Day O'Connor's Husband Dies."
5. Thomas, *First*, 240–41, 341.
6. SCOTUS, "Sandra Day O'Connor."

Biblical Insight: How to Recognize a Wise Person

by Seth Grotzke

It is difficult to read of the life and legacy of Sandra Day O'Connor and not consider the threads of wisdom which are woven throughout. Those who framed the US Constitution walked the path of wisdom, choosing to distribute power instead of consolidate it. President Reagan demonstrated wisdom in selecting a woman who would go on to serve in such a manner. O'Connor herself exemplified wisdom through her studies, career, and service to both her country and family. We recognize wisdom when we see it because "wisdom is vindicated by her deeds."[7]

Yet as easy as it is to recognize a wise choice in hindsight, we still find ourselves frustrated every day with decisions which need to be made based on limited knowledge. We are frustrated with ourselves or others when we thought a wise choice was made, but it ended with disastrous results. Perhaps we prayed about it and consulted others. Perhaps we studied the facts and took into account as many variables as we could imagine, yet in spite of our best intentions, the decision turned out to be the wrong one.

There is a genre of Scripture dedicated to wisdom which forms a significant part of our Bibles. In both the Old Testament and the New Testament we hear the call of Wisdom to all those who seek life. The books of Proverbs, Ecclesiastes, and Job are the most common place to turn for examples of wisdom literature.

In Proverbs we meet Wisdom, who is sure and consistent. Through pithy statements and general principles, we are called to a life which recognizes God as Creator and King, and his laws as the path of life. God is fair and just. But as we turn to Ecclesiastes the Preacher presents a different shade of wisdom. Sometimes life is unpredictable. Like a vapor which disappears, or smoke which dissipates, so life cannot be grasped. Sometimes we can't even comprehend it. Wisdom helps, but is inadequate.

Finally, the book of Job brings color to how we are to live out the wise life. Is life unpredictable? Absolutely. Job has lost everything even though he has committed no obvious sin to deserve his ill fortune. So, then: Is God fair, his world consistent? The end of Job clearly states yes. As Job cannot comprehend the universe and its working as God questions him,

---

7. Luke 7:35; cf. Prov 8.

so we cannot imagine judging God's ways. Wisdom is demonstrated when we trust our heavenly Father in the times of both blessing and devastation.

It is then in the New Testament that we find the pinnacle of wisdom, not in a decision or a plan but in a person. Jesus himself is Wisdom, and what he communicates to the world is the offer that Wisdom makes to the simple: "Heed my call and find life, or disregard my words and find death" (see Matt 7:24–27). And despite your circumstance, no matter if life is working for or against you, "Trust God. He will care for you" (see Matt 6:25–34).

We can recognize a wise choice by its immediate or long-term consequences. We can recognize a wise person by their consistent choices over a lifetime. But Jesus tells us there is a quality of wisdom which can only be seen from eternity's perspective. A truly wise person is the one who hears his words and lives by them.

49

The Supreme Court
Equal Justice Under Law

MOST AMERICANS ARE FAMILIAR with Lady Justice being depicted as blindfolded, a set of scales suspended from one hand, and a sword in the other. The scales represent the weighing of evidence upon which she measures the support and opposition of a case. The blindfold represents impartiality without regard to power, wealth, or status. The sword represents the idea that justice can be swift and final.[1] But sometimes laws have been wrongly applied or justice has been denied. That's when Americans can seek equal justice under the law in the courts.

Above the main entrance to the United States Supreme Court Building is the motto "Equal Justice under Law."[2] The Supreme Court is the final arbiter of the law and functions as a last resort since its rulings cannot be appealed. The Court also decides on cases dealing with the interpretation of the United States Constitution and can overturn a law passed by Congress which the Court determines is unconstitutional.

The Judiciary Act of 1789 passed by the first United States Congress established the Supreme Court.[3] The country's highest judicial tribunal was to sit in the nation's Capital and would initially be composed of a chief justice and five associate justices. Creating this third branch of government was brilliant as the judicial branch serves as a system of checks and balances on the executive and legislative branches. James Madison,

---

1. "Lady Justice Explained."
2. SCOTUS, "About the Court."
3. Drexler, "Judiciary Act of 1789."

one of the founders, said about this novel idea of a third branch, "We are in a wilderness without a single footstep to guide us."[4]

The Supreme Court held its inaugural session from February 2 through February 10, 1790, at the Royal Exchange in New York City, then the US capital.[5] As the American writer and historian Fergus Bordewich describes:

> Symbolically, the moment was pregnant with promise for the republic—this birth of a new national institution whose future power, admittedly, still existed only in the mind's eye of a few farsighted Americans. Bewigged and swathed in their robes of office, Chief Justice John Jay and his three associate justices sat before a throng of spectators and waited for something to happen, but nothing did. They had no cases to consider. After a week of inactivity, they adjourned and went home.[6]

Over time, the Supreme Court has had plenty of cases to consider. Receiving anywhere from 7,000 to 8,000 new cases each term, actual rulings are issued on only eighty to ninety cases per year.[7] The US Reports have published a total of over 30,800 Supreme Court opinions, covering the decisions handed down from February 1790 to March 2020.[8]

After moving to the new United States Capital in Philadelphia in 1790, and then to Washington DC in 1800, the Supreme Court finally had its own building in 1935, 146 years after it was established. Article II, Section 2, Clause 2 of the United States Constitution, known as the Appointments Clause, empowers the president to nominate and, with the confirmation of the United States Senate, to appoint public officials, including justices of the Supreme Court.

Congress initially established a six-member Supreme Court, but the size was reduced to five members in 1801. In 1807, the number grew to seven, then nine in 1837, and ten in 1863. Finally, in 1869, the Circuit Judges Act set the number of justices to nine, where it has since remained.[9] President Franklin D. Roosevelt attempted to expand or "pack" the Court

---

4. Rutland, *James Madison*, 65.
5. Hodak, "February 2, 1790."
6. Bordewich, "Political Rhetoric over SCOTUS," 310.
7. Millhiser, "Supreme Court's Enigmatic 'Shadow Docket' Explained," para. 15.
8. "Supreme Court," para. 72.
9. Roos, "Why Do 9 Justices Serve?"

in 1937.[10] His proposal envisioned the appointment of one additional justice for each incumbent justice who reached the age of 70 years 6 months and refused retirement, up to a maximum bench of fifteen justices. The plan was rejected by Congress and the American people because they realized as each political party gained power there would be no end to adding additional justices.

Since the Supreme Court was established in 1789, presidents have submitted 163 justice nominations, and of those, 126 justices were confirmed by the U.S. Senate.[11] President George Washington appointed nine justices to the Supreme Court. Franklin Roosevelt appointed eight. Andrew Jackson and William Howard Taft each appointed five justices. Presidents Nixon, Reagan, and Trump each appointed three.

There have been many notable justices. Oliver Wendell Holmes is the oldest at ninety years old and one of the most oft-cited Supreme Court justices ever to sit on the court. President William Howard Taft is the only President to have also served on the Supreme Court. He left the White House in 1913 after one term as President and was appointed in 1921 as Chief Justice. Thurgood Marshall became the first Black justice appointed to the Supreme Court after being nominated by President Lyndon B. Johnson. Marshall once described his approach to legal matters as, "you do what you think is right and let the law catch up."[12]

Jurists are often categorized in legal and political circles as being judicial conservatives or liberals. Conservatives that support originalism interpret the Constitution based on the original understanding "at the time it was adopted." They might consider Thurgood Marshall's approach as judicial activism or legislating from the bench. "Judicial activism is usually a pejorative term, implying that judges make rulings based on their own political agenda rather than precedent and take advantage of judicial discretion."[13]

Supreme Court justices are not elected, have a lifetime appointment, and are paid over a quarter of a million dollars a year even after they retire[14]—all of which are notions which are counterintuitive or at odds with the idea of a representative government accountable to the people. But the

10. Davis, *FDR*, 46–68.
11. United States Senate, "Supreme Court Nominations: present–1789," para. 1.
12. Walsh, *Gavel and Sickle*, 67.
13. Fahner, *Judicial Deference*, 6.
14. "Judicial Compensation."

Supreme Court was designed to allow jurists to make unpopular decisions and not be subject to political fallout, especially in cases that Americans feel passionately about or that profoundly impact their daily lives, such as abortion, same-sex marriage, immigration, health care, and state sovereignty. Even with all the shortcomings and human frailties involved in governing, adding the Supreme Court to create a three-branch system of checks and balances has served America's democratic republic well.

Winston Churchill is credited as saying "Many forms of Government have been tried, and will be tried in this world of sin and woe. No one pretends that democracy is perfect or all-wise. Indeed it has been said that democracy is the worst form of Government except for all those other forms that have been tried from time to time . . ."[15]

Biblical Insight: God's Law, Man's Law, My Law

by Ronald Ian Phillips

Judges are expected to have wisdom, impartiality, judicial temperament, and independence. But when today's judges are often appointed by political parties, influenced by special-interest groups or have their personal agenda, some fall short. Modern judges might do well to emulate the judges in the Bible. Well, maybe not all the twelve judges found in the book of Judges.

Samson was the last of the judges of the ancient Israelites mentioned in the book of Judges before the institution of the monarchy in Israel. The story of Samson and Delilah and the Philistines told in Judges 13–16 has become a favorite Bible story for children. But it is also a cautionary tale for adults and especially for those in leadership roles.

An angel announces Samson's birth not once, but twice. An angel appears to Samson's mother before he is born and tells her she is going to bear a son (Judg 13:3). The angel then tells her, "You are childless but you will give birth to a son. No razor shall come upon his head, for the boy shall be a Nazirite to God from birth, and he shall save Israel from the hand of the Philistines" (Judg 13:5) When she tells her husband, Manoah, he prays that God will send the angel again to "teach us how to bring up the boy" (Judg 13:8). The angel does return, repeats to Manoah what he already told his wife, and then Manoah asks the angel's name. The angel

---

15. Garber, "Churchill On Democracy," para. 5.

refuses to say, because the name "Is too wonderful" or beyond understanding and then the angel ascends toward Heaven in the blazing flame from Manoah's altar sacrifice (Judg 13:18–20).

So Samson's birth was announced by an angel, he had a God-given mission, and he was given supernatural power. But with great power comes great responsibility. As a Nazirite, Samson was bound by three vows: never to drink wine, never to touch a corpse, and never to cut his hair. Before he died, Samson broke all three vows. It's actually one of the saddest chapters in the whole Bible when we consider Samson's tremendous potential and colossal failures. Yet there are lessons to be learned.

In the beginning, there was God's law, from Adam to Moses to Samson. Deuteronomy 30:19–20 (NIV) implores us even today to make the right choice and follow God's law when we read, "This day I call the heavens and the earth as witnesses against you that I have set before you, life and death, blessings and curses. Now choose life, so that you and your children may live and that you may love the Lord your God, listen to His voice, and hold fast to Him." But there are seven cycles of apostasy and revival described in the book of Judges. Seven times Israelis abandoned God's law and rebelled against him, resulting in the hostile occupation of their lands by the Philistines.

The United States of America is remarkably blessed to have had "man's laws" that protected religious freedom among other inalienable rights. This was not the case in Israel at the time of the judges. The longer the Israelis lived under the pagan Philistines, the more they adopted their pagan ways, intermarried, and worshiped their gods. As recorded in Deuteronomy 7:3–4, they were warned, "Do not intermarry with them. Do not give your daughters to their sons or take their daughters for your sons, for they will turn your children away from following me to serve other gods." Soon the savagery and unimaginable cruelty of the Philistines were also seen in much of Israel.

When God's laws are disregarded, moral depravity soon follows. When a just system of man's laws is ignored and broken there is a total breakdown in society. It's every person for themself. "In those days there was no king in Israel: every man did that which was right in his own eyes" (Judg 21:25). In the time of judges, Israel slipped into total anarchy. Mayhem and lawlessness ensued as they gave in to their own personal desires and personal sense of justice. Into this world, Samson was called to be the deliverer from the Philistines and restore Israel to God. But Samson too often followed his personal laws and gave into his personal wants, letting anger and desires of the flesh ruin him (Gal 5:17–21).

Samson's fraternizing with the Philistines who were out to subjugate Israel and destroy him should be a cautionary tale for us. "He who walks with wise men will be wise, but the companion of fools will be destroyed" (Prov 13:20). This story demonstrates how a person gradually makes moral compromises that could lead to their destruction. It also shows we cannot abuse the gifts God has given us but should use them to bring glory to God. Samson stands as a warning about the dangers of moral compromise; and yet at the same time, a reminder that God's grace is greater than all our sin (Rom 5:21).

50

Endless Wars

ON JULY 4, 1776, the Second Continental Congress unanimously adopted the Declaration of Independence and a new nation was born. But America would be at war for seven more years until Great Britain finally recognized the independence of the United States with the Treaty of Paris on September 3, 1783. Avoiding wars has been a struggle for America ever since. From 1776 until today, America has been at war 93 percent of the time with less than twenty full years of peace.[1]

Throughout history, people of the world have longed for peace. The Kellogg-Briand Pact signed by sixty-three nations in 1928 actually outlawed war.[2] Nations that signed the Pact included the future World War II Axis nations of Germany, Italy, and Japan. It failed because there were no provisions for enforcement and nations were still permitted to fight in self-defense. A little more than a decade after the Kellogg-Briand Pact outlawed war, World War II began, which was the deadliest and most destructive war in history.

In 1996, economist Thomas Friedman came up with what is known as the Golden Arches Theory of Conflict Prevention. The premise is that no two countries with McDonald's franchises have ever gone to war with each other because as Friedman states, "countries with middle classes large enough to sustain a McDonald's have reached a level of prosperity

---

1. Oord, "Believe It or Not," para. 1.
2. Hathaway and Shapiro, "Outlawing War?"

and global integration that makes warmongering risky and unpalatable to its people."[3] Although generally true, there have been countries with McDonald's that still have an appetite for war.

Some military conflicts have been very short lived. The Bay of Pigs Invasion, in which American-backed insurgents tried to topple Fidel Castro's Communist Cuba, lasted only three days. In response, the Soviet Union placed nuclear weapons in Cuba just ninety miles off America's shores, which prompted President John F. Kennedy to demand that the nuclear missiles be removed. The ensuing Cuban Missile Crisis in October of 1962 lasted twelve days as the world teetered on the brink of nuclear war.

Following the September 11, 2001 terrorist attacks on the World Trade Center and the Pentagon by Osama bin Laden's Al-Qaeda organization, the United States entered into a war in Afghanistan against Al-Qaeda and the Taliban. With nineteen years and ten months of fighting before the US withdrawal, the Afghanistan war is America's longest war.[4]

Some wars have been popular, like the Spanish-American War, nicknamed "The Splendid Little War." Yellow journalists like Joseph Pulitzer and William Randolph Hearst sensationalized the war for Cuban independence from Spain and, without evidence, blamed Spain for the explosion of the USS Maine in Havana Harbor in Cuba, leading to US intervention. The Spanish-American War only lasted 114 days, had relatively few casualties, made national heroes out of Teddy Roosevelt and the Rough Riders, and allowed the United States to acquire Puerto Rico, Guam, and the Philippine Islands from Spain.

The Vietnam War became unpopular for myriad reasons. On December 1, 1969, for the first time since 1942, a lottery was held to draft young American men.[5] This followed the Tet Offensive of 1968, which showed America was not winning the Vietnam War, and the Pentagon Papers, which revealed US government officials were lying to the American public. Many objectors saw the Vietnam War as a civil war instead of a larger global conflict between the superpowers. Public opinion steadily turned against the war, and by 1970, two-thirds of

---

3. Veseth, *Globaloney*, 26.
4. Glaser and Mueller, "Overcoming Inertia."
5. "Draft lottery (1969)."

Americans believed the US had made a mistake by sending troops to fight in Vietnam.[6]

World War I (1914–18), also known as "The Great War," was perhaps the most idealistic war. It was to be "the war to end all wars" and a war "to make the world safe for democracy." It did neither. The First World War became one of the deadliest conflicts in history, with an estimated 9 million combatant deaths and 13 million civilian deaths as a direct result of the war.[7] The harsh Versailles Treaty, ending the war on the eleventh hour of the eleventh day of the eleventh month of 1918, was never signed by the United States. Armistice Day, on November 11th, became Veterans Day to honor all the American men and women who have patriotically served in the military.

After World War I, America withdrew from world affairs and became self-absorbed with the Roaring 20s and The Great Depression of the 1930s. The aftermath of World War I saw the rise of Communism in Russia, Fascism in Germany and Italy, and led to World War II, the deadliest of all wars, just over twenty years later.

The United States has not been very good at staying out of wars and even worse at what some consider nation-building. Most agree that war should be a last resort. And some argue that America should not be like the queen on a chess board, checking everyone. There are many alternatives to war, including economic incentives, diplomacy, collaborating with other nations, sanctions, or tariffs.

But what will happen when America is attacked from the ever-increasing arsenal of nuclear, biological, and electromagnetic pulse weapons of mass destruction?[8] Or called on to prevent genocide or to stop a rogue nation from developing weapons of mass destruction? Delaying war would allow the enemy to advance their military capabilities or solidify their hold on another country's territory they invaded.

Being prepared to defend the United States and knowing when to show restraint is a challenge even for the wealthiest and most powerful nation in the world. America walks a fine line, knowing when to defend civilization and basic human rights, keep trade lanes open for commerce, and provide world leadership—all while avoiding wars.

---

6. Hagopain, *Vietnam War in American History*, 13–14.

7. Royde-Smith, "World War I," para. 4.

8. Miller, *Cold War*, 76–77.

Biblical Insight: Neither Will They Learn War Anymore

by Ronald Ian Phillips

History students learn a lot about wars which are often used as benchmarks in the story of mankind. Learning about past and present human conflicts result in many of us today living in constant anxiety and fear. However, it's not just wars on a global scale that we fear but also the day-to-day battles and sudden troubles we face in our own lives.

Imagine if you could live without fear or anxiety. The most recurrent instruction in the Bible is "Fear not," which is repeated over 300 times. Psalm 27:1 tells us, "The Lord is my light and my salvation; whom shall I fear? The Lord is the strength of my life; of whom shall I be afraid?" We either live by fear or we live by faith.

At the height of Jesus' ministry, he stood at the Sea of Galilee and spoke for hours to a great multitude that had gathered. As evening approached, we learn in Mark 4:35 that Jesus said, "Let us cross over to the other side." Keep in mind that the Sea of Galilee is eight miles wide. When a terrible storm suddenly came up and the raging tempest and crashing waves threatened to sink their small boat, the disciples were terrified.

His disciples had witnessed Jesus healing the sick, casting out demons, and many other miracles. But now Jesus was sound asleep, and their boat was sinking. The disciples woke him and said, "Teacher, don't you care if we drown?" (Mark 4:38). You have to wonder what the disciples expected Jesus to do. Did they forget they were talking to the Son of God? But they were panic-stricken and were only focused on themselves.

Before we are too critical of the disciples, we should realize they had done nothing wrong to deserve this life-threatening moment. They were in the perfect will of God. When relationship conflicts, financial problems, sickness, or injuries suddenly come upon us, we may have done nothing wrong, but we can be certain our faith will be tested. We might think, "Why is this happening to me again? Is Jesus sleeping? Why doesn't He answer my cries for help?" But God's word tells us in Deuteronomy 31:8, "And the Lord, He is the One who goes before you. He will be with you, He will not leave you nor forsake you; do not fear nor be dismayed."

Maybe the disciples in a sinking boat wanted Jesus to help bail water, but instead he did what God so often does in our times of trouble—Jesus did something spectacular and unimaginable. Mark 4:39–41 tells us, "Then He arose and rebuked the wind, and said to the sea, 'Peace, be still!' And the wind ceased and there was a great calm. And then Jesus asked the disciples, 'Why are you so fearful? How is it that you have no faith?' And they feared exceedingly, and said to one another, 'Who can this be, that even the wind and the sea obey Him!'"

A year or so later, on the Sea of Galilee, in a yet another storm, Peter saw Jesus walking on the water. When Jesus assured Peter he could join him, Peter began walking on the water toward Jesus. "But when he saw that the wind was boisterous, he was afraid; and beginning to sink, he cried out, saying, 'Lord, save me!' And immediately Jesus stretched out His hand and caught him, and said to him, 'O you of little faith, why did you doubt?'" (Matt 14:30–31 NKJV).

In both incidences, the disciples took their eyes off of Jesus and only saw the peril around them. Notice that Peter started sinking after he became afraid. Faith and fear do not go together. When we are fearful, we take our eyes off the Savior because we lack faith. But when we have faith, Jesus will catch and rescue us. Hebrews 13:5–6 tells us, "God has said, 'Never will I leave you; never will I forsake you.' So we say with confidence, The Lord is my helper; I will not be afraid," and two verses later we are reminded that "Jesus Christ is the same yesterday and today and forever" (Heb 13:8).

The disciples knew the Messiah was physically with them but didn't trust in his power. Just the reverse is true today. We say we believe in the power of prayer and God's supernatural attributes but don't believe he is there in our times of need. When sudden troubles arise, we are afraid because we don't know how long they will last or how much worse they will get. We only focus on solving our immediate problems and lose sight of our ultimate destination. It's a good reminder that we walk *through* and not just *into* the valley of the shadow of death. The disciples did get to the other side. As Christians, our eternal destination is assured. Jude 1:24 (NKJV) says, "Now to Him who is able to keep you from stumbling, And to present you faultless before the presence of His glory with exceeding joy."

Neither the battles waged around the world nor the ones fought in our personal lives will end until Jesus Christ comes to earth and establishes the kingdom of God over which he will reign as King of kings. Over 700 years before the birth of Jesus, the prophet Isaiah wrote about the future when Jesus Christ the Messiah returns to earth to set up his kingdom during the millennium. Our hope and future is found in the words of Isaiah 2:4: "And He shall judge among the nations . . . nation shall not lift up sword against nation, neither shall they learn war anymore."

51

In God We Trust

THERE WAS OFTEN LITTLE freedom of religion in the early colonies as they teetered on becoming a theocracy or having an official state religion where there was no separation between church and state. Eight of the thirteen British colonies in America had official, or established, churches, and in those colonies, dissenters who sought to practice or proselytize a different version of Christianity or a non-Christian faith were sometimes persecuted.[1]

A tax to support the established religion was collected in the colonies. Many state constitutions also required officeholders and voters to take an oath stating they would follow the major tenets of the established faith. The Congregational Church was established by early puritans, mainly in the New England states. The Anglican of England, or Episcopal, Church was predominant in the Southern states, and the Quakers controlled the middle states.

As a result of The Great Awakening Protestant revival in the mid-1700s, American colonies rejected the established church's authority in matters of religion. Colonists questioned the government's right to meddle in personal religious beliefs. Support for the separation of church and state grew stronger, as did the desire of individual Americans to worship God and exercise their religious free will.

---

1. "Religion in Colonial America."

When the First Amendment was ratified in 1791, the establishment clause prohibited the creation of a national church. The first clause in the Bill of Rights states that, "Congress shall make no law respecting an establishment of religion." But official state churches still existed in many states. Laws in states with an official religion mandated that everyone attend a house of worship and pay taxes that funded the salaries of ministers of that established religion.[2]

A balance in America had to be struck between the separation of church and state, and acknowledging the role of religion in representative government. On March 5, 1984, Chief Justice Burger of the Supreme Court stated, "There is an unbroken history of official acknowledgment by all three branches of government of the role of religion in American life."[3] Courts in the United States have a long legacy of ruling that government should not ignore the significance of the fact that a vast portion of Americans believe in and worship God and respect the need to recognize the religious heritage of our nation's history.

So what role should the United States government have in matters of religion? There are countless examples of how the rich heritage of religion in America is integrated into the very fabric of American society, from our money to our national anthem, from our motto to the pledge of allegiance. Far from being hostile toward worship, the United States government has, in the past, recognized the importance of God to most Americans. Local, state, and federal governments celebrate the vital history of stating that we are one nation under God.

The Continental Congress, a legislative body that governed the United States from 1774–89, contained an extraordinary number of deeply religious men. The inclusion of a prayer before the opening of each session of both the United Stated House and the Senate traces its origins back to the days of the Continental Congress, and the official recommendation of Benjamin Franklin on June 28, 1787. Franklin said: "I have lived, Sir, a long time, and the longer I live, the more convincing proofs I see of this truth: that God Governs in the affairs of men. And if a sparrow cannot fall to the ground without his notice, is it probable that an empire can rise without his aid?"[4]

---

2. "Religion in Colonial America," paras. 1–5.

3. Adamson, *Freedom of Religion*, 154.

4. Office of the Chaplaincy, United States House of Representatives, "Benjamin Franklin Speech," 3.

The lyrics to "The Star-Spangled Banner" come from a poem written by a thirty-five-year-old lawyer, Francis Scott Key, after witnessing the bombardment of Fort McHenry by British ships in the War of 1812. In the fourth verse of Key's poem, and now America's national anthem, are the words, "And this be our motto—In God is our trust! And the Star-Spangled Banner in triumph shall wave, O'er the land of the free and the home of the brave."[5]

A prayer room was established in 1854 for the United States Senate and House of Representatives. The room includes a stained glass window of George Washington kneeling in prayer, with the words from Psalm 16:1, "Preserve me, O God, for in Thee do I put my trust." The words from President Abraham Lincoln's Gettysburg Address, "This Nation Under God," are also displayed in the Congressional Prayer Room.[6] The words "under God" were added to The Pledge of Allegiance on Flag Day in 1954.

On April 22, 1864, Congress passed the Coinage Act, which authorized "In God We Trust" to be printed on the two-cent coin. President Theodore Roosevelt, in November 1907, objected to God's name being printed on money as he believed it was irreverent and sacrilegious.[7] However, on July 30, 1957, the 84th United States Congress passed a law with President Dwight Eisenhower's approval that the phrase "In God We Trust" must appear on American currency and declared the phrase as the national motto.[8]

According to a 2003 joint poll taken by *USA Today*, *CNN*, and *Gallup*, 90 percent of Americans support the inscription "In God We Trust" on US coins.[9] Legal challenges continue today over this cherished right of personal religious freedom. What makes America unique is not only its separation of church and state, but its need to include God in its governing and acknowledge the nation's religious heritage.

---

5. Ferris, *Star-Spangled Banner*, 19, 20, 188.

6. Office of the Chaplaincy, United States House of Representatives, "Congressional Prayer Room."

7. Schulz, "Teddy Roosevelt's Letter."

8. Ferris, *Star-Spangled Banner*, 19, 20, 188.

9. "In God We Trust Explained," para. 3.

Biblical Insight: Whom Can We Trust?

by David Grotzke

In a world that is forever searching for something or someone to trust in, or hope in, the motto on our money is a good reminder of where hope needs to be placed. Not in the money, because its value rises and falls. Not in our jobs, because they come and go. Not in our government, because it is a fallible human institution. Not in our friends, because their means are limited. Not in ourselves, because "our hearts are deceitful above all things and desperately wicked" (Jer 17:9). Rather, it is "In God We Trust."

The psalmist recognized so many benefits that come to those individuals or nations that put their trust in God. The motto for American currency comes from Psalm 16:1. It is recognizing our country's reliance upon Israel's God. In the KJV, the phrase, "in thee do I put my trust," is translated other places as "in you I take my refuge." God is a place we can go for protection. He is a fortress that cannot be broken down, burned down, or penetrated in any way. He deserves our reliance.

Psalm 16:2 says he provides me with good things and with good friends. The ESV translates the last of Psalm 16:2 as, "I have no good apart from you." Even when things do not appear to be going well for believers, we can be assured that the Lord is working things out for his good. Our reliance is rewarded by his excellence, excellent things, and excellent friends, saints that friends can delight in. Those saints the New Testament calls "beloved brethren" (Col 4:7; Jas 1:16; Phm 16).

Psalm 16:5 (ESV) reminds us we can rely upon his sustenance, the "chosen portion," "my cup" and "my lot." These are all descriptions of things that are provided by someone greater than ourselves. In this case, it is the Lord, not some earthly power. Jesus talks of this in Matthew 6:30–31: "Wherefore, if God so clothe the grass of the field, which today is, and tomorrow is cast into the oven, shall he not much more clothe you, O ye of little faith? Therefore take no thought, saying what shall we eat? Or what shall we drink? Or where with all shall we be clothed?"

God provides sustenance for today, referred to as "boundary lines... in pleasant places" (Ps 16:6 ESV), and maintenance of my future, or "my lot" and a goodly heritage. This is not just my future in this life, but also my future life with God.

Psalm 16:7 expresses the psalmist's gratitude for God's guidance. His counsel applies both in the day as well as the night. It applies in both the light as well as in the dark. It applies in the good times and in the bad times. Solomon would later express it by saying, "in all thy ways acknowledge him and he will direct thy paths" (Prov 3:6). He will give you counsel and guidance.

Psalm 16:8 is about endurance, line-backers, foundations, cornerstones, and roots: things that do not move, but endure. Keep your eyes on the Lord, your Bible in hand, and the Holy Spirit filling you, and you "shall not be moved."

Psalm 16:9 is a picture of exuberance. Not just a smile and a nod. Not a mumbled "Thank You," but a "foot stomping, heel clicking, arms waving, 'Thank you, Jesus!'" The moment when a person rejoices with their whole being: Exuberance!

Psalm 16:10 recognizes the permanence of this relationship. There is no abandonment, even at death. No more than God the Father could leave the Son to decay in a grave. God will not abandon his own.

Psalm 16:11 shows God's desire to lead us through a life of abundance, "fullness of joy" and "pleasures forevermore." This may only be experienced fully when we come into the very presence of our God.

Unfortunately, a caution was also given in Psalm 16:4 that warns of a grievance against those who "hasten after another god." Not just the promise of an uncomfortable situation, but "multiplied" sorrows, extreme sorrows. Is this the fate of our own country? We see the push to remove anything that acknowledges the God of Scripture and wonder at the hopelessness growing in this country. Nothing and no one can replace the psalmist's God. Our forefathers recognized what our present fathers are ignoring. We cannot survive the multiplied sorrows for long unless "In God We Trust!"

52

A Journey to the Heavens

AMERICA'S NUCLEAR MONOPOLY HAD ended when the Soviets successfully tested their first nuclear device on August 29, 1949. Nikita Khrushchev was the leader of the Soviet Union in 1956 when he said to America, "We will bury you."[1] Most Americans interpreted Khrushchev's outburst as a nuclear weapons threat. When Khrushchev pounded his shoe on the table during a 1960 United Nations General Assembly meeting in New York City, Americans worried these angry tirades could lead to nuclear annihilation.

In 1956, the United States developed a siren warning and radio broadcast system in the event of a nuclear attack. Both private and public fallout shelters, designed to protect occupants from radioactive debris or fallout from a nuclear explosion, sprung up across the country.

Schoolchildren had atom bomb air raid drills, and were taught to "duck and cover" under their school desks as a method of personal protection against the effects of a nuclear explosion. In 1951, the New York City schools allocated $159,000 for 2.5 million student dog tags to be used in identifying the bodies of children in case of a nuclear war, according to historian JoAnne Brown.[2]

The space race began in earnest when the Soviet Union launched the 184-pound Sputnik 1 into low orbit on October 4, 1957. America's

---

1. Reuters Staff, "False Claim," paras. 9–15.
2. Gass-Poore, "From Toys to Tags and Terror," paras. 1–3.

answer to Sputnik was the Vanguard rocket which attempted to place a 3-pound satellite in outer space two months later. It reached an altitude of three feet eleven inches before exploding on the Cape Canaveral launch pad. The top of the rocket landed in the bushes near the pad, and began transmitting signals, leading American columnist Dorothy Kilgallen to remark, "Why doesn't somebody go out there, find it, and shoot it?"[3] The American press called it Kaputnik, Flopnik, Stayputnik.[4] Of the eleven Vanguard rockets which the project attempted to launch, three of them successfully placed satellites into orbit.

Project Mercury was developed to launch an American astronaut into orbit and return him safely to Earth. Seven men with "the right stuff" were chosen and trained for this goal.[5] On the night of May 18, 1959, these seven men gathered at Cape Canaveral to watch their first rocket launch, which was similar to the one that would carry them into orbit. A few minutes after liftoff, it spectacularly exploded. The astronauts were stunned. Alan Shepard turned to John Glenn and said: "Well, I'm glad they got that out of the way."[6]

On April 12, 1961, the Soviet cosmonaut Yuri Gagarin became the first human to journey into outer space. Less than a month later, Alan Shepard became the first American to travel into space. "When reporters asked Shepard what he thought about as he sat atop the Redstone rocket, waiting for liftoff, he replied, 'The fact that every part of this ship was built by the lowest bidder.'"[7] But Shepard's flight only lasted fifteen minutes and it would be up to John Glenn to attempt an orbit.

Allowing the "Red Menace" to conquer the world and now outer space was unacceptable for Americans. With each Soviet success in the space race, Americans became more desperate to find a hero who could show the United States was winning the Cold War. On February 20, 1962, as millions watched on television, John Glenn became that hero when he was the first American to orbit the Earth from space. The American author Tom Wolfe described John Glenn as, "The last true national hero America has ever had."[8]

3. Military Wiki Editors, "Vanguard (Rocket)," para. 7.
4. "60 Years Ago."
5. Reuters Editors, "U.S. Astronaut John Glenn Laid to Rest," paras. 4, 6.
6. Glenn and Taylor, *John Glenn*, 321.
7. Kranz, *Failure Is Not an Option*, 200–201.
8. Reuters Editors, "U.S. Astronaut John Glenn Laid to Rest," para. 2.

A Journey to the Heavens 241

Before John Glenn became one of the seven Project Mercury astronauts, he was one of the best United States Marine Corps fighter pilots in World War II and Korea. Glenn flew 149 dangerous-combat missions, returning with 250 holes in his aircraft. Then, in 1957, Glenn set a supersonic, transcontinental-flight record of 725 mph in just three hours and twenty-three minutes, flying faster than a forty-five-caliber bullet.[9]

In 1962, John Glenn made three orbits of Earth, traveling at 17,500 mph, on a spaceflight lasting five hours. As he passed over the Australian city of Perth in the dark, the residents turned on all their lights which he could see from space. "His odds of not surviving this were about one in six," astronaut Steve Lindsey said of John Glenn's flight aboard Friendship 7. As engineer O'Malley pressed the button to launch the spacecraft he said, "The good Lord ride all the way," and then capsule communicator Scott Carpenter uttered the famous phrase "Godspeed, John Glenn."[10]

Upon a successful return to Earth, John Glenn received the Space Congressional Medal of Honor from President John Kennedy. In 1974, Glenn won election to the United States Senate and served for the next twenty-four years. In 1998, Senator Glenn became the oldest person to date to fly in space as a member of the Discovery space shuttle mission. In 2012 he received the Presidential Medal of Freedom.

John Glenn's observations after a journey beyond the confines of Earth have been echoed by many other astronauts. He marveled at the size of the universe saying, "Our galaxy is some 100,000 light years in diameter . . . we realize how difficult it is to visualize the tremendous scale of the universe beyond our solar system." The closest star to our own, Proxima Centauri, is 4.3 light years away, but that is still 100 million times farther than a trip to the moon. To reach it by spaceship would take at least 25,000 years.[11] Glenn explained, "To look out at this kind of creation and not believe in God is to me impossible," John Glenn told reporters in 1998, just after returning from his final trip to space at age seventy-seven. "It just strengthens my faith."[12]

On Christmas Eve 1968, three Apollo 8 astronauts—Frank Borman, James Lovell, and William Anders—read from the book of Genesis as

---

9. Glenn and Taylor, *John Glenn*, 220–21.
10. Wilford, "At Cape Canaveral," 22.
11. Bryson, *Short History of Nearly Everything*, 24–36.
12. Denison, "John Glenn's Greatest Mission," para 5.

they orbited the moon.[13] Anders said, "We came to explore the moon and what we discovered was the Earth."[14] From 240,000 miles away, William Anders photographed the brilliant blue-and-white oasis of Earth from the vast darkness of space and the lifeless moon. *Earthrise,* his color photo, has inspired so many to reflect on the uniqueness and preciousness of the planet Earth. Frank Borman ended the Christmas Eve broadcast from the moon with, "And from the crew of Apollo 8, we close with good night, good luck, a Merry Christmas, and God bless all of you—all of you on the good Earth."[15]

Biblical Insight: Heaven

by David Grotzke

John Glenn viewed the second heaven, the stars, and the planets, and his faith in God was strengthened. As a person envisions the third Heaven, where God dwells, excitement about the future grows. If the first heaven, where the birds fly, and the clouds float is amazing; and the second heaven, where planets and galaxies exist astounds the astronauts; then the third Heaven, God's abode, must be beyond anything we could describe. First Corinthians 2:9 explains, "But as it is written, Eye hath not seen, nor ear heard, neither have entered into the heart of man, the things which God hath prepared for them that love him."

But three contemporary ideas about heaven have recently developed that can make believers sometimes wonder what the excitement is all about. These beliefs include: it is the final abode for everyone; all inhabitants are some sort of cloud potatoes who spend their time strumming their harps and polishing their haloes; and they will be sitting in eternal church services. Most people struggle to keep awake during an hour-long worship service, much less an ever and ever service.

None of these ideas are biblically accurate and thankfully it is not the description of Heaven we get from God's word. Revelation 21 gives us a physical description of the third Heaven, which is a great city called New Jerusalem. Revelation 21:10 explains, "And he carried me away in the spirit to a great and high mountain, and shewed me that great city,

---

13. Benson and Faherty, *Moonport,* 457.
14. Anders, quoted in "Celebrate Apollo," para. 1.
15. Benson and Faherty, *Moonport,* 457.

the holy Jerusalem, descending out of Heaven from God." This city seems to be a cube 1,500 miles long, wide and high (v. 16), with twelve levels (v. 14). It is filled with the glory of God, (v. 11) beautiful colors and precious stones, with twelve gates made of single pearls, which far exceeds the one our astronauts saw from outer space.

In Revelation 7:16 we read, "They shall hunger no more, neither thirst anymore; neither shall the sun light on them, nor any heat. For the Lamb which is in the midst of the throne shall feed them, and shall lead them unto living fountains of waters: and God shall wipe away all tears from their eyes."

The Bible shares the wonderful news by saying, "and there shall be no more death, neither sorrow, nor crying, neither shall there be any more pain: for the former things are passed away" (Rev 21:4). The Scriptures go on to say there will be a river of life flowing from the throne of God through the middle of the street and a tree of life which yields fruit each month. There will be no more night or need of light or sun, "for the Lord God will be their light, and they will reign forever and ever" (Rev 22:1–5).

Not everyone will be there: only those who have had their sins forgiven, the children of God. His people will be there. God can dwell with humanity because his Son Jesus paid the cost for our sin. "But nothing unclean will ever enter it, nor anyone who does what is detestable or false, but only those who are written in the Lamb's book of life" (Rev 21:27 ESV).

This city can be our city. "He that overcometh shall inherit all things; and I will be his God, and he shall be my son" (Rev 21:7). He wants to be our God and wants us to be his sons and daughters. God wants us to be with him. Jesus said in John 14:3, "If I go and prepare a place for you, I will come again and receive you unto myself, that where I am, there ye may be also." Heaven can be your city, but you must decide to ask God to forgive you and save you. That is why Jesus died.

Because this great and holy city can be our city, it is natural for us to want to know something about our future home. Understanding that we will be with God and other Christians in a place of forgiveness and extraordinary beauty makes us more excited than ever to reach our final home. The more we read God's word, the more we will be able to visualize Heaven, and the more we will join with John Glenn in saying, "It just strengthens my faith."

Bibliography

"10 Things You Really Ought to Know about George Washington." https://www.mountvernon.org/george-washington/10-things-you-really-ought-to-know-about-george-washington

"1918 Pandemic (H1N1 Virus)." *CDC* (March 20, 2019). https://www.cdc.gov/flu/pandemic-resources/1918-pandemic-h1n1.html.

"60 Years Ago: Vanguard Fails to Reach Orbit." *NASA* (December 6, 2017). https://www.nasa.gov/feature/60-years-ago-vanguard-fails-to-reach-orbit.

Ackerman, Kenneth D. *Boss Tweed: The Rise and Fall of the Corrupt Pol Who Conceived the Soul of Modern New York.* New York: Carroll & Graf, 2005.

Adamson, Barry. *Freedom of Religion, the First Amendment, and the Supreme Court: How the Court Flunked History.* New Orleans: Pelican, 2007.

Alabama Scenic Byways. "Selma to Montgomery Historic Trail." https://www.alabamabyways.com/2012/06/26/selma-to-montgomery-historic-trail/.

Alexander, John K. *Samuel Adams: America's Revolutionary Politician.* Lanham, MD: Rowman & Littlefield, 2002.

Ambrose, Stephen E. *Americans at War.* Jackson: University Press of Mississippi, 1997.

———. *Eisenhower: Soldier, General of the Army, President-Elect (1893–1952).* New York: Simon & Schuster, 1983.

———. *Eisenhower: The President (1952–1969).* New York: Simon & Schuster, 1984.

———. *Undaunted Courage: Meriwether Lewis, Thomas Jefferson, and the Opening of the American West.* New York: Simon & Schuster, 1996.

"American Bison." https://en.wikipedia.org/wiki/American_bison.

American Experience. "Annie Oakley in Europe." *PBS.org* (2021). https://www.pbs.org/wgbh/americanexperience/features/oakley-europe/.

———. "Carrie Nation." *PBS.org* (2021). https://www.pbs.org/wgbh/americanexperience/features/other-notable-people/.

American Legends: The Life of Billy Graham. Scotts Valley, CA: Charles River, 2015.

American National Red Cross. "Clara Barton: Visionary Leader and Founder of the Red Cross." https://www.redcross.org/about-us/who-we-are/history/clara-barton.html.

Andrews, Evan. "10 Little-Known Facts about the Lewis and Clark Expedition." *History.com* (September 3, 2018). https://www.history.com/news/10-little-known-facts-about-the-lewis-and-clark-expedition.

———. "10 Things You Should Know about Prohibition." *History.com* (February 22, 2019). https://www.history.com/news/10-things-you-should-know-about-prohibition.

Archbold, Rick, and Robert D. Ballard. *The Lost Ships of Robert Ballard*. San Diego: Thunder Bay 2005.

Asbury, Herbert. *Carry Nation*. New York City: Knopf, 1929.

Austin, Suzanne Alchon. *A Pest in the Land: New World Epidemics in a Global Perspective*. Albuquerque: University of New Mexico Press, 2003.

Avrich, Paul. *The Haymarket Tragedy*. Princeton, NJ: Princeton University Press, 1986.

Bain, David Howard. *Empire Express: Building the First Transcontinental Railroad*. New York: Viking Penguin, 1999.

Bardhan-Quallen, Sudipta. *Franklin Delano Roosevelt: A National Hero*. New York: Sterling, 2007.

Barnum, Phineas. *The Life of P. T. Barnum*. Buffalo, NY: Courier, 1888.

Barretta, Lisa. *The Street Smart Psychic's Guide to Getting a Good Reading*. Woodbury, MN: Llewellyn, 2009.

Bartelt, William E. *There I Grew Up: Remembering Abraham Lincoln's Indiana Youth*. Indianapolis: Indiana Historical Society, 2008.

BBC News. "Home by Christmas—October 1950 to January 1951." (May 26, 2010). https://www.bbc.com/news/10162993.

Beach, Randall. "The Life of Barnum Gets Another Look." *The New York Times* (September 9, 1990). https://www.nytimes.com/1990/09/09/nyregion/the-life-of-barnum-gets-another-look.html.

Beggs, Scott. "10 Fascinating Facts about Huey Long." *Mental Floss* (April 27, 2018). https://www.mentalfloss.com/article/538463/facts-about-huey-long.

Begos, Kevin. "125 Years after Johnstown: Facts about the Flood." *The Tribune-Democrat* (May 28, 2014). https://www.tribdem.com/news/local_news/125-years-after-johnstown-facts-about-the-flood/article_f53f09ce-5513-5b7f-84be-893235edd958.html

Bell, James B. *Empire, Religion and Revolution in Early Virginia, 1607–1786*. London: Palgrave Macmillan, 2013.

Bell, James B., and Richard L. Abrams. *In Search of Liberty: The Story of the Statue of Liberty and Ellis Island*. Garden City, NY: Doubleday, 1984.

Benko, Ralph. "The Biggest Recession You've Never, Ever Heard of." *Forbes* (February 2, 2015). https://www.forbes.com/sites/ralphbenko/2015/02/02/the-biggest-recession-youve-never-ever-heard-of/?sh=34528cee3619.

Bennett, William. *America: The Last Best Hope*. Nashville: Thomas Nelson, 2006.

Benson, Charles D., and William Faherty. *Moonport: A History of Apollo Launch Facilities and Operations*. Washington, DC: National Aeronautics and Space Administration, 1978.

Benton, Michael. "Samuel Adams." *John Adams* (November 6, 2013). http://johnadamsinfo.com/samuel-adams/94/.

Bergreen, Laurence, *Capone—The Man and the Era*. New York: Simon & Schuster, 1994.

Bibliography

Berton, Pierre. *Klondike Fever: The Life and Death of the Last Great Gold Rush*. New York: Carroll & Graf, 2004.

Beschloss, Michael R. *Presidential Courage: Brave Leaders and How They Changed America, 1789–1989*. New York: Simon & Schuster, 2008.

Binghamton University. "U.S. Civil War Took Bigger Toll than Previously Estimated, New Analysis Suggests." *ScienceDaily* (September 24, 2021). www.sciencedaily.com/releases/2011/09/110921120124.htm.

Biography.com Editors. "Harry Houdini Biography." (April 15, 2021). https://www.biography.com/performer/harry-houdini.

———. "Norman Rockwell Biography." (December 1, 2021). https://www.biography.com/artist/norman-rockwell.

Birchall, Frederick T. "100,000 Hail Hitler; U.S. Athletes Avoid Nazi Salute to Him." *The New York Times* (August 2, 1936) https://www.nytimes.com/1936/08/02/archives/100000-hail-hitler-us-athletes-avoid-nazi-salute-to-him-frantic.html.

Black, Harry. *Canadian Scientists and Inventors: Biographies of People Who Made a Difference*. Markham, ON: Pembroke, 1997.

Black Hills & Badlands Tourism Association. "Mount Rushmore National Memorial." https://www.blackhillsbadlands.com/parks-monuments/mount-rushmore-national-memorial.

BlackPast. "(1963) George Wallace, 'Segregation Now, Segregation Forever.'" *BlackPast* (January 22, 2013). https://www.blackpast.org/african-american-history/speeches-african-american-history/1963-george-wallace-segregation-now-segregation-forever/.

Blazeski, Goran. "Annie Oakley Shot a Cigarette Out of the Kaiser's Mouth, Had She Hit Him, She Could Have Prevented WWI." *The Vintage News* (March 5, 2017). https://www.thevintagenews.com/2017/03/05/annie-oakley.

Bloom, Ken, and Frank Vlastnik. *Broadway Musicals: The 101 Greatest Shows of All Time*. New York: Black Dog & Leventhal, 2004.

Blum, Deborah. "The Chemist's War." *Slate* (Feb 19, 2010). https://slate.com/technology/2010/02/the-little-told-story-of-how-the-u-s-government-poisoned-alcohol-during-prohibition.html.

Blumhofer, Edith. *Her Heart Can See: The Life and Hymns of Fanny J. Crosby*. Grand Rapids: Eerdmans, 2005.

Bordewich, Fergus M. "Political Rhetoric over SCOTUS Nominee Is Historically Unhinged." (May 3rd, 2016). http://www.fergusbordewich.com/blog/?p=310.

Brammer, Robert. "The Sinking of the Lusitania." *Library of Congress* (May 29, 2015). https://blogs.loc.gov/law/2015/05/the-sinking-of-the-lusitania/.

Branch, Taylor. *Parting the Waters: America in the King Years 1954–63*. New York: Simon & Schuster, 1988.

Brands, H. W. *The General vs. the President: MacArthur and Truman at the Brink of Nuclear War*. New York: Doubleday, 2017.

———. *The Man Who Saved the Union: Ulysses S. Grant in War and Peace*. New York: Doubleday, 2012.

Bredhoff, Stacey. *American Originals*. Seattle: University of Washington Press, 2001.

Britton, Tamara L. *Dwight D. Eisenhower*. Minneapolis: ABDO, 2009.

Bruce, Robert V. *Alexander Bell and the Conquest of Solitude*. Ithaca, NY: Cornell University Press, 1990.

Bryner, Jeanna. "Did Abe Lincoln Have Smallpox?" *NBC News* (May 17, 2007). https://www.nbcnews.com/id/wbna18727435.

Bryson, Bill. *A Short History of Nearly Everything*. New York: Crown, 2003.

"California Gold Rush, 1848–1864." *LearnCalifornia.org* (July 27, 2011). http://www.learncalifornia.org/doc.asp?id=118.

Calkins, Carroll, ed. *The Story of America*. New York: Readers Digest Association, 1975.

Campbell, W. Joseph. *Getting It Wrong: Ten of the Greatest Misreported Stories in American Journalism*. Berkeley: University of California Press, 2010.

Carlson, Darren K. "Americans Weigh in on Evolution vs. Creationism in Schools." *Gallup* (May 24, 2005). https://news.gallup.com/poll/16462/americans-weigh-evolution-vs-creationism-schools.aspx.

Caulkins, Alice. "Nast on Broadway: His Grand Caricaturama of 1868." *HarpWeek* (2005). https://thomasnast.com/Activities/NastCaricaturama/subpages/CommentaryPage.asp?Commentary=01Intro-01NastOverview.

"Celebrate Apollo: Exploring the Moon, Discovering Earth." https://www.nasa.gov/pdf/323298main_CelebrateApolloEarthRise.pdf.

Census Bulletin. "Census of Population and Housing, 1890." United States Census Office. https://www.census.gov/prod/www/decennial.html.

Chappell, Bill. "Norman Rockwell's 'Saying Grace' Sells for $46 Million at Auction." *NPR* (December 4, 2013). https://www.npr.org/sections/thetwo-way/2013/12/04/248790682/norman-rockwells-saying-grace-sells-for-46-million-at-auction

Charles, Eleanor. "Westchester Guide: Fanny Crosby's Day." *The New York Times* (August 30, 1992) https://www.nytimes.com/1992/08/30/nyregion/westchester-guide-609692.html.

"Charles H. Spurgeon." https://www.wholesomewords.org/biography/biospurgeon6.html.

Chen, James. "Full Faith and Credit." *Investopedia* (July 31, 2021). https://www.investopedia.com/terms/f/full-faith-credit.asp.

Chernow, Ron. *Alexander Hamilton*. New York: Penguin, 2005.

———. *Grant*. New York: Penguin, 2017.

———. *Titan: The Life of John D. Rockefeller, Sr.* New York: Vintage, 1998.

———. *Washington: A Life*. New York: Penguin, 2010.

Christianity.com staff. "Fanny Crosby: America's Hymn Queen." *Christianity.com* (April 28, 2010). https://www.christianity.com/church/church-history/timeline/1801-1900/fanny-crosby-americas-hymn-queen-11630385.html.

Circus Ring of Fame Editors. "Phineas Taylor Barnum." https://circusringoffame.org/barnum-phineas-taylor/.

"Civil War Casualties." https://www.historynet.com/civil-war-casualties.

Clark, Ella E., and Margot Edmonds. *Sacagawea of the Lewis and Clark Expedition*. Berkeley: University of California Press, 1983.

CNN Editorial Research. "World War II Fast Facts." *CNN* (September 2, 2018). https://edition.cnn.com/2013/07/09/world/world-war-ii-fast-facts/index.html

Cody, David. "Child Labor." *The Victorian Web* (April 26, 2019). http://www.victorianweb.org/history/hist8.html.

Cohn, Samuel K., Jr. "The Black Death: End of a Paradigm." *The American Historical Review* 107.3 (June 2002) 703–38. https://doi.org/10.1086/ahr/107.3.703.

Cole, Mark. "Mark Cole: Five Tools for Communicating Vision." *John C. Maxwell* (November 15, 2019). https://www.johnmaxwell.com/blog/mark-cole-five-tools-for-communicating-vision/.

Bibliography

Cooper, Bruce C. *Riding the Transcontinental Rails: Overland Travel on the Pacific Railroad, 1865–1881*. Philadelphia: Polyglot, 2005.

Corbett, Christopher. "The Pony Express: Riders of Destiny." *Historynet*. https://www.historynet.com/pony-express.

Corning, Howard M. *Dictionary of Oregon History*. Hillsboro, OR: Binfords & Mort, 1989.

"Coronavirus Cases." *Worldometers*. https://www.worldometers.info/coronavirus.

Crawford, Ace. "Thousands Celebrate at the Shrine of Democracy." *National Park Service* (July 6, 2011). https://www.nps.gov/moru/learn/news/thousands-celebrate-at-the-shrine-of-democracy.htm.

Crosby, Alfred W. *America's Forgotten Pandemic: The Influenza of 1918*. Cambridge: Cambridge University Press, 2003.

Crow, Melinda. "Journey through American History in Montgomery, Alabama." *Newsweek* (March 5, 2019). https://www.newsweek.com/montgomery-alabama-travel-1351256.

D'Ambra, Duke. "Glenn Cunningham." *The Kansas Historical Society*. https://www.kshs.org/index.php?url=km/facets/view/facets:385,622,4961.

Davis, Kenneth, S. *FDR: Into the Storm, 1937–1940*. New York: Random House, 1993.

Denison, Jim. "John Glenn's Greatest Mission." *Christian Headlines* (December 9, 2016). https://www.christianheadlines.com/columnists/denison-forum/john-glenn-s-greatest-mission.html.

Denworth, Lydia. *Toxic Truth: A Scientist, a Doctor, and the Battle Over Lead*. Boston: Beacon, 2009.

The Dexter Avenue King Memorial Baptist Church. "History." https://www.dexterkingmemorial.org/about/history/.

Donald, David Herbert. *Lincoln*. New York: Simon & Schuster, 1996.

"Donner Party, Westward Movement." http://www.seecalifornia.com/history/donner-party.html.

Donovan, James. *A Terrible Glory: Custer and the Little Bighorn—The Last Great Battle of the American West*. Boston: Little, Brown, 2008.

Douglas, Ann. *Terrible Honesty—Mongrel Manhattan in the 1920s*. New York: Farrar, Straus, & Giroux, 1995.

"Draft Lottery (1969)." https://en.wikipedia.org/wiki/Draft_lottery_(1969).

Drexler, Ken. "Judiciary Act of 1789: Primary Documents in American History." *Library of Congress*. https://guides.loc.gov/judiciary-act.

Duffy, Jim. "The Story Behind Wild West Sharpshooter Annie Oakley's Time on the Eastern Shore." *Secrets of the Eastern Shore* (November 1, 2015). https://www.secretsoftheeasternshore.com/annie-oakley-house/.

Dumas, Alexandre. "Alexandre Dumas Quotes." https://www.alexandredumasworks.com/alexandre-dumas-quotes/.

Earhart, Amelia. *Last Flight*. New York: Harcourt, Brace, 1937.

Eckers, Michael. *The Boys of Wasioja*. Dodge Center, MN: Community News, 2010.

Egan, Timothy. *The Worst Hard Time: The Untold Story of Those Who Survived the Great American Dust Bowl*. Boston: Mariner, 2005.

Ellis, Joseph J. *American Creation*. New York: Knopf, 2007.

———. *Founding Brothers: The Revolutionary Generation*. New York: Knopf, 2000.

Emery, David. "Did the 1938 Radio Broadcast of 'War of the Worlds' Cause a Nationwide Panic?" *Snopes.com* (October 28, 2016). https://www.snopes.com/fact-check/war-of-the-worlds/.

Evers, Stan K. "George Whitefield—Revival Preacher." *Banner of Truth* (June 7, 2005). https://banneroftruth.org/us/resources/articles/2005/george-whitefield-revival-preacher/.

"The Evolution of the American Flag (1776–2014)." USFlagStore.com (2014). https://www.usflagstore.com/american_flag_history_1776_to_present_s/2205.htm.

"Facts about the 1889 Flood." https://www.jaha.org/attractions/johnstown-flood-museum/flood-history/facts-about-the-1889-flood/

Fahner, Johannes Hendrik. *Judicial Deference in International Adjudication: A Comparative Analysis (Studies in International Law)*. Oxford: Hart, 2022.

"Fanny Crosby." *FamPeople* (May 17, 2019). https://fampeople.com/cat-fanny-crosby_20.

Felix, Chad. "Harry Houdini and the Case against Fortune-Telling in American Politics." *Melville House Books* (October 13, 2016). https://www.mhpbooks.com/harry-houdini-and-the-case-against-fortune-telling-in-american-politics/.

Ferling, John E. *The Ascent of George Washington: The Hidden Political Genius of an American Icon*. London: Bloomsbury, 2009.

———. *Setting the World Ablaze: Washington, Adams, Jefferson, and the American Revolution*. Oxford: Oxford University Press, 2000.

Fernández-Armesto, Felipe. *Amerigo: The Man Who Gave His Name to America*. New York: Random House, 2007.

Ferris, Marc. *Star-Spangled Banner: The Unlikely Story of America's National Anthem*. Baltimore: Johns Hopkins University Press, 2014.

Fields, Joseph E. *Worthy Partner: The Papers of Martha Washington*. Westport, CT: Greenwood, 1994.

Fink, Kenneth, dir. *The Vernon Johns Story*. New York: Big Apple Films, 1994.

Fischer, David Hackett. *Paul Revere's Ride*. New York: Oxford University Press, 1994.

———. *Washington's Crossing*. New York: Oxford University Press, 2004.

Fleming, Esther. "Is There Still Damage from the Dust Bowl?" *SidmartinBio* (December 14, 2018). https://www.sidmartinbio.org/is-there-still-damage-from-the-dust-bowl/.

Foner, Eric. *The Fiery Trial: Abraham Lincoln and American Slavery*. New York: Norton, 2011.

Foner, Eric, and John Garraty. *The Reader's Companion to American History*. Boston: Houghton Mifflin, 1991.

Frankel, Todd C. "New NASA Data Show How the World Is Running Out of Water." *The Washington Post*. (June 16, 2015). https://www.washingtonpost.com/news/wonk/wp/2015/06/16/new-nasa-studies-show-how-the-world-is-running-out-of-water/.

"Franklin D. Roosevelt: The Second Term." https://www.sparknotes.com/biography/fdr/section10/.

Fraser, Steve. *The Age of Acquiescence: The Life and Death of American Resistance to Organized Wealth and Power*. Boston: Little, Brown, 2015.

Friedman, Thomas L. "Foreign Affairs Big Mac I." *The New York Times* (December 8, 1996). https://www.nytimes.com/1996/12/08/opinion/foreign-affairs-big-mac-i.html.

Frost, Robert. "Mending Wall." *Poetry Foundation*. https://www.poetryfoundation.org/poems/44266/mending-wall.

Garber, Larry. "Churchill On Democracy: Lessons for Today." *Lobe Log* (January 17, 2019). https://lobelog.com/churchill-on-democracy-lessons-for-today/.

Garcia, Jesus, et al. *Creating America: A History of the United States, Beginnings Through World War I*. Evanston, IL: McDougal Littell, 2007.

Garrett, Charlie. "Ruth 1:1–5 (Famine and Heartache)." *The Superior Word* (August 10, 2014). https://superiorword.org/ruth-1-1-5-famine-and-heartache/.

Garrow, David J. *Bearing the Cross: Martin Luther King Jr. and the Southern Christian Leadership Conference*. New York: Morrow, 1986.

Gass-Poore, Jordan. "From Toys to Tags and Terror . . ." *Dailymail.Com* (August 10, 2017). https://www.dailymail.co.uk/news/article-4776328/US-pupils-wore-dog-tags-ID-bodies-Cold-War.html.

"General Tom Thumb & the "Fairy Wedding." *Barnum-Museum.org* (February 27, 2018). https://barnum-museum.org/general-tom-thumb-fairy-wedding/.

Gienapp, William. *Abraham Lincoln and Civil War America*. Oxford: Oxford University Press, 2002.

Gilbert, Martin. *A History of the Twentieth Century, 1900–1933, Vol. 1*. 3 vols. New York: Morrow, 1997.

Glaeser, Edward. *Triumph of the City: How Our Best Invention Makes Us Richer, Smarter, Greener, Healthier, and Happier*. New York: Penguin, 2011.

Glaser, John, and John Mueller. "Overcoming Inertia: Why It's Time to End the War in Afghanistan." *Cato Institute* (August 13, 2019). https://www.cato.org/publications/policy-analysis/overcoming-inertia-why-its-time-end-war-afghanistan.

"Glenn Cunningham, US, Olympian." https://www.365christianmen.com/podcast/glenn-cunningham-us-olympian/.

Glenn, John, and Nick Taylor. *John Glenn: A Memoir*. New York: Bantam, 1985.

Goff, John S. *Robert Todd Lincoln: A Man in His Own Right*. Manchester Center, VT: Friends of Hildene, 1990.

Going, Jonathan. *The Christian Library*. Volume 2. 6 vols. Gloucester, UK: Thomas George, Jr., 1835.

Goldin, Claudia. *The Race between Education and Technology*. Cambridge: Harvard University Press, 2008.

Good, Cassandra. "That Time When Alexander Hamilton Almost Dueled James Monroe." *Smithsonian Magazine* (October 26, 2015). https://www.smithsonianmag.com/history/time-when-alexander-hamilton-almost-dueled-james-monroe-180957045/.

Gordon, John Steele. "John Rockefeller Sr." *Philanthropy Roundtable*. https://www.philanthropyroundtable.org/almanac/people/hall-of-fame/detail/john-rockefeller-sr.

Grace, Michael L. "Cruise Ship History–Cunard Line's RMS Berengaria (Formerly the SS Imperator) Was Sailing from England to New York When the 1929 Wall Street Crash Hit—Passengers Went from Millionaires to Paupers While at Sea." *The Past and Now* (September 6, 2008). https://www.cruiselinehistory.com/cruise-ship-history-%E2%80%93-cunard-line%E2%80%99s-rms-berengaria.

"Grant Administration Scandals." https://en.wikipedia.org/wiki/Grant_administration_scandals.

"Great Chicago Fire Begins." https://www.history.co.uk/this-day-in-history/08-october/great-chicago-fire-begins#.

Greenhouse, Linda. "O'Connor Has Breast Surgery to Stop Cancer." *The New York Times* (October 22, 1988). https://www.nytimes.com/1988/10/22/us/o-connor-has-breast-surgery-to-stop-cancer.html.

Grizzard Frank E. Jr. *George Washington: A Biographical Companion*. Santa Barbara, CA: ABC-CLIO, 2002.

Grosvenor, Edwin S., and Morgan Wesson. *Alexander Graham Bell: The Life and Times of the Man Who Invented the Telephone*. New York: Abrams, 1997.

Grunwald, Michael. *The Swamp: The Everglades, Florida, and the Politics of Paradise*. New York: Simon & Schuster, 2007.

Gullotta, Daniel N. "The Great Awakening and the American Revolution." *Journal of the American Revolution* (August 10, 2016). https://allthingsliberty.com/2016/08/great-awakening-american-revolution/.

Guinness World Records. "Best-Selling Book." https://www.guinnessworldrecords.com/world-records/best-selling-book-of-non-fiction.

Guttman, Jon. "Soapy Smith: Con Man's Empire." *Historynet*. https://www.historynet.com/soapy-smith-con-mans-empire.htm.

Hagopain, Patrick. *The Vietnam War in American Memory*. Amherst: University of Massachusetts Press, 2009.

Halberstam, David. *The Fifties*. New York: Villard, 1993.

Hall, Jacob Henry. *Biography of Gospel Song and Hymn Writers*. New York: Revell, 1914.

Hammond, Gabriela. "Statue of Liberty Meaning: What She Stands For." *Statue of Liberty Tour* (March 25, 2021). https://www.statueoflibertytour.com/blog/statue-of-liberty-meaning-what-she-stands-for/.

Hammond, Joshua, and James Morrison. *The Stuff Americans Are Made of: The Seven Cultural Forces That Define Americans*. New York: Macmillan, 1996.

Hanson, David J. "Carry Nation Biography (Carrie Nation, Carry A. Nation): Prohibitionist & Temperance Activist." https://www.alcoholproblemsandsolutions.org/carry-nation-biography-carrie-nation/.

Hantula, Richard. Jonas Salk: Trailblazers of the Modern World. Milwaukee: Stevens, 2004.

Hargreaves, Steve. "The Richest Americans in History: John D. Rockefeller." *CNN* (June 2, 2014). https://money.cnn.com/gallery/luxury/2014/06/01/richest-americans-in-history.

Harris, Jonathan. *A Statue for America: The First 100 Years of the Statue of Liberty*. New York: Four Winds, 1985.

Harris, Neil. "The Gilded Age Revisited: Boston and the Museum Movement." American Quarterly 14.4. (Winter 1962) 545–66.

Haskew, Michael E. *West Point 1915: Eisenhower, Bradley, and the Class the Stars Fell On*. Minneapolis: Zenith, 2014.

Hatfield, Mark O., et al. "Vice Presidents of the United States 1789–1993." U.S. Senate Historical, U.S. Government Printing Office Washington Office (1997). Edited by Wendy Wolff. https://www.govinfo.gov/content/pkg/CDOC-104sdoc26/pdf/CDOC-104sdoc26.pdf.

Hathaway, Oona, and Scott Shapiro. "Outlawing War? It Actually Worked." *The New York Times* (September 2, 2017). https://www.nytimes.com/2017/09/02/opinion/sunday/outlawing-war-kellogg-briand.html.

Hawkinson, Don. *Character for Life: An American Heritage: Profiles of Great Men and Women of Faith Who Shaped Western Civilization*. Green Forest, AR: New Leaf, 2005.

Hazen, Kendra. "Episode 6: Early Maps of Florida." *A History of Central Florida*, (February 12, 2014). Podcast video, 14:27. http://stars.library.ucf.edu/ahistoryofcentralfloridapodcast/6.

Heiligman, Deborah. *Charles and Emma: The Darwins' Leap of Faith*. New York: Square Fish, 2011.

Heitmann, John. *The Automobile and American Life*. Jefferson, NC: McFarland, 2009.

Herman, Arthur. *Freedom's Forge: How American Business Produced Victory in World War II*. New York: Random House, 2012.

Hersey, Mark D. "Cunningham Calls It a Career." *KU History*. https://kuhistory.ku.edu/articles/cunningham-calls-it-career.

Hesselberg, Erik. "Remembering Lusitania a Century Later." *Hartford Courant* (May 9, 2015). https://www.courant.com/news/connecticut/hc-lusitania-100-years-later-connecticut-20150509-story.html.

Hietala, Thomas R. *Manifest Design: American Exceptionalism and Empire*. Ithaca, NY: Cornell University Press, 2003.

Hill, Draper, and John Adler. *Doomed by Cartoon: How Cartoonist Thomas Nast and the New York Times Brought Down Boss Tweed and His Ring of Thieves*. New York: Morgan James, 2008.

Hills, Waring. "Norman Rockwell at the Charleston Navy Yard." *Patriots Point Naval & Maritime Museum* (June 9, 2010). https://www.patriotspoint.org/news-and-events/norman-rockwell-at-the-charleston-navy-yard/.

History.com editors. "Abigail Adams Urges Husband to 'Remember the Ladies.'" *History.com* (March 30, 2020). https://www.history.com/this-day-in-history/abigail-adams-urges-husband-to-remember-the-ladies.

———. "First Airplane Flies." *History.com* (December 15, 2021). https://www.history.com/this-day-in-history/first-airplane-flies.

———. "The Gettysburg Address." *History.com* (August 24, 2010). https://www.history.com/topics/american-civil-war/gettysburg-address.

———. "Huey Long." *History.com* (March 7, 2019). https://www.history.com/topics/crime/huey-long.

———. "Klondike Gold Rush." *History.com* (August 21, 2018). https://www.history.com/topics/westward-expansion/klondike-gold-rush.

———. "Over 2,000 Die in the Johnstown FFFF." *History.com* (July 14, 2020). https://www.history.com/this-day-in-history/the-johnstown-flood.

———. "Scopes Monkey Trial Begins." *History.com* (July 8, 2021). https://www.history.com/this-day-in-history/monkey-trial-begins.

———. "Theodore Roosevelt's Wife and Mother Die." *History.com* (February 11, 2021). https://www.history.com/this-day-in-history/theodore-roosevelts-wife-and-mother-die.

———. "World War I Battles: Timeline." *History.com* (April 8, 2021). https://www.history.com/topics/world-war-i/battle-of-cambrai.

Hodak, George. "February 2, 1790: Supreme Court Holds Inaugural Session." *ABA Journal* (February 1, 2011). https://www.abajournal.com/magazine/article/february_2_1790_supreme_court_holds_inaugural_session.

Hoehling, A. A., and Mary Hoehling. *The Last Voyage of the Lusitania*. Seattle: Madison 1996.

Holmes, David L. "The Founding Fathers, Deism, and Christianity." https://www.britannica.com/topic/The-Founding-Fathers-Deism-and-Christianity-1272214.

Horgan, John. "Justinian's Plague (541–42 CE)." *World History Encyclopedia* (December 26, 2014). https://www.worldhistory.org/article/782/justinians-plague-541–42-ce/.

Howell, Thomas. "Alexander Hamilton and the Coast Guard Navy." *Coast Guard (blog)*, U.S. Naval Institute (February 2, 2018). https://blog.usni.org/posts/2018/02/02/alexander-hamilton-and-the-coast-guard.

Huckabee, Mike, and Steve Feazel. *The Three Cs That Made America Great: Christianity, Capitalism, and the Constitution*. Meadville, PA: Trilogy Christian, 2020.

Huddleston, John. *Killing Ground: The Civil War and the Changing American Landscape*. Baltimore: Johns Hopkins University Press, 2002.

Humes, Edward. *Over Here: How the G.I. Bill Transformed the American Dream*. New York: Diversion, 2014.

Hunter, George William. *A Civic Biology*. New York: American, 1914.

Hutcheson, Edwin. *Floods of Johnstown: 1889-1936-1977*. Johnstown, PA: Cambria County Tourist Council, 1989.

"'I Can't Tell a Lie, Pa,' George Washington and the Cherry Tree Myth." George Washington's Mount Vernon. https://www.mountvernon.org/george-washington/facts/myths/george-washington-and-the-cherry-tree-myth/.

"Immigration to the United States, 1851–1900." https://www.loc.gov/classroom-materials/united-states-history-primary-source-timeline/rise-of-industrial-america-1876-1900/immigration-to-united-states-1851-1900/.

Infectious Diseases Society of America. "Aspirin Misuse May Have Made 1918 Flu Pandemic Worse." *ScienceDaily* (October 3, 2009). www.sciencedaily.com/releases/2009/10/091002132346.htm.

"In God We Trust Explained." *Everything.Explained.Today*. https://everything.explained.today/In_God_We_Trust/.

International Olympic Committee. "The XIth Olympic Games—Berlin, 1936." https://olympics.com/en/olympic-games/berlin-1936.

Jackson, Donald. *Thomas Jefferson & the Stony Mountains: Exploring the West from Monticello*. Norman: University of Oklahoma Press, 2002.

James, Dorris Clayton. *The Years of MacArthur: Triumph and Disaster 1945–1964*. Boston: Houghton Mifflin, 1985.

"The Jazz Age: The American 1920s." https://www.digitalhistory.uh.edu/disp_textbook_print.cfm?smtid=2&psid=3399.

Jinwoochong. "Buried Under Flushing Meadows Is the 1939 World's Fair Time Capsule, to Be Opened in 5000 Years." *Untapped New York* (April 13, 2005). https://untappedcities.com/2015/04/13/buried-under-flushing-meadows-is-the-1939-worlds-fair-time-capsule-to-be-opened-in-5000-years/.

Johnson, Caleb. "John Howland." http://mayflowerhistory.com/howland.

Johnson, Charles. *Pirates: A General History of the Robberies and Murders of the Most Notorious Pirates*. London: Chrysalis, 2002.

Jones, Jeffrey M. "Who Had the Lowest Gallup Presidential Job Approval Rating?" https://news.gallup.com/poll/272765/lowest-gallup-presidential-job-approval-rating.aspx.

Josephson, Matthew. *The Robber Barons: The Great American Capitalists, 1861–1901*. San Diego: Harcourt, 1962.

"Judicial Compensation." https://www.uscourts.gov/judges-judgeships/judicial-compensation.

Kalan, Elliott. "The Original Futurama: The Legacy of the 1939 World's Fair." *Popular Mechanics* (March 11, 2010). https://www.popularmechanics.com/technology/design/a5322/4345790/.

Kalush, William, and Larry Sloman. *The Secret Life of Houdini: The Making of America's First Superhero*. New York: Atria, 2007.

Kamen, Al, and Marjorie Williams. "How Sandra Day O'Connor Became the Most Powerful Woman in 1980s America." *The Washington Post* (March 29, 2016). https://www.washingtonpost.com/news/arts-and-entertainment/wp/2016/03/29/how-sandra-day-oconnor-became-the-most-powerful-woman-in-1980s-america/.

Kamensky, Jane, et al. *A People and a Nation: A History of the United States*. 11th ed. Boston: Cengage Learning, 2017.

Kansas Historical Society. "Carry A. Nation." (August 2017). https://www.kshs.org/kansapedia/carry-a-nation/15502.

———. "Turkey Red Wheat." (April 2015). https://www.kshs.org/kansapedia/turkey-red-wheat/16789.

Kazin, Michael. *A Godly Hero: The Life of William Jennings Bryan*. New York: Knopf, 2006.

Kelly, Barbara M. *Expanding the American Dream: Building and Rebuilding Levittown*. Albany, NY: State University of New York Press, 1993.

Kennedy, David. *Freedom from Fear: The American People in Depression and War, 1929–1945*. Oxford: Oxford University Press, 1999.

Kennedy, Lesley. "Most Immigrants Arriving at Ellis Island in 1907 Were Processed in a Few Hours." *History.com* (March 7, 2019). https://www.history.com/news/immigrants-ellis-island-short-processing-time.

Kennedy, Roger G. *Burr, Hamilton, and Jefferson: A Study in Character*. Oxford: Oxford University Press, 2000.

Keyes, Alexa. "Top 7 Foreign Gifts to the U.S." *ABC News* (April 13, 2012). https://abcnews.go.com/Politics/top-foreign-gifts-us/story?id=16132444.

Khan Academy. "The Eisenhower Era Unit 8." https://www.khanacademy.org/humanities/us-history/postwarera/1950s-america/a/the-eisenhower-era.

Kirby, Doug, et al. "Cardiff Giant." https://www.roadsideamerica.com/story/2172.

Kitman, Jamie Lincoln. "The Secret History of Lead." The Nation. (March 20, 2000). https://www.thenation.com/article/archive/secret-history-lead/.

Klein, Christopher. "10 Things You May Not Know about Alexander Graham Bell." *History.com*. (March 26, 2020). https://www.history.com/news/10-things-you-may-not-know-about-alexander-graham-bell.

———. "10 Things You May Not Know about Annie Oakley." *History.com* (July 13, 2021). https://www.history.com/news/10-things-you-may-not-know-about-annie-oakley.

———. "10 Things You May Not Know about John Adams." *History.com* (September 1, 2018). https://www.history.com/news/10-things-you-may-not-know-about-john-adams#:~:text=8.

———. "The Scandalous Romance That May Have Saved the British Monarchy." *History.com* (December 10, 2019). https://www.history.com/news/the-scandalous-romance-that-may-have-saved-the-british-monarchy.

———. "When Teddy Roosevelt Was Shot in 1912, a Speech May Have Saved His Life." *History.com* (July 21, 2019). https://www.history.com/news/shot-in-the-chest-100-years-ago-teddy-roosevelt-kept-on-talking.

Klingaman, William K. *Abraham Lincoln and the Road to Emancipation*. New York: Viking Adult, 2001.

Knecht, Clare. "Historical Progression." https://issuu.com/clareknecht/docs/residual_farmland/s/10489532.
Kohler, Ron. *Gettysburg*. Meadville, PA: Christian Faith, 2021.
Kolbert, Elizabeth. "The Big Sleazy: How Huey Long Took Louisiana." *The New Yorker* (June 4, 2006). https://www.newyorker.com/magazine/2006/06/12/the-big-sleazy
Kosak, Hadassa. "Triangle Shirtwaist Fire." *The Shalvi/Hyman Encyclopedia of Jewish Women* (December 31, 1999). https://jwa.org/encyclopedia/article/triangle-shirtwaist-fire.
Kotlikoff, Laurence. "Is the United States Bankrupt?" *Review* 88 (July 2006) 235–50. https://econpapers.repec.org/article/fipfedlrv/y_3a2006_3ai_3ajul_3ap_3a235-250_3an_3av.88no.4.htm.
Kovarik, Bill. "Charles F. Kettering and the 1921 Discovery of Tetraethyl Lead in the Context of Technological Alternatives." *Evisa* (1994). http://www.speciation.net/Database/Links/Charles-F-Kettering-and-the-1921-Discovery-of-Tetraethyl-Lead-In-the-Context-of-Technological-Alternatives-;i1863.
Kranz, Gene. *Failure Is Not an Option: Mission Control from Mercury to Apollo 13 and Beyond*. New York: Simon & Schuster. 2000.
Kunhardt, Jr., Philip B., et al. *P. T. Barnum: America's Greatest Showman*. New York: Knopf, 1995.
Lacayo, Richard. "Suburban Legend William Levitt." *TIME* (December 7, 1998). http://content.time.com/time/magazine/article/0,9171,989781,00.html.
"Lady Justice Explained." *Everything.Explained.Today*. https://everything.explained.today/Lady_Justice/.
Lange, Brenda. *The Triangle Shirtwaist Factory Fire*. New York: Chelsea House, 2008.
"Later Years." *Paul Revere Heritage Project* (2007). http://www.paul-revere-heritage.com/biography/later-years.html.
Lawrence, Tom. "Adding Fifth Face to Mount Rushmore National Memorial Has Been Political Football for Decades." *Argus Leader* (June 26, 2020). https://www.argusleader.com/story/news/2020/06/26/south-dakota-mount-rushmore-national-memorial-national-park-service-can-add-face/3243967001/.
Lawson, Edward W. *The Discovery of Florida and Its Discoverer Juan Ponce de León*. Whitefish, MT: Kessenger, 1946.
Lawson, Russell M., and Benjamin A. Lawson. *Race and Ethnicity in America: From Pre-contact to the Present*. 4 vols. Santa Barbara, CA: Greenwood, 2019.
Leepson, Marc, and Nelson DeMille. *Flag: An American Biography*. New York: St. Martin's, 2006.
"Letter from Charles Dickens on Ragged Schools." https://www.bl.uk/collection-items/letter-from-charles-dickens-on-ragged-schools-from-the-daily-news.
Levin, Phyllis Lee. *Edith and Woodrow: The Wilson White House*. New York: Scribner, 2001.
Levine, Alexandra S. "If Martin Luther King Had Sneezed." *The New York Times* (January 12, 2017). https://www.nytimes.com/2017/01/12/nyregion/new-york-today-martin-luther-king-sneeze-izola-ware-curry-ive-been-to-the-mountaintop-speech.html.
Levinson, Sanford. "The Twelfth Amendment." *National Constitution Center*. https://constitutioncenter.org/interactive-constitution/interpretation/amendment-xii/interps/171.
Levy, Leonard. *Seasoned Judgments: The American Constitution, Rights, and History*. Piscataway, NJ: Transaction, 1995.

Lewis, Jack. "Lead Poisoning: A Historical Perspective." *US Environmental Protection Agency* (September 16, 2016). https://archive.epa.gov/epa/aboutepa/lead-poisoning-historical-perspective.html.

Library of Congress. "On These Walls: Inscriptions and Quotations in the Buildings of the Library of Congrss." https://www.loc.gov/loc/walls/madison.html.

Licht, Walter. *Working for the Railroad: The Organization of Work in the Nineteenth Century.* Princeton, NJ: Princeton Legacy Library, 1983.

Lincoln, Abraham. *The Collected Works of Abraham Lincoln: Volume 1, 1824–1848.* 9 vols. New Brunswick, NJ: Rutgers University Press, 1953.

Linder, Douglas O. "Scopes 'Monkey' Trial (1925)." https://famous-trials.com/scopesmonkey.

Little, Becky. "The Statue of Liberty Has Long Been a Magnet for Protest." *History.com* (August 23, 2018). https://www.history.com/news/statue-of-liberty-protest-history-immigration-suffrage-vietnam-war.

Long, Elgen M., and Marie K. Long, *Amelia Earhart: The Mystery Solved.* New York: Simon & Schuster, 1999.

Long, Huey. *Every Man a King: The Autobiography of Huey P. Long.* Boston: Da Capo, 1996.

Longfellow, Henry W. "I Heard the Bells on Christmas Day." *Hymnary* (1864). https://hymnary.org/text/i_heard_the_bells_on_christmas_day

———. "Paul Revere's Ride." *Paul Revere House.* https://www.paulreverehouse.org/longfellows-poem/.

Lovell, Mary S. *The Sound of Wings: The Life of Amelia Earhart.* New York: St. Martin's, 1989.

Lovett, Leslie Anne. "The Jaybird-Woodpecker War: Reconstruction and Redemption in Fort Bend County, Texas, 1869–1889." Master's thesis, Rice University, 1994. https://hdl.handle.net/1911/13861.

Lowell, James Russell. "The Present Crisis." https://poets.org/poem/present-crisis.

MacLeod, Elizabeth. *Alexander Graham Bell: An Inventive Life.* Toronto, ON: Kids Can, 1999.

Magat, Richard. "The Forgotten Roles of Two New York City Teachers in the Epic Scopes Trial." *Science & Society* 70.4 (October 2006) 541–49.

Mansky, Jackie. "P.T. Barnum Isn't the Hero the 'Greatest Showman' Wants You to Think." *Smithsonian Magazine* (December 22, 2017). https://www.smithsonianmag.com/history/true-story-pt-barnum-greatest-humbug-them-all-180967634/.

Marquis, Alice Goldfarb. "Written on the Wind: The Impact of Radio During the 1930s." *Journal of Contemporary History* 19.3 (July 1984) 385–415. https://doi.org/10.1177/002200948401900302.

Martinez, J. Michael. *Coming for to Carry Me Home: Race in America from Abolitionism to Jim Crow.* Lanham, MD: Rowman & Littlefield, 2016.

Matray, James I. "Truman's Plan for Victory: National Self-Determination and the Thirty-Eighth Parallel Decision in Korea." *Journal of American History* 66.2 (September 1979) 314–33.

McCarthy, Andy. "A Brief Passage in U.S. Immigration History." *New York Public Library* (July 1, 2016). https://www.nypl.org/blog/2016/07/01/us-immigration-history.

McCullough, David. *John Adams.* New York: Simon & Schuster, 2001.

———. *The Johnstown Flood.* New York: Simon & Schuster, 1987.

McNeill, J. R. *Something New Under the Sun: An Environmental History of the Twentieth-Century World.* New York: Norton, 2001.

McPherson, James M. *Battle Cry of Freedom: The Civil War Era*. Oxford: Oxford University Press, 2003.

McTavish T. J. *A Theological Miscellany*. Nashville: Thomas Nelson, 2005.

Meier, Michael T. "Civil War Draft Records: Exemptions and Enrollments." Prologue Magazine 26.4 (Winter 1994). https://www.archives.gov/publications/prologue/1994/winter/civil-war-draft-records.html.

Mettler, Suzanne. "Bring the State Back in to Civic Engagement: Policy Feedback Effects of the G.I. Bill for World War II Veterans." *American Political Science Review* 96.2 (June 2002) 351–65. https://www.jstor.org/stable/3118030.

———. "How the GI Bill Built the Middle Class and Enhanced Democracy." *Scholars Strategy Network* (January 1, 2012). https://scholars.org/contribution/how-gi-bill-built-middle-class-and-enhanced-democracy.

Meyer, Diana Lambdin. *Kansas Myths and Legends: The True Stories behind History's Mysteries (Legends of the West)*. Guilford, CT: TwoDot, 2017.

Mieder, Wolfgang. *Making a Way Out of No Way Martin Luther King's Sermonic Proverbial Rhetoric*. Bern: Lang, 2010.

Mikkelson, David. "Did Houdini Die from a Punch to the Stomach?" *Snopes.com* (May 2, 2001). https://www.snopes.com/fact-check/death-of-houdini/.

Military Wiki Editors. "Vanguard (Rocket)." https://military-history.fandom.com/wiki/Vanguard_(rocket).

Millard, Candice. *The River of Doubt: Theodore Roosevelt's Darkest Journey*. New York: Doubleday, 2006.

Miller, David. *The Cold War: A Military History*. New York: Dunne, 1999.

Miller, Donald L. *City of the Century: The Epic of Chicago and the Making of America*, New York: Rosetta, 2014.

Miller, Nathan. *Theodore Roosevelt: A Life*. New York: Morrow, 1992.

Miller, Spencer. "If You See a Good Fight . . . Get in It." *Faithlife* (2013). https://sermons.faithlife.com/sermons/122982-if-you-see-a-good-fight . . . get-in-it.

Millhiser, Ian. "The Supreme Court's Enigmatic 'Shadow Docket,' Explained." *Vox Media* (Aug 11, 2020). https://www.vox.com/2020/8/11/21356913/supreme-court-shadow-docket-jail-asylum-covid-immigrants-sonia-sotomayor-barnes-ahlman.

Milner, Connor, et al. *The Oxford History of the American West*. New York: Oxford University Press, 1994.

Moe, Richard. *The Last Full Measure: The Life and Death of the First Minnesota Volunteers*. Saint Paul: Minnesota Historical Society, 2001.

Monk, Craig. *Writing the Lost Generation: Expatriate Autobiography and American Modernism*. Iowa City: University of Iowa Press, 2004.

Moore, Mark H. "Actually, Prohibition Was a Success." https://alcap.thrive.am/files/66/Themes/Prohibition%20was%20a%20success%202.pdf.

Morain, Tom. "The Great Depression Hits Farms and Cities in the 1930s." https://www.iowapbs.org/iowapathways/mypath/great-depression-hits-farms-and-cities-1930s.

Moreno, Barry. *The Statue of Liberty Encyclopedia*. New York: Simon & Schuster, 2000.

Morgan, Robert J. *100 Bible Verses Everyone Should Know by Heart*. Nashville: B&H, 2010.

Morison, Samuel Eliot. *Admiral of the Ocean Sea: A Life of Christopher Columbus*. New York: MJF, 1970.

Nash, Gary B. *The American People: Creating a Nation and a Society.* New York: Pearson Education, 2008.

National Academy of Sciences. *Science and Creationism: A View from the National Academy of Sciences.* 2nd edition. Washington, DC: National Academies Press, 1999.

National Archives (NARA). "Letter to President William McKinley from Annie Oakley." https://www.archives.gov/research/recover/example-02.html.

National Park Service. "Abolition." https://www.nps.gov/stli/learn/historyculture/abolition.htm.

———. "Carving History." https://www.nps.gov/moru/learn/historyculture/carving-history.htm.

———. "Theodore Roosevelt the Rancher." https://www.nps.gov/thro/learn/historyculture/theodore-roosevelt-the-rancher.htm.

———. "Why These Four Presidents?" https://www.nps.gov/moru/learn/historyculture/why-these-four-presidents.htm.

Nevins, Allan. *The Emergence of Modern America, 1865–1878.* Dorset, UK: Reprint Services Corp, 1935.

Newport, Frank. "Politics in U.S., 46% Hold Creationist View of Human Origins." *Gallup* (June 1, 2012). https://news.gallup.com/poll/155003/hold-creationist-view-human-origins.aspx.

"Norman Rockwell: A Brief Biography." *Norman Rockwell Museum.* https://www.nrm.org/about/about-2/about-norman-rockwell/.

"North American Tall Grass Prairie." https://wrangle.org/ecotype/north-american-tall-grass-prairie.

NPR Editors. "'Out of Order' at the Court: O'Connor on Being the First Female Justice." *Fresh Air.* (March 5, 2013). https://www.npr.org/2013/03/05/172982275/out-of-order-at-the-court-oconnor-on-being-the-first-female-justice.

NWS Editors. "Inauguration Weather." *National Weather Service* (January 21, 2017). https://www.weather.gov/lwx/events_Inauguration.

NYC Parks. "Flushing Meadows Corona Park." https://www.nycgovparks.org/parks/flushing-meadows-corona-park.

Office of the Chaplaincy, United States House of Representatives. "Benjamin Franklin, from a Speech to the Constitutional Convention, June 28, 1787." https://chaplain.house.gov/chaplaincy/chaplain_brochure.pdf.

———. "Congressional Prayer Room." https://chaplain.house.gov/religion/prayer_room.html.

OhRanger.com. "Making Mount Rushmore." http://www.ohranger.com/mount-rushmore/making-mount-rushmore.

OlyMadMen. "Glenn Cunningham." https://www.olympedia.org/athletes/78288.

"'One Third of a Nation.' FDR's Second Inaugural Address." http://historymatters.gmu.edu/d/5105/.

Oord, Christian. "Believe It or Not: Since Its Birth the USA Has Only Had 17 Years of Peace History." *War History Online* (March 19, 2019). https://www.warhistoryonline.com/instant-articles/usa-only-17-years-of-peace.html.

Ornig, Joseph R. *My Last Chance to Be a Boy: Theodore Roosevelt's South American Expedition of 1913–1914.* Baton Rouge: Louisiana State University Press, 1998.

Orse, Joseph Andrew. *The Lives of Chang & Eng: Siam's Twins in Nineteenth-century America.* Raleigh: North Carolina State University Press, 2014.

Osbeck, Kenneth W. *Amazing Grace: 366 Inspiring Hymn Stories for Daily Devotions*. Grand Rapids: Kregel, 2010.

O'Shea, Stephen. *Back to the Front*. Vancouver: Douglas and McIntyre, 2012.

Paine, Albert Bigelow. *Thomas Nast: His Period and His Pictures*. Princeton, NJ: Pyne, 1974.

Palumbo, Arthur E. *The Authentic Constitution: An Originalist View of America's Legacy*. New York: Algora, 2009.

Parrish, Michael E. *Anxious Decades: America in Prosperity and Depression, 1920–1941*. New York: Norton. 1994.

PBS. "James Gregory Interview." https://www.pbs.org/fmc/interviews/gregory.htm.

———. "Monkey Trial, WGN Radio Broadcasts the Trial." https://www.pbs.org/wgbh/americanexperience/features/monkeytrial-wgn-radio-broadcasts-trial/.

———. "Mount Rushmore." *American Experience* (aired January 20, 2002). https://www.pbs.org/wgbh/americanexperience/films/rushmore/.

Pennsylvania Department of Health. "Polio Fact Sheet." https://www.health.pa.gov/topics/Documents/Diseases%20and%20Conditions/Polio%20.pdf.

Perkins, Sid. "Johnstown Flood Matched Volume of Mississippi River." *Science News* 176.11 (October 20, 2009) https://www.sciencenews.org/article/johnstown-flood-matched-volume-mississippi-river.

Perry, Elisabeth Israels, and Karen Manners Smith. *The Gilded Age & Progressive Era: A Student Companion*. New York: Oxford University Press, 2006.

Peters, Arthur K. *Seven Trail West*. New York: Abbeville, 1996.

Petrie, A. Roy. *Alexander Graham Bell*. Don Mills, ON: Fitzhenry & Whiteside, 1975.

Philbrick, Nathaniel. *Mayflower: A Story of Courage, Community, and War*. New York: Viking, 2006.

Phillips, Jeff. *The Military History of Private Charles Samuel Phillips: 7th Battalion, Duke of Cornwall's Light Infantry The Battle of Cambrai*. Rochester, MN: self-published, 2020.

Phillipson, Donald J. C. "Alexander Graham Bell." *The Canadian Encyclopedia* (August 30, 2017). https://www.thecanadianencyclopedia.ca/en/article/alexander-graham-bell.

Piper, Henry Dan. "Fitzgerald's Cult of Disillusion." *American Quarterly* 3.1 (1951) 69–80. https://doi.org/10.2307/3031187.

"Poll Taxes in the United States Explained." *Everything.Explained.Today*. http://everything.explained.today/Poll_taxes_in_the_United_States/.

Pooley, Jefferson, and Michael J. Socolow. "The Myth of the *War of the Worlds* Panic." *Slate* (October 28, 2013). https://slate.com/culture/2013/10/orson-welles-war-of-the-worlds-panic-myth-the-infamous-radio-broadcast-did-not-cause-a-nationwide-hysteria.html.

Post Editors. "The Rockwell Files: Best Job Ever." https://www.saturdayeveningpost.com/sep-keyword/rockwell/.

———. "Rockwell Video Minute: Saying Grace." *Saturday Evening Post Society* (November 25, 2019). https://www.saturdayeveningpost.com/2019/11/rockwell-video-minute-saying-grace/.

Potter, Lee Ann, and Wynell Schamel. "The Homestead Act of 1862." *Social Education* 61.6 (October 1997) 359–64.

"President George Washington's Farewell Address." http://www.ourdocuments.gov/doc.php?doc=15.

"Presidential Historians Survey 2017." *C-SPAN* (2017). https://www.c-span.org/presidentsurvey2017/?page=overall.

Preston, Diana. *Wilful Murder: The Sinking of the "Lusitania."* New York: Doubleday, 2002.

Ptacin, Mira. "How Harry Houdini Became the Champion of Mother's Day: Mira Ptacin on Magic, Mediums, and Mothers." *Literary Hub* (May 8, 2020). https://lithub.com/how-harry-houdini-became-the-champion-of-mothers-day.

Rather, Dan, and Mark Sullivan. *Our Times—America at the Birth of the Twentieth Century.* New York: Scribner, 1996.

Ray, Brian D. "Research Facts on Homeschooling." *NHERI* (September 9, 2021). https://www.nheri.org/research-facts-on-homeschooling/.

Ray, Charles. *A Marvelous Ministry: The Story of C. H. Spurgeon's Sermons, 1855–1905.* Cleveland: Pilgrim, 1985.

"The Real Story of Revere's Ride." *The Paul Revere House.* https://www.paulreverehouse.org/the-real-story/.

Regis, Margaret. *When Our Mothers Went to War: An Illustrated History of Women in World War II.* Seattle: Nav, 2008.

Reid, John Phillip. *Constitutional History of the American Revolution: The Authority to Tax.* Madison: University of Wisconsin Press, 1987.

Reiss, Benjamin. *The Showman and the Slave: Race, Death, and Memory in Barnum's America.* Cambridge: Harvard University Press, 2001.

"Religion and the Founding of the American Republic." *Library of Congress.* https://www.loc.gov/exhibits/religion/rel02.html.

"Religion in Colonial America: Trends, Regulations, and Beliefs." https://www.facinghistory.org/nobigotry/religion-colonial-america-trends-regulations-and-beliefs.

"Remembering the 1911 Triangle Factory Fire." https://trianglefire.ilr.cornell.edu/.

Remey, Oliver E., et al. *The Attempted Assassination of Ex-President Theodore Roosevelt.* Canton, OH: Pinnacle, 2017.

Rensberger, Boyce. "Clues from the Grave Add Mystery to the Death of Huey Long." *The Washington Post* (June 29, 1992). https://www.washingtonpost.com/archive/politics/1992/06/29/clues-from-the-grave-add-mystery-to-the-death-of-huey-long/cbdd5297-27a1-4534-96bb-68175daf3573/.

Reuters Editors. "U.S. Astronaut John Glenn Laid to Rest at Arlington National Cemetery." *Reuters* (April 6, 2017). https://www.reuters.com/article/people-johnglenn-idINKBN1782AL

Reuters Staff. "False Claim: Nikita Khrushchev 1959 Quote to the United Nations General Assembly." *Reuters* (May 11, 2020). https://www.reuters.com/article/ukfactcheck-khrushchev-1959-quote/false-claim-nikita-khrushchev-1959-quote-to-the-united-nations-general-assembly-idUSKBN22N25D.

Richard Nixon Foundation. "A Final Salute to General Eisenhower." March 30, 2016. https://www.nixonfoundation.org/2016/03/47-years-ago-president-nixon-celebrates-life-general-eisenhower/

Riley, Glenda. *The Life and Legacy of Annie Oakley.* Norman: University of Oklahoma Press, 1994.

Ritchie. Donald A. *American Journalists: Getting the Story.* Oxford: Oxford University Press, 2007.

Roach, David. "For Pilgrims, Thanksgiving Was a Way of Life." *Christianity Today* (November 23, 2020). https://www.christianitytoday.com/ct/2020/november-web-only/thanksgiving-pilgrim-thankfulness-faith-providence-belief.html.

Roberts, Sam. "An Immigrant's Contribution to Mount Rushmore Is Recognized, 75 Years Later." *The New York Times* (June 28, 2016). https://www.nytimes.com/2016/06/29/nyregion/luigi-del-bianco-mount-rushmore.html.

Roberts, Warren. *A Place in History: Albany in the Age of Revolution, 1775–1825*. Albany: State University of New York Press, 2010.

Robertson, Frank C., and Beth Kay Harris. *Soapy Smith: King of the Frontier Con Men*. New York: Hastings House, 1961.

Rockwell, Abigail. "Norman Rockwell: Artist or Illustrator?" (August 24, 2015). https://americanillustration.org/wp-content/uploads/2016/05/15.08.25_AbigailRockwell.pdf.

"The Rockwell Files: Best Job Ever." *The Saturday Evening Post* (December 17, 2020). https://www.saturdayeveningpost.com/

Rogers. Kevin. "Amelia Earhart Disappears Near Howland Island." https://worldhistoryproject.org/1937/7/2/amelia-earhart-disappears-near-howland-island.

Roos, Dave. "Why Do 9 Justices Serve on the Supreme Court?" *History.com* (September 24, 2020). https://www.history.com/news/supreme-court-justices-number-constitution.

Roosevelt, Theodore. *The Strenuous Life: Essays and Addresses*. New York: Century, 1900.

Rose, Mark. "When Giants Roamed the Earth." *Archaeology* 58.6 (November–December 2005). https://archive.archaeology.org/0511/etc/giants.html.

Rosen, William. *Justinian's Flea: Plague, Empire, and the Birth of Europe*. New York: Viking, 2007.

Rosenberg, Jennifer. "Franklin D. Roosevelt Quotes." *ThoughtCo* (March 11, 2020). https://www.thoughtco.com/quotes-by-franklin-d-roosevelt-1779836.

Rottinghaus, Brandon, and Justin Vaughn. "New Ranking of U.S. Presidents Puts Lincoln at No. 1; Obama at 18; Kennedy Judged Most Overrated." *The Washington Post* (February 16, 2015). https://www.washingtonpost.com/news/monkey-cage/wp/2015/02/16/new-ranking-of-u-s-presidents-puts-lincoln-1-obama-18-kennedy-judged-most-over-rated/.

Royde-Smith, John Graham. "World War I—Killed, Wounded, and Missing." *Encyclopedia Britannica*. https://www.britannica.com/event/World-War-I/Killed-wounded-and-missing.

Russell, Jeffrey Burton. *Inventing the Flat Earth: Columbus and Modern Historians*. New York: Praeger, 1991.

Rutland, Robert Allen. *James Madison: The Founding Father*. New York: Macmillan, 1987.

Saxena, Jaya. "130 Years Ago, Elephants Solved Panic on the Brooklyn Bridge." *New-York Historical Society* (May 29, 2014). http://behindthescenes.nyhistory.org/elephants-panic-brooklyn-bridge-.

Scannell, Nancy. "Cunningham Still Running His Race." *The Washington Post* (May 11, 1979). https://www.washingtonpost.com/archive/sports/1979/05/11/cunningham-still-running-his-race/6651faf6-d0dc-4025-9127-ee1611c6550f/.

Schulz, Jeff. "Teddy Roosevelt's Letter on His Reverential Reason for 'Dropping In God We Trust' from Money." https://www.newspapers.com/clip/41216216/teddy-roosevelts-letter-on-his/.

Schwartz, A. Brad. *Broadcast Hysteria: Orson Welles's War of the Worlds and the Art of Fake News*. New York: Hill and Wang, 2015.
Schwartz, Shelly. "Biography of Harry Houdini: The Great Escape Artsist." *ThoughtCo* (January 22, 2020). https://www.thoughtco.com/harry-houdini-1779815.
"The Scopes Trial Excerpts from the Textbook John Scopes Used in Class." https://www.digitalhistory.uh.edu/disp_textbook.cfm?smtID=3&psid=1134.
"Scopes Trial, Humor." https://en.wikipedia.org/wiki/Scopes_Trial.
SCOTUS. "About the Court." The Supreme Court of the United States. https://www.supremecourt.gov/about/about.aspx.
———. "Sandra Day O'Connor, First Woman on the Supreme Court." https://www.supremecourt.gov/visiting/sandradayoconnor.aspx.
Segall, Grant. *John D. Rockefeller: Anointed With Oil*. Oxford: Oxford University Press, 2001.
"Seminary Park." https://www.co.dodge.mn.us/departments/parks_and_trails/seminarypark.php.
Senate Historical Office. "John Adams, 1st Vice President (1789–1797)." (November 11, 2020). https://www.senate.gov/about/officers-staff/vice-president/VP_John_Adams.htm.
Severance, Diane. "What Was the Great Awakening?" (2010). https://www.christianity.com/church/church-history/timeline/1701-1800/the-great-awakening-11630212.html.
Shakespeare, William. *As You Like It*. London: Macmillan International, 2010.
Shapiro, Fred R. *The Yale Book of Quotations*. New Haven: Yale University Press, 2006.
Shapiro, Stanley. "The Celebrity of Charles Lindbergh." *Air Power History* 56.1 (Spring 2009) 20–33. https://www.jstor.org/stable/26275716.
Shi, David E., and George Brown Tindall. *America: A Narrative History*. New York: Norton, 2012.
"The Shot Heard Round the World: The Battles of Lexington and Concord." https://www.constitutionfacts.com/us-declaration-of-independence/the-shot-heard-round-the-world/.
Sides, Hampton. *Blood and Thunder: The Epic Story of Kit Carson and the Conquest of the American West*. New York: Doubleday, 2007.
Sielicki, Jim. "Robert G. Heft: Designer of America's Current National Flag." https://www.chamberofcommerce.org/usflag/flagdesigner.html.
"Significance of the Great Awakening: Roots of Revolution." (2020). http://www.great-awakening.com/roots-of-revolution/.
Simonsen, Lone et al. "Pandemic Versus Epidemic Influenza Mortality: A Pattern of Changing Age Distribution." *The Journal of Infectious Diseases* 178 (July 1, 1998) 53–60.
Sky History. "#ThisDayinHistory 1938, Orson Welles began a US radio broadcast that would shock the nation. #WarOfTheWorlds." (October 30, 2018). https://twitter.com/HISTORYUK/status/1057313957365669889.
Sladen, Douglas. *Younger American Poets, 1830–1890*. London: Griffith, Farran, Okeden & Welsh, 1891.
Smith, Jean Edward. *Grant*. New York: Simon & Schuster, 2002.
Smith, Jeff. *Alias Soapy Smith: The Life and Death of a Scoundrel*. Juneau, AK: Klondike Research, 2009.
Snyder, Robert E. "Huey Long and the Presidential Election of 1936." *Louisiana History* 16.2. (1975) 117–43. http://www.jstor.org/stable/4231456.

Solomon, Deborah. *American Mirror: The Life and Art of Norman Rockwell.* New York: Farrar, Straus and Giroux, 2013.
Sotos, John G. *The Physical Lincoln Sourcebook.* Mt. Vernon, VA: Mount Vernon Book Systems, 2008.
"The South Secedes." https://www.ushistory.org/us/32e.asp.
Specter Michael. "After Ebola." *The New Yorker* (August 1, 2014). https://www.newyorker.com/news/daily-comment/whats-ebola.
Spurgeon, Charles Haddon. "Now." *The Spurgeon Center* (December 4, 1864). https://www.spurgeon.org/resource-library/sermons/now/#flipbook/.
Stephanson, Anders. *Manifest Destiny: American Expansion and the Empire of Right.* New York: Hill and Wang, 1996.
Steward, David O. *Madison's Gift: Five Partnerships That Built America.* New York: Simon & Schuster, 2016.
St. Hill, Thomas Nast. "The Life and Death of Thomas Nast: His Grandson Recalls." *American Heritage* 22.6 (October 1971). https://www.americanheritage.com/life-and-death-thomas-nast.
Stolark, Jessie. "Fact Sheet: A Brief History of Octane in Gasoline: From Lead to Ethanol." *Environmental and Energy Study Institute* (March 30, 2016). https://www.eesi.org/papers/view/fact-sheet-a-brief-history-of-octane.
Strachan, Hew. *The First World War.* London: Penguin, 2005.
Sullivan, Jerry, et al. *The Passenger Pigeon: Once There Were Billions.* Chicago: Field & Street, 2004.
Sullivan, Patricia. "Sandra Day O'Connor's Husband Dies." *The Washington Post* (November 11, 2009). http://voices.washingtonpost.com/postmortem/2009/11/sandra-day-oconnors-husband-di.html.
"Supreme Court of the United States Published Opinions." https://en.wikipedia.org/wiki/Supreme_Court_of_the_United_States.
Swanson Jay. "Huey Long and the Power of Populism." *Current Affairs* (November 27, 2019). https://www.currentaffairs.org/2019/11/huey-long-and-the-power-of-populism.
Tanner, Beccy. "Kansas Track Star Glenn Cunningham Overcame Burn Injuries to Set Records." *The Wichita Eagle* (January 19, 2014). https://www.kansas.com/news/article1132020.html.
Tassava, Christopher. "The American Economy During World War II." *EH.Net* (February 10, 2008). http://eh.net/encyclopedia/the-american-economy-during-world-war-ii/.
Taylor, Alan. *American Colonies: The Settling of North America.* London: Penguin, 2001.
Tellier, Luc-Normand. *Urban World History: An Economic and Geographical Perspective* 2nd ed. New York: Springer, 2019.
Terry, Allison. *How a Senate Tradition Keeps George Washington's Words Alive.* Boston: Christian Science Monitor, 2013.
"Theodore Roosevelt: Assassination Attempt, 1912." *Doctor Zebra.* https://doctorzebra.com/prez/z_x26a_g.htm.
Theodore Roosevelt Center at Dickinson State University. "The Man in the Arena." https://www.theodorerooseveltcenter.org/Learn-About-TR/TR-Encyclopedia/Culture-and-Society/Man-in-the-Arena.aspx.
———. "The River of Doubt." https://www.theodorerooseveltcenter.org/Learn-About-TR/TR-Encyclopedia/Strenuous-Life/River-of-Doubt.

Thomas, Evan. *First: Sandra Day O'Connor.* New York: Random House, 2019.
"Thomas Nast." https://www.illustrationhistory.org/artists/thomas-nast
Thompson, Todd A. "Astronomy 161: An Introduction to Solar System Astronomy." http://www.astronomy.ohio-state.edu/~thompson/161/measearth.html.
Timberlane Regional Schools. "The Industrial Revolution: The Rise of Immigration." https://libguides.timberlane.net/c.php?g=745727&p=5340829.
Time Editors. "Eisenhower: Soldier of Peace." *TIME* (April 4, 1969). https://time.com/81343/eisenhower-soldier-of-peace/.
———. "Heroes: Battle of Washington." August 8, 1932. *TIME* (October 25, 2008). http://content.time.com/time/subscriber/article/0,33009,744107,00.html.
———. "Time 100 Persons of the Century." *TIME* (June 6, 1999). http://content.time.com/time/magazine/article/0,9171,26473,00.html.
Torricelli, Robert, and Andrew Carroll, eds. *In Our Own Words: Extraordinary Speeches of the American Century.* New York: Washington Square. 2008.
Towne, Charles Hanson. *The Rise and Fall of Prohibition: The Human Side of What the Eighteenth Amendment Has Done to the United States.* New York: Macmillan, 1923.
Traub, James. *John Quincy Adams: Militant Spirit.* New York: Basic, 2016.
"The Triangle Shirtwaist Factory Fire." https://www.osha.gov/aboutosha/40-years/trianglefactoryfireaccount.
Tucker Carol. "The 1950s—Powerful Years for Religion." *USC News* (June 16, 1997). https://news.usc.edu/25835/The-1950s-Powerful-Years-for-Religion/.
Uldrich, Jack. *Into the Unknown: Leadership Lessons from Lewis & Clark's Daring Westward Adventure.* New York: Amacom, 2004.
Unger, Harlow Giles. *The French War against America: How a Trusted Ally Betrayed Washington and the Founding Fathers.* Hoboken, NJ: Wiley, 2005.
United Nations. "Global Humanitarian Response Plan Covid-19." https://www.who.int/health-cluster/news-and-events/news/GHRP-COVID-19-July-2020-final.pdf?ua=1.
United States Senate. "Supreme Court Nominations: present–1789." https://www.senate.gov/pagelayout/reference/nominations/Nominations.shtml.
U.S. Department of Commerce. *Statistical Abstract of the United States, 1957.* Washington DC: U.S. Bureau of the Census, 1957.
U.S. Deptartment of Labor: "Chapter 3: The Department in the New Deal and World War II 1933–1945." https://www.dol.gov/general/aboutdol/history/dolchp03
U.S. Department of State: Office of the Historian. "Biographies of the Secretaries of State: John Quincy Adams (1767–1848)." https://history.state.gov/departmenthistory/people/adams-john-quincy.
U.S. Gov. Printing. *Memorial Services in the Congress of the U. S. House Document No. 91–195.* Washington, DC: U.S. Government Printing Office, 1970.
Van der Vat, Dan. *The Pacific Campaign World War II: The U.S.-Japanese Naval War 1941–1945.* New York: Simon & Schuster, 1991.
Vergano, Dan. "1918 Flu Pandemic That Killed 50 Million Originated in China, Historians Say." *National Geographic* (January 24, 2014). https://www.nationalgeographic.com/adventure/article/140123-spanish-flu-1918-china-origins-pandemic-science-health.
Veseth, Michael. *Globaloney: Unraveling the Myths of Globalization.* Washington, DC: Rowman & Littlefield, 2006.

Vinciguerra Thomas. "The Truce of Christmas, 1914." *The New York Times* (December 25, 2005). https://www.nytimes.com/2005/12/25/weekinreview/the-truce-of-christmas-1914.html.

von Drehle, David. *Triangle: The Fire That Changed America.* New York: Grove, 2004.

Wade, Nicholas. "Europe's Plagues Came From China, Study Finds." *The New York Times* (October 31, 2010). https://www.nytimes.com/2010/11/01/health/01plague.html#:~: text=The%20great%20waves%20of%20plague,harmfully%20in%20the%2019th%20century.

Wagner, Ella. "Triangle Shirtwaist Factory (Brown Building)."https://www.nps.gov/places/triangle-shirtwaist-factory-brown-building.htm.

Walbert, David. "The Depression for Farmers." http://www.davidwalbert.com/pdf/learnnc/the-depression-for-farmers-p5955.pdf.

Wallace, Chris. *Character: Profiles in Presidential Courage.* New York: Rugged Land, 2004.

Wallenfeldt, Jeff. "'We Shall Overcome': LBJ and the 1965 Voting Rights Act." *Encyclopedia Britannica.* https://www.britannica.com/event/Selma-March/We-Shall-Overcome-LBJ-and-the-1965-Voting-Rights-Act.

Walsh, Anthony. *The Gavel and Sickle: The Supreme Court, Cultural Marxism, and the Assault on Christianity.* Wilmington, DE: Vernon, 2017.

Walvin, James. *A Child's World. A Social History of English Childhood, 1800–1914.* New Orleans: Pelican. 1982.

Waugh, Joan. "Ulysses S. Grant: Life Before the Presidency." *Miller Center, University of Virginia.* https://millercenter.org/president/grant/life-before-the-presidency.

Waxman, Olivia B. "The Troubling History of the Fight to Honor Leif Erikson—Not Columbus—as the Man Who 'Discovered America." *Time* (October 4, 2019). https://time.com/5414518/columbus-day-leif-erikson-day/.

Weingroff, Richard F. "Federal-Aid Highway Act of 1956: Creating the Interstate System." Public Roads 60.1 (Summer 1996). https://highways.dot.gov/public-roads/summer-1996/federal-aid-highway-act-1956-creating-interstate-system.

Weintraub, Stanley. *15 Stars—Eisenhower, MacArthur, Marshall—Three Generals Who Saved the American Century.* New York: Free Press, 2007.

Weir, Robert. *Class in America: An Encyclopedia, Volume 3: Q-Z.* 3 vols. Westport, CT: Greenwood, 2007.

Welch, Jerry. *The Encyclopedia of Your Observations: A Creed for Living Life.* Bloomington, IN: Trafford, 2015.

White, Richard D. *Kingfish: The Reign of Huey P. Long.* New York: Random House. 2006.

White, Ronald C. *American Ulysses: A Life of Ulysses S. Grant.* New York: Random House, 2016.

Whiting, Jim. *What's So Great about Annie Oakley?* Hallandale Beach, FL: Mitchell Lane, 2007.

"Why Is 'Freon' Being Phased Out?" *United States Environmental Protection Agency.* (March 15, 2021). https://www.epa.gov/ods-phaseout/homeowners-and-consumers-frequently-asked-questions.

Wilford, John Noble. "At Cape Canaveral, Reliving the Grand Highs of '62." *The New York Times* (October 28, 1998). https://www.nytimes.com/1998/10/28/us/at-cape-canaveral-reliving-the-grand-highs-of-62.html.

Wills, Chuck. *DK Biography: Annie Oakley.* London: Dorling Kindersley, 2007.

Wilson, Linda D. "Nation, Carry Moore, (1846–1911)." *The Encyclopedia of Oklahoma History and Culture* https://www.okhistory.org/publications/enc/entry.php?entry=NA006.

Windsor, The Duke of. *A King's Story by H.R.H. The Duke of Windsor*. London: Cassell, 1951.

Winter, Jay, and Blaine Baggett. *The Great War and the Shaping of the 20th Century*. New York: Penguin, 1996.

Wishart, David J. "One-Room Schoolhouses." *Encyclopedia of the Great Plains* (2011). http://plainshumanities.unl.edu/encyclopedia/doc/egp.edu.032.xml.

Withey, Lynne. *Dearest Friend: A Life of Abigail Adams*. New York: Atria, 1981.

Wood, Gordan. *Empire of Liberty*. Oxford: Oxford University Press, 2009.

Woodger, Elin, and Brandon Toropov. *Encyclopedia of the Lewis and Clark Expedition*. New York: Infobase, 2009.

Wordsworth, William. "Rob Roy's Grave." https://www.bartleby.com/371/437.html.

Young, Alexander. *Chronicles of the Pilgrim Fathers of the Colony of Plymouth from 1602 to 1625*. New York: Little and Brown, 1841.

Zarefsky, David. *Lincoln, Douglas, and Slavery: In the Crucible of Public Debate*. Chicago: University of Chicago Press, 1993.

Ziegler, Philip. *King Edward VIII: The Official Biography*. New York: Knopf, 1991.

Zinn, Howard. *A People's History of the United States*. New York: Harper Perennial Modern Classics, 2005.

www.ingramcontent.com/pod-product-compliance
Lightning Source LLC
Chambersburg PA
CBHW050842230426
43667CB00012B/2116